British Aerospace
Harrier and Sea Harrier

British Aerospace
Harrier and

ROY BRAYBROOK

Sea Harrier

OSPREY AIR COMBAT

Published in 1984 by Osprey Publishing Limited
12–14 Long Acre, London WC2E 9LP
Member company of the George Philip Group
© Roy Braybrook 1984

Sole distributors for the USA

Publishers & Wholesalers Inc
Osceola, Wisconsin 54020, USA

British Library Cataloguing in Publication Data

Braybrook, Roy
    British Aerospace Harrier and Sea Harrier.—(Osprey air
combat series.
    1. Harrier (Jet fighter plane)   2. Sea Harrier
    (Jet fighter plane)
    I. Title
    623.74′64   UG1242.F5
ISBN 0-85045-561-8

Editor Dennis Baldry
Designed by Joy Fitzsimmons
Printed in Spain

Contents

Preface 7

Introduction 9

1 The Challenge 10

2 Hawker P.1127 to Harrier 36

3 Production Aircraft 70

4 The Falklands Conflict 102

5 Harrier Derivatives – AV-8B and
   Beyond 176

Acknowledgements 192

Abbreviations 192

Appendices 194

Index 199

This book is dedicated to pilots such as 'Bill' Bedford, John Farley, 'Dave' Morgan, and Peter Squire, who tested, demonstrated, or went to war (or otherwise risked their necks) in, the Harrier family of V/STOL combat aircraft.

Preface

The Harrier family of V/STOL (vertical or short take-off and landing) aircraft began life as the Hawker Aircraft P.1127 project of 1957, designed by Ralph Hooper. While I was on leave from the RAF late that summer, I went back to the Hawker project office in Canbury Park Road, Kingston-on-Thames, to find out what had been happening while I was away on National Service. During that visit, Bob Marsh, who had recently superseded Vivian Stanbury as head of the office, showed me in confidence a three-view drawing of the P.1127. It was a blunt little aeroplane, supported at the hover (he explained) by jets from four rotatable nozzles on its Bristol Aero Engines BE.53 turbofan, the arrangement of the jets about the aircraft centre of gravity (CG) giving a ground cushion effect under the centre fuselage.

Seen in the context of the P.1103 supersonic fighter on which the project team had been working in the previous year, the P.1127 appeared to be merely a technical oddity, not at all the kind of design that Hawker Aircraft manufactured. Indeed, having served my postgraduate apprenticeship on the Hunter, which was beautiful, but built like a battleship and with a structure weight to match, I doubted very much whether ours was the right company to be looking at an aircraft that depended completely for its success on being light in weight. Possibly it was right for Folland, which company had produced the lightweight Gnat, but certainly not 'Harry's'.

There was no way that anyone in the Hawker project office could have foreseen at that time that the P.1127 and its BE.53 engine would reach fruition only many years in the future as the Hawker Siddeley Aviation (HSA)/British Aerospace (BAe) Harrier with Rolls-Royce (R-R) Pegasus engine, entering RAF service in 1969, then as the USMC AV-8A of 1971, the RN Sea Harrier of 1979, and (in extensively modified form) as the McDonnell Douglas (MDC) AV-8B Harrier II or Harrier GR.5 of the mid-1980s.

In terms of my own connection with the programme, I certainly never imagined that on returning to Hawker employment in 1958, I would spend ten years in the project office, partly trying to launch a more advanced V/STOL aircraft based on the single-engine vectored-thrust concept, and another equally frustrating decade working with the marketing department, vainly attempting to sell the Harrier family abroad.

Even less likely would have been the idea that, a quarter-century after my first sight of the P.1127 general arrangement drawing, I would be a freelance writer, interviewing RAF and RN pilots who were 'over the moon', having just operated the project's offspring with a success that staggered even them, in a war with Argentina.

This book attempts to review the highlights of the Harrier programme, and to place the whole matter of V/STOL aircraft in clearer perspective. Any views expressed are my own, and they are advanced partly to encourage further discussion of the subject. Unless Britain and her NATO allies give more serious consideration during the 1980s to the whole V/STOL concept and its proper place in the military inventory, then all the work that the manufacturers and operators put into achieving a technological lead for the West may well have been in vain.

Roy Braybrook
Kingston-upon-Thames, England
1984

Introduction

The history of the BAe Harrier and its R-R Pegasus engine has two principal aspects. In terms of V/STOL technology, it is basically a story of how we British, through a combination of good luck and inventiveness, won our only current world lead in aviation, then sat back and waited for others (not only the Americans and the Russians; but possibly even the Japanese) to take this lead from us. In terms of the practical application of this revolutionary concept, the principal story concerns a small band of RN and RAF pilots and engineers, who went to a war in the South Atlantic with Sea Harriers and Harrier GR.3s. They flew from aircraft carriers, helicopter pads, and what is almost certainly the world's shortest military airstrip, providing an effective first line of air defence for the British task force, and close support for our troops fighting on East Falkland.

A quarter-century after the P.1127 was conceived, Britain discovered in the acid test of war that there really is a case for a major air arm to have a V/STOL aircraft component, simply for the operational flexibility that such systems provide.

No other country in the world could have reinforced its naval air arm with fixed-wing aircraft from its air force. Or flown such aircraft from a helicopter platform on a container ship. Or had air force pilots (who had never even *seen* an aircraft carrier before) make their first deck landings in the middle of a war zone and fly their first operational missions the very next day. Or have operated fixed-wing air force aircraft from 850 ft (260 m) of aluminium planking beside the amphibious landing area. Or refuelled air defence fighters on board assault ships, with dozens of emergency landing sites available in the form of helicopter pads and short grass airfields. No other nation on earth could have done what Britain did in this 'Operation Corporate' by virtue of V/STOL aircraft.

In the Falklands conflict the Harrier family achieved an unquestionable triumph. If there had been no Sea Harrier, there could have been no Task Force, and the Falklands would now be 'Las Malvinas'. However, both the Sea Harrier and the RAF Harrier GR.3 performed far better than our politicians and Whitehall warriors had any right to expect. The effectiveness of these aircraft was largely due to outstanding efforts by engineers in both services and industry, and to the emphasis that Fleet Air Arm squadron commanders had placed on air combat training long before the conflict erupted.

If the Falklands episode proved anything beyond the fact that the British services and industry respond magnificently to the demands of war, it is surely that in this country defence needs have sunk too low in the order of priorities. Time and again, major problems arose in the South Atlantic because essential equipment and facilities had been deleted from successive budgets as 'below-the-line' items.

In regard to the Harrier family, the principal difficulty was that only 34 Sea Harriers had been funded to provide two operational squadrons, plus one training unit and attrition reserves. Considering that any further replacement aircraft would take the best part of three years to build, this situation was ludicrous, as the RN knew (and protested) from the outset of the programme. Regarding the RAF Harrier, there appear to have been no contingency plans to operate GR.3s from RN carriers. To have done so would have required modifications and additional equipment, and that again would have cost money.

At the outbreak of the fighting, neither the Sea Harrier nor the GR.3 had provisions to dispense chaff or flares (as we could see Israeli aircraft doing on television most evenings), and neither was cleared to use laser-guided bombs. These shortcomings were rectified, but at time of writing it appears that neither aircraft yet has ECM (jamming) equipment or provisions for medium-range air-air missiles or anti-radar air-surface missiles.

Britain's attitude to defence spending needs to change, and it is not sufficient merely to bring existing equipment up to modern international standards. Equally important is the need to start work with America on a new generation of V/STOL combat aircraft to replace the Sea Harrier and Harrier II around the turn of the century.

Chapter 1
The Challenge

Even today, more than 20 years after the Hawker P.1127's first historic transitions between jetborne and wingborne flight, a display of V/STOL (vertical or short take-off and landing) by a member of the Harrier family is still a showstopper. The idea that a modern combat aircraft capable of near-sonic speed in level flight can also hover like a helicopter (albeit considerably more noisily) still catches the attention of the crowds.

The Western World's only operational high performance V/STOL aircraft – a title it has held since 1969 – the Harrier has demonstrated its practical value in air defence and surface attack in the Falklands conflict, hence it is clearly more than just a circus act for airshows. Its advocates claim that the V/STOL fighter as a broad concept warrants inclusion as an element in every major air force, and that it has the potential to revolutionize naval air warfare. Such claims demand examination. If they are true, then the West should now be spending far more on improving V/STOL technology, to safeguard the present lead.

Dramatic and important as V/STOL may be, there is little general understanding of the basic concept, although the idea of an engine with rotatable nozzles appears to be simplicity in the extreme. Few people appreciate why it took so long to produce a high performance aircraft with the ability to hover, and thus largely dispense with runways in the conventional sense. Few understand why the Harrier family has appealed to only a handful of air arms, and why the repeatedly forecast world-wide switch to V/STOL has not materialized.

In the following pages the history of Harrier development, the current marketing failure and future prospects are all discussed. However, firstly we look at the nature of the technical challenge, and of the problems that delayed the practical achievement of V/STOL for well over half a century after the first CTOLs (conventional take-offs and landings) by the Wright brothers.

How Manned Flight Began

In discovering a means to fly, man imitated the birds, first apeing the gliding flight of the more efficient soaring birds, then adding thrust to make possible sustained level flight. None of this was easy, because the birds had the benefit of millions of years of evolution, in the course of which they had developed lightweight bone structures, aerodynamically efficient wings, muscles of high power/weight ratio, and a control system that allowed operation over a wide attitude range. They also had many other advanced features, such as automatic leading edge slats and variable-camber wings – concepts we are still endeavouring to reproduce mechanically.

The birds were thus able to combine lightweight, unbraced monoplane airframes of excellent aerodynamic efficiency with a powerplant that (in the majority of cases) could give flying speed from a standing start. On completion of a sortie, the bird's low wing loading (weight per unit wing area) gave a slow stall, and the reciprocating movement of the wings made it possible to kill the remaining airspeed by means of a highly effective airbrake action, and thus achieve a vertical landing.

Lacking the birds' advantages, men began by using biplanes or wire-braced monoplanes to achieve rigid, lightweight structures, despite the drag penalties involved. They reasoned (correctly) that if a flying machine glided at an angle of (for instance) one-in-ten, then its drag was being overcome by its own weight component down the glide path, and that level flight could therefore be attained by a powerplant giving an equivalent thrust. In this example, thrust need be equal to only one tenth of aircraft weight.

However, obtaining even this modest level of thrust without an excessively heavy engine was not

A conventional aircraft in this attitude so close to the ground would be in serious trouble. This Rolls-Royce photograph shows the first DB Harrier beginning its rocket climb at the Hannover Air Show

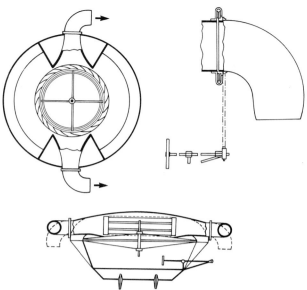

Porter's vectored-thrust concept of 1910 with rotating nozzles

The Wibault Gyroptère V/STOL concept of 1956 featured a rear-mounted engine driving four centrifugal blowers

The Wibault/Lewis V/STOL patent of 1956 incorporated a number of refinements, with the core of the engine mounted near the CG, and an extension shaft running a forward mounted fan which featured separate intakes. Interestingly, the patent included the possibility of incorporating two V/STOL nozzles at the end of the jetpipe

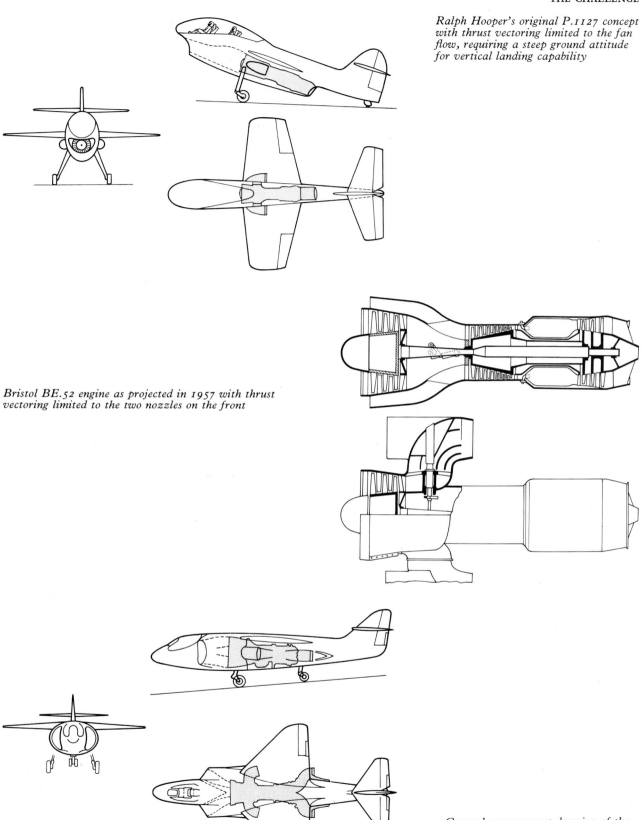

Ralph Hooper's original P.1127 concept with thrust vectoring limited to the fan flow, requiring a steep ground attitude for vertical landing capability

Bristol BE.52 engine as projected in 1957 with thrust vectoring limited to the two nozzles on the front

General arrangement drawing of the P.1127 in June 1957 with the four-nozzle BE.53 engine, stuby delta wing and mid-mounted flat tailplane

Conventional flight is achieved because the wing acts as a thrust-magnification device. This Lockheed TR-1 can probably generate a lifting force equal to 25 times its drag, hence little thrust is required.

easy. Once the basic ideas of stability and control were understood from gliding experiments, manned flight depended for further development on engines of high power/weight ratio and on efficient propellers. The point to be grasped is that man finally achieved sustained flight through the use of a wing as a force-magnification device, reducing thrust demands to manageable proportions.

In the above example, the aircraft would be capable of generating a lifting force equal to *ten times* the thrust required to sustain it in forward flight. If pioneer aviators had simply pointed their propellers at the sky and tried for VTO, their vehicles might have lifted on their undercarriages slightly, but they would have had to wait until at least the 1940s for progress in powerplants to catch up with their ambitions. With the level of technology available in the early decades of the century, man would have remained bound to the earth, had it not been for the lighter-than-air balloon and the thrust-magnification effect of the moving wing.

Unfortunately, wing lift requires airspeed, hence if the wing is fixed rigidly to the aircraft, the whole machine has to move forwards for aerodynamic lift to support the aircraft's weight. Whereas most birds can reach flying speed virtually instantly, the conventional aircraft has a relatively low acceleration and a comparatively high unstick speed, hence take-off requires both time and distance. Most current aircraft take 10–40 seconds to unstick, and, when allowances are made for aborted take-offs and partial power failures, they require runways of the order of 8,000–10,000 ft (2,500–3,000 m).

To put some numbers to the thrust-magnification capability of a wing, a typical fighter airframe can generate lift equal to around 10 times its drag. In the case of a subsonic transport aircraft this L/D ratio may go as high as 20 (about

half that of a good sailplane). For various practical reasons the thrust installed by the manufacturer is considerably more than these figures may imply. In the case of a transport aircraft, sea level static thrust is typically 25–35 per cent of gross weight, to satisfy take-off demands and to make possibly cruise at high altitude. In a combat aircraft, the thrust installed is proportionally higher, to achieve the desired manoeuvrability, acceleration and climb rate. Going back to the time when the P.1127 was designed, a ground attack aircraft would typically have had a static thrust equal to 40 per cent of gross weight, and in a fighter thrust would have equalled perhaps 75 per cent of gross.

It is only with the latest generation of American fighters that conventional aircraft have been given a static thrust of the same order of magnitude as their weights, and this improvement has required a major advance in the thrust/weight ratio (T/W) of engines. Throughout most of the history of fighter development, it has been impossible to install enough thrust to achieve take-off purely by means of jet lift, since to have allocated so much weight to the powerplant would have left no scope for the aircraft to carry fuel. In essence, V/STOL as we know it today had to wait until it was possible to produce engines that generated a thrust equal to seven or eight times their weight, or for the advent of some form of thrust-magnification device.

The use of jet lift for V/STOL requires that the aircraft powerplant has a nominal (testbed) thrust in the region of 80–125 per cent of take-off weight. Taking the example of a Harrier with a Pegasus engine of 21,500 lb (9,750 kg) testbed thrust, at a weight of 26,875 lb (12,188 kg) it would have a T/W of only 0.8, but it could still perform STO. At the opposite extreme, at a weight of 17,200 lb (7,800 kg) it has a T/W of 1.25 and can use VTO. The reasons it requires a nominal T/W in excess of 1.00 are mainly that net thrust is reduced by recirculation of hot gases to the intake, that intake efficiency (unlike that on the testbed) is less than 100 per cent, that air is bled from the engine for the reaction control system, there are power offtakes to the gearbox for hydraulic and electrical services, etc, there may be an aerodynamic download on the airframe, and that some thrust margin is required to accelerate the aircraft upwards.

At more conventional thrust/weight ratios, some improvement in take-off performance can be produced through the use of jet lift, but the effect is less than dramatic. This was illustrated by the case of the Grumman A2F-1 Intruder, which first flew in April 1960, with provision for the pilot to

Only in the very latest fighters, instanced here by a General Dynamics F-16 Fighting Falcon, has the thrust installed exceeded the aircraft weight. Stood on its tail, the F-16 could in principle achieve VTO

The first true fixed-wing VTO aircraft was the rocket-powered Bachem Natter. This rare photograph from the Deutsches Museum shows a model test (M17) from a 39.4 ft (12 m) launch rail in 1944

select a downward jet deflection angle of 30 degrees to reduce approach speed. This produced a jet lift component equal to half the thrust, and (given enough drag, to allow full thrust to be used) in theory this should have effectively reduced the weight of the aircraft by around a quarter. In practice, it appears that less than full thrust could be used in the approach, and speed was reduced by a mere six knots (11 km/hr). The Intruder's jet deflection system was accordingly deleted on the fifth and subsequent aircraft.

Tail-Sitters

In one area at least, engine technology reached the stage at which jet lift could have practical application during WWII, with the development of liquid-fuel rocket motors in Germany. Such engines gave a thrust/weight ratio of around 15:1, perhaps ten times higher than contemporary turbojet engines, although high fuel consumption more than offset the saving in powerplant weight in all projects except those intended for flights of very short duration. Germany's Bachem Ba 349 *Natter* (Adder) was a rocket-powered tail-sitter

interceptor that took off vertically from a ramp, but at the outset (at least) it was more akin to a manned surface-air missile or a zero-length launch fighter (ie, one blasted up an inclined ramp to flying speed by rocket boost motors) rather than the V/STOL aircraft as we know it today.

The *Natter* initially had no special means of control for low speeds, which led to problems as it came off the ramp, hence the tail surfaces were enlarged, and it was decided to place water-cooled control vanes in the rocket efflux. After completing the interception, the idea was that the pilot would bale out, and the aircraft would be parachuted to earth. Despite a fatal first manned launch on 28 February 1945, six successful test flights were made. Nonetheless, the *Natter* was dropped from the *Jägernotprogramm* (Emergency Fighter Programme) in favour of the relatively conventional Me 263.

The *Natter* is believed to have been the first of the 'tail-sitters', which – given effective low-speed controls and less exotic powerplants – make VTOL possible in an aircraft that differs from a conventional design basically in having a special form of undercarriage to suit vertical attitude launch and recovery. In terms of practical flying hardware, the first examples were the Lockheed XFV-1 and Convair XFY-1, naval fighters powered by a 5,850 shp Allison T40 turboprop driving a pair of three-bladed contra-rotating propellers. Both aircraft flew in the mid-1950s, but in 1956 the US Navy terminated these programmes. In view of the fact that the service had been operating conventional jet fighters (the North American Fury, McDonnell Banshee, and Grumman Panther) since the late 1940s, it seems likely that the tail-sitter developments were seen from the outset only as technology demonstrators. The US Navy nonetheless retained a strong interest in V/STOL, and is today one of the principal driving forces behind advanced developments in this field.

The Convair and Lockheed tail-sitters, which began development in 1951, might be regarded conceptually as having used propellers as thrust-augmentors for small turbine engines. However, even at that time straightforward turbojets were already approaching the stage (in T/W terms) at which tail-sitting VTOL research aircraft could be produced without any form of thrust augmentation. The Ryan X-13 Vertijet began development in 1953 under USAF funding, using a single Rolls-Royce Avon similar to that fitted to the Hawker Hunter. The X-13 made CTOL

The Lockheed XFV-1 tail-sitter was a technology demonstrator for a carrier-borne fighter. The landing gear looks somewhat fragile, and it may be significant that CTOL tests were made using a jury undercarriage

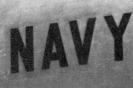

The Convair XFY-1 'Pogo' was the first VATOL aircraft to complete transitions between thrustborne and wingborne flight. The pilot was 'Skeets' Coleman and the time November 1954. The tufting indicates flow separations

LEFT
The practical problems of obtaining access to the cockpit and powerplant are illustrated by this photograph of the Convair XFY-1 'Pogo'. The pilot's seat could be tilted through 45 degrees to minimize orientation problems

Operating from a vertical ramp, the Rolls-Royce Avon-powered Ryan X-13 was the world's first jet-powered VATOL aircraft to demonstrate successful transitions. However, the tail-sitter was superseded by the flat-riser

flights in late 1955 using a jury undercarriage, and followed with vertical attitude operations from 28 May 1956. Whereas the XFV-1 and XFY-1 sat with four small wheels on the ground, the X-13 operated from a vertical ramp, to which it was attached by hooks.

In the case of designing a fighter that requires a T/W of around 1.25 for combat performance, a tail-sitter design can provide VTOL with minimum weight penalty and virtually no change to the powerplant. In principle, the only weight penalty relative to a conventional aircraft of similar T/W is that of the low-speed control system, which may be more than offset by the saving in undercarriage weight.

The Rolls-Royce 'Flying Bedstead' of 1953 was powered by two Nene turbojets mounted back-to-back to eliminate gyroscopic effects. Incapable of wingborne flight, it provided guidance on puffer and autostabilizer requirements

One disadvantage of the tail-sitter is that, unless afterburner or some form of rocket boost is held in reserve (neither of which options is likely to be acceptable), this class of aircraft is unable to take off at higher weights than normal. The CTOL aircraft may be designed for one specific take-off weight, but always has the capacity for an overload take-off, simply through the use of an extended ground run. At a time when defence economies are bringing demands for ever-increasing operational flexibility, the rigid weight limit on tail-sitter take-off weight is a major drawback for this concept.

In addition, the pilot of the tail-sitter has a severe orientation problem during transition, unless (as in some designs) his seat is rotated to preserve a relatively conventional attitude. This requires an enlarged cockpit, and the instruments and controls should really move with the pilot. The task of loading external stores makes it virtually essential that the tail-sitter is operated from a tilting platform and 'bombed up' in a horizontal attitude.

Notwithstanding these very real problems, the tail-sitter is so close in powerplant, structure and systems to a conventional fighter that it still has some attraction in the context of a dedicated fighter of which no surface attack capability is required. In view of this and the possibility of developing reliable automatic systems to control an aircraft during take-off and landing (something that the Yak-36 *Forger* already appears to make use of), the tail-sitting VTOL aircraft may yet reach service status in the longer term, probably for naval operation.

Flat Risers

Despite successful demonstrations by the Ryan X-13, even in the mid-1950s VTOL was still only marginally feasible. The tail-sitter with its off-the-shelf engine and minimum weight penalty was a relatively easy way to gain VTOL experience, but pilot orientation problems and general lack of operational flexibility then stifled further development. However good the experimental tail-sitters look on film, they really only served to prove what many designers had said from the outset, namely that what was needed if V/STOL was to progress was a 'flat-riser'. Such an aircraft would eliminate pilot orientation problems, and would be able also to use STOL, so that aerodynamic wing lift could assist jet lift, allowing take-off at much higher weights when necessary.

The Lockheed XV-4B Hummingbird or VZ-10 was powered by two P&W JT12 turbojets, exhausting through jet augmentors. It was later converted to house a battery of lift engines in the centre fuselage

There was no shortage of ideas for V/STOL flat-risers. General Electric developed the concept of buried fans, spun by peripheral turbines driven by high energy gases diverted during take-off and landing from the propulsion engines. This form of thrust augmentation was tested with some success on the Ryan XV-5A, which was powered by two GE J85s and first flew on 25 May 1964 under US Army funding. However, aside from the obvious weight and stowage penalties associated with large cut-outs in the wing and fuselage, there was also the problem of the momentum drag of the air drawn through the fans, which limited STO performance. It was therefore later proposed (in applying the buried fan concept to strike fighters) to have smaller, retractable fuselage-mounted fans that could be tilted to improve STO performance at high weights.

Another form of thrust magnification is the 'jet-augmentor', in which engine exhaust gases expand through nozzles mounted in a specially shaped duct, the main jets inducing additional air to flow through the duct and thus create suction on upward facing surfaces. In simple, small-scale

laboratory tests it is possible to demonstrate thrust augmentations in excess of 50 per cent. The concept also has the attraction that the extra thrust is produced by means of low-cost sheets of metal, rather than expensive rotating machinery.

In full-scale trials, however, jet-augmentors have been disappointing. The principle was tested in the mid-1960s with the Lockheed XV-4B Hummingbird, which had fuselage-mounted jet-augmentors, but reports suggest that little or no thrust augmentation was produced. The jet-augmentor concept was also to have been used in the Rockwell XFV-12A during the 1970s, with augmentors in both wing and foreplane, but this programme was terminated before flight was attempted.

To date, few forms of thrust augmentation have worked at full-scale. In experiments with military STOL transports under USAF funding, upper surface blowing (USB) was tested on the Boeing YC-14, and externally-blown flaps (EBF) on the McDonnell Douglas YC-15, but such schemes are basically means of thrust deflection or vectoring, rather than augmentation. Jumping ahead in the story of V/STOL development, it is probably true to say that so far the only really practical means of thrust augmentation has proved to be the direct addition of a large fan to a turbojet. In effect, this is what Bristol Aero Engines did in developing the

The Rockwell XFV-12A was proposed as a technology demonstrator for a supersonic VTOL fighter for the US Navy. The efflux from a P&W F401 turbofan was to be ducted to jet augmentors in the wing and foreplane

This artist's impression of the Rockwell XFV-12A project shows the augmentor ducts open. The grille behind the cockpit was an auxiliary inlet for the F401 engine, which was mounted in the rear fuselage

BE.53. The result was a massive increase in static thrust for proportionally little extra weight, ultimately producing a T/W of 7.0 in terms of short lift engine rating and dry engine weight.

Military Needs

To summarize, the achievement of V/STOL in a fixed-wing aircraft required much more installed thrust than normal (before fighters such as the F-15), and for practical service use it was generally agreed that the aircraft had to be a flat-riser. To provide the large thrust required amounted in the mid-1950s to inventing some new form of powerplant.

It was at this stage that military demands in Europe began to emphasize the need for NATO tactical aircraft to be capable of dispersing away from conventional air bases. The Soviet Union had developed first generation nuclear warheads for ballistic missiles some years previously, hence in the mid-1950s it was felt in the West that the Russians would soon have small tactical warheads available in large numbers, able to destroy all major NATO airfields on the Central Front during the first few days of war. Without air cover, NATO armies could not hope to withstand a Warsaw Pact thrust, so (the argument ran) Western combat aircraft must be able to fly from

smaller operating sites in wartime.

The first credible technical response to these demands came from Rolls-Royce (R-R), at that time a public company and the principal rival to Bristol Aero Engines in the British engine market. Engineers working for R-R at Derby suggested that specialized lift engines which were operated for only a few minutes during take-off and landing could produce far higher T/W values than normal engines that had to operate over a wide range of conditions. Turbojets were then achieving a T/W of 4:1 or 5:1, but these lift engines were to give 8:1 initially, 16:1 in the second generation, and ultimately 24:1. Although it was found in practice that these small engines were associated with unusually high installation factors (ie, there was a disproportionate weight penalty due to structural cut-outs, inlet and exit doors, etc), these engines were still sufficiently light to be added to a conventional aircraft to make possible V/STOL operation. Given eight or more of these engines, it was even possible that an engine failure in hovering flight could be allowed for.

What became known as the 'Rolls-Royce concept' of a composite powerplant, with separate engines for jet lift and forward propulsion found several supporters, notably Short Bros in the UK and Dassault Aviation in France. However, other manufacturers (including Hawker Aircraft) felt

The Boeing YC-14 STOL tactical transport had two GE CF6 engines exhausting over the upper surface of the wing, so that deflection of trailing edge flaps would turn the attached jets, vectoring the thrust

Like the YC-14, the McDonnell Douglas YC-15 was designed to meet the USAF AMST (Advanced Medium STOL Transport) target. In this case thrust vectoring was achieved by having the jets blow directly at the flaps

The Shorts SC.1 had four RB.108 lift engines in the centre fuselage and one RB.108 in the rear as a propulsion engine. The first transition between wingborne and jetborne flight occurred on 6 April 1960

that the resulting complexity was incompatible with dispersed operation, and that a Mach 2 fighter (which was the ultimate aim) could not accept the in-flight performance penalty resulting from the sheer bulk of the battery of lift engines.

The Rolls-Royce concept was tested in the Shorts SC.1 and the Dassault Balzac and Mirage IIIV. It worked, although reports indicate that there was a significant loss of lift due to the induced downwash over the airframe, that there was an embarrassing increase in dihedral effect (rolling moment due to sideslip) in partially-jetborne flight, that supersonic acceleration of the Mirage IIIV was less than remarkable, and that the gyroscopic effects of the two engine sets required autostabilization of relatively high authority.

What might be regarded conceptually as a half-way house to the Rolls-Royce concept was tested in the 1960s in the Soviet Union. In essence, a row of two or three lift engines was mounted in the centre fuselage of a fighter to support perhaps half its weight and thus reduce unstick and landing

speeds. This alternative to the use of variable-sweep wings for STOL was demonstrated in flight at Domodedovo in 1967, in the form of the MiG-21 *Fishbed G*, the Mikoyan *Faithless* (a delta-wing equivalent of the MiG-23), and the Su-15 *Flagon B*. It appears that the jet lift approach to STOL was subsequently abandoned in favour of the variable-sweep wing, possibly because the latter also provides improved acceleration, reduced gust response, and longer high altitude loiter.

The idea of applying just sufficient jet lift that stall speed was significantly reduced, yet reaction controls were not required, is nonetheless an interesting one. Whatever its shortcomings, this programme left the Soviet Union with a fully developed lift engine that was available off-the-shelf for later V/STOL aircraft, notably the Yak-36 *Forger*. Before leaving the lift engine concept, it should be noted that, despite its limitations in the fighter field, such engines will almost certainly provide at least part of the jet lift for any future military transport aircraft (they tend to be too noisy for civil applications), and that it is a major advantage for any V/STOL proposal to be based on standard engines that have a wide range of possible applications.

The basic Rolls-Royce concept of completely separate powerplants for jet lift and propulsion

Dassault's Balzac was what would now be termed a technology demonstrator for a supersonic strike fighter, based on the Rolls-Royce concept of a composite powerplant of lift and propulsion engines

was not only probably too complex for a tactical fighter, but also wasteful in the sense that the thrust available for forward flight was not used to provide jet lift. A more efficient approach (and probably the best in terms of the minimum combined weight of powerplant and fuel) for a strike fighter was developed in Germany separately by Focke-Wulf and Entwicklungsring-Süd (later to become integrated in VFW and MBB respectively). In this approach the propulsion powerplant was optimized in size and operating cycle for the cruise phase, thus giving the minimum fuel consumption. Its thrust was deflected downwards at low speeds, and supplemented with just enough lift engines to achieve V/STOL. The result was an aircraft less safe in the event of an engine failure during partially jetborne flight than the Mirage IIIV (with its eight centrally-mounted lift engines), but it resulted in the lightest aircraft for a given mission. This conclusion was later accepted by the Dassault team during the course of Franco–German collaboration, but this was yet another V/STOL programme that did not reach fruition.

The 'German concept' was the basis of the ill-fated VJ101D, but the broad principle was demonstrated in the VJ101C, which combined two

The Dassault Mirage IIIV is claimed to have been the first V/STOL aircraft capable of Mach 2.0. It was powered by eight Rolls-Royce RB.162 lift engines and one SNECMA/P&W TF-306 propulsion engine

fixed lift engines with four engines in tilting, tip-mounted pods, and in the VFW 1262, which had a central Bristol-type vectored-thrust engine and two lift engines mounted in the fuselage. The Yak-36 *Forger* might be regarded conceptually as a derivative of the VFW 1262.

The Single Vectored-Thrust Engine

In discussing the ways in which lift engines could be used to achieve V/STOL, various examples have been quoted from later years to illustrate the form that such aircraft might take. On the one hand there was the Mirage IIIV, offering safety in jetborne flight at the expense of considerable complexity, and on the other there were projects such as the VJ101D offering minimum weight penalty and some relaxation of complexity, but with an increased probability of engine failure and doubtful security in the event of that happening.

In designing a fighter for dispersed operation, there were clear attractions in using a single engine that could provide both jet lift and propulsive thrust. Such an aircraft would be comparatively simple to maintain, and it could offer a reasonable degree of security in jetborne flight, provided the engine was highly reliable. What was needed was an engine with a thrust line that could be turned to any angle between the horizontal and the vertical, what the Bristol patent termed *'orientatable thrust'*. All the available thrust could then be used in STO to accelerate the aircraft

Soviet VTOL technology has culminated (operationally at least) in the Yak-36 Forger. These Forger-As were photographed on the carrier Minsk (see below) during a Pacific deployment in November 1982. All three aircraft have dorsal strakes, and the nearest has a 23 mm gun pod mounted underwing

As proposed in 1969 by HSA's Hatfield division, the HS.141 VTOL commercial transport would have had 16 Rolls-Royce RB.202 lift engines mounted in long fairings along the sides of the fuselage

BELOW
Conceptually a forerunner of the German VJ101C, the Bell D-188 fighter project (shown here in mockup form) was to have had four engines in tilting wingtip pods, and two in the rear fuselage

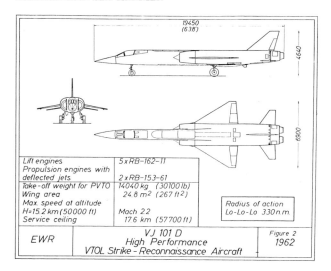

Lift engines	5 x RB-162-11	
Propulsion engines with deflected jets	2 x RB-153-61	
Take-off weight for PVTO	14040 kg (30100 lb)	
Wing area	24.8 m² (267 ft²)	
Max. speed at altitude H=15.2 km (50000 ft)	Mach 2.2	Radius of action Lo-Lo-Lo 330 n.m.
Service ceiling	17.6 km (57700 ft)	

EWR	VJ 101 D High Performance VTOL Strike - Reconnaissance Aircraft	Figure 2 1962

along the ground, and deflected downward (typically through 60 degrees) for unstick, to provide a combination of jet lift and propulsive thrust. Having lifted off at well below its normal stall speed, the aircraft would then accelerate to wingborne flight, and the thrust rotated back to the horizontal. For landing, the aircraft would be much lighter, hence wing lift would not be required to assist jet lift. The aircraft could thus be brought to the hover with jets vertical, as in lightweight VTO.

Professor Theodore von Karman was later to coin the term '*vectored-thrust*' for such engines, and the expression caught on. In mathematics, a vector is something with both magnitude and direction, hence 'vectored' thrust implied that both of these quantities could be changed at will. For performance purposes, a V/STOL engine such as

TOP LEFT
Remarkably similar in configuration to Britain's TSR.2, the Entwicklungsring-Süd VJ101D was to have augmented the lift of five RB.162s by bending the jetpipes of the two RB.153 propulsion engines

Dornier played a leading role in early V/STOL developments. This Do 29 (left) was one of the first vectored-thrust aircraft. It was powered by two 270 hp Lycoming engines, and first flew in December 1958

Designed by Prof Gero Madelung, the EWR VJ101C had two lift engines in the fuselage and four engines in rotatable pods. The 'translating' intakes made possible jet lift at quite high forward speeds

the R-R Pegasus differs from a conventional powerplant only in the sense that the *direction* of its thrust can be varied, hence the term was not really appropriate. For marketing purposes, it was to prove a bad choice, since 'vectored-thrust' seems to be difficult to translate into most foreign languages.

In understanding how vectored-thrust was finally achieved, it is important to appreciate that its success depended on two conditions being satisfied. Firstly, as the thrust line was rotated between the horizontal and the vertical, it had to continue to pass approximately through the aircraft CG. To merely deflect the jets emerging at the rear of a conventional design would produce a very strong pitch control, which could be useful in air combat (and possibly in STO), but it could not produce an aircraft that could hover or perform V/STOL.

Secondly, it was vital that the engine CG should not be substantially ahead of the aircraft CG. In a conventional fighter such as the Hunter, it is approximately true to say that the weight of the engine in the rear fuselage counterbalances that of the pilot, cockpit and operational equipment in the front fuselage. Hence, if the engine were to be placed for any reason in the front fuselage, a normal aircraft layout would be ruled out, since it is impossible to put sufficient equipment in the rear fuselage to balance both the cockpit and the powerplant in front. Had it not been for this restriction on engine location, the single-engined V/STOL fighter might well have appeared some years earlier, since no major invention would have been called for.

Early Concepts

The basic idea of thrust vectoring for V/STOL goes back far beyond the first practical jet engine. On 24 August 1909, less than six years after the Wright brothers' first powered flight, *The Aero* published a letter from Mr C Edgar Simpson, suggesting that aircraft should be powered by fans forcing air through 'curved draught funnels' on either side. For short take-off the two side funnels would be directed toward the earth (Simpson failed to appreciate the need for maximum acceleration), while a fan at the rear would force the machine forwards, the side funnels then lifting it from the ground after a run of a few yards. After reaching a safe height, the side funnels would be turned toward the rear to assist in propulsion, and for landing they would again be directed downwards. Simpson ended his specification by saying that if birds alighted in the manner of existing aeroplanes, they would break their legs or turn over!

What may well have been the first suggestion of vectored-thrust for V/STOL went unheeded, but

The first prototype EWR VJ101C in conventional flight, with wingtip engines horizontal and lift engines closed down. The second aircraft (X-2) had afterburning propulsion engines and marginally exceeded Mach 1.0

in the following year Mr James Robertson Porter applied for a patent covering what we would now call vectored-thrust for airships and maritime vessels. The basic idea was no great advance on Simpson's letter, but the fan was replaced by a radial-flow compressor that discharged air (or water in the case of a ship) through rotatable curved pipes on either side, so that the jets could generate a force in whatever direction was required.

In engineering terms, Porter's scheme was no great invention, but at least the originator (unlike Simpson) understood that the thrust available was so small in relation to the mass of the vehicle that vectored thrust could at that stage have a significant effect on take-off and landing performance (or manoeuvring, for a ship) only in the case of a machine largely supported by some form of buoyancy. There appears to be no evidence that Porter's proposal was ever applied to an airship, but at least one early dirigible (the Vickers HMA N09) had vectored-thrust, the complete powerplants (ie, engines with propellers) being tilted to provide both forward propulsion and low-speed height control. This form of thrust vectoring is still in use today in the Skyship series developed by Airship Industries in the UK.

In his Chadwick Memorial Lecture of 1974, Ralph Hooper (as originator of the P.1127) referred to a letter published in *Flight* in 1911, in which the correspondent suggested that, if the Wright brothers' *Flyer* had had two large flexible ducts mounted behind the propellers, and the ducts were bent through a right angle to point downward, then the aircraft could have taken off vertically. Once again, the concept showed a lack

of understanding of the very modest T/W ratios of aircraft then current, but the idea of thrust vectoring for lift and propulsion was quite clear.

Interest in vectored-thrust then appears to have waned, possibly because the depressing realities of the T/W situation became better appreciated. However, the development of practical turbojet engines in the early 1940s brought renewed endeavours. Here at last were powerful, concentrated jets of gases, that could be turned at will to produce a thrust line to suit any particular phase of flight.

In Germany in 1944 von Wolff made a provisional patent application for thrust vectoring, using 'lattice-like, interconnected turning vanes' or 'swinging, overlapping, ring-shaped pipe segments'. Aside from shortening take-off and landing runs, von Wolff also foresaw the use of thrust vectoring to enhance manoeuvrability. With the ending of the war, the application was taken no further, and it can be argued in the light of earlier publications that it would never have survived the rigorous examination of Munich's *Patentamt*. A collection of patent application extracts subsequently produced by the Allied Control Commission referred to von Wolff's jet thrust vectoring by means of turning vanes on the rear end of the engine, but there is no indication that this extract or the original document had any influence on postwar V/STOL developments.

The Dornier Do 31 V/STOL transport combined two Pegasus vectored-thrust engines with batteries of RB.162 lift engines in wingtip pods. In the production version, the Spey would have replaced the Pegasus

RIGHT
Canadair was a pioneer in tilt-wing V/STOL aircraft. The CL-84 prototype first flew in 1965, and was followed by three CL-84-1s, which were used for operational evaluation by the CAF and US Navy

The VFW 1262 had a centrally-mounted Bristol BS.94 vectored-thrust engine and two RB.162 lift engines. In service it would have operated from special grids, but it is shown here using debris guards

Although there is some doubt whether it completed transitions, the Bell ATV pioneered jet vectoring, with two tilting engines under the wing. A separate engine drove a compressor for reaction controls

Although Hitler's Germany provided the setting for a vast array of advanced aircraft projects, some of which still stagger the imagination, the writer knows of no jet-powered fixed-wing V/STOL flat-riser design before the end of the war. One VTOL flat-riser was under development in 1943 for maritime applications, to provide air defence for merchant ships, but this aircraft was destroyed in an air raid and subsequently abandoned. Designated Focke-Achgelis Fa 269, it was to have been powered by a single BMW 801 radial engine (as used in the Fw 190 fighter), producing 1,900 hp and driving two wing-mounted pusher propellers by means of shafts and gear boxes. For take-off and landing the propellers were to swing down below the wing. The Fa 269 was to have been equipped with two 30 mm MK-108 cannon, and a maximum level speed of 300 kt (556 km/hr) was predicted. In view of the successes achieved by Focke-Achgelis in the helicopter field, the concept might well have worked, although the proximity of the wing to the large-diameter

propellers could have led to vibration problems during transitions and at the hover. A comparable scheme was developed in the postwar years by Dornier, in the form of the Do 29.

Propeller-driven vectored-thrust aircraft were to appear in many forms in the mid-1960s: the Curtiss-Wright X-19A had tilting propellers on the tip of the wing and foreplane, the Bell X-22A had tilting ducted fans, and the Vought XC-142A and Canadair CL-84 had turboprop engines on a tilting wing. However, the world's first jet-powered vectored-thrust aircraft left the ground on 1954 in the form of the Bell ATV (air test vehicle), which had trunnion-mounted J44 engines on either side of the fuselage, under a high-set wing.

The Bell ATV was only a crude technology demonstrator, and it received little publicity, which may suggest that it never completed transitions between jetborne and wingborne flight. In any event, it was soon to be superseded by the same company's X-14, which was a much more practical research tool.

To reduce development costs, the X-14 wing and fuselage were based on those of the Beech Bonanza, and the tail was that of the Beech T-34 Mentor. The powerplant initially consisted of two

It would be difficult to overstate the importance of the Bell X-14 in demonstrating the practicality of thrust vectoring without autostabilizer. It had two engines, exhausting via rotatable cascades

1,750 lb (795 kg) BSE Viper turbojets, but these were later replaced by 2,450 lb (1,110 kg) GE J85s. The first hover was made on 19 February 1957, and the first transition on 24 May 1958.

The engines were mounted side-by-side in the lower front fuselage, their jets emerging under the aircraft CG through two sets of turning vanes mounted at 45 degrees to the engine axis. By rotating the rear set of vanes, the thrust could be vectored between the horizontal and the vertical, turning through an arc that gave each engine an outboard thrust component at intermediate angles. This system of vectoring thus required two engines, so that lateral thrust components could be cancelled out.

The location of the turning vanes below the CG limited pitching moments during transition to acceptable levels, but the fact that the engines were well ahead of the CG severely restricted the development potential of the X-14 concept. To make the aircraft balance properly, the cockpit had to be located well aft, providing a layout that was

incompatible with the design of a high performance combat aircraft. The X-14 could, however, have been developed to the level of a tactical reconnaissance aircraft, and it was later copied in the Yakovlev *Freehand*, two examples of which were shown at Domodedovo in July 1967.

The thrust-vectoring mechanism used on the Russian aircraft appeared to be closer to Pegasus-type nozzles than the twin cascades of the X-14, but *Freehand* retained the limitations inherent in the forward engine location. The aircraft was reportedly tested on the half-deck carrier *Moskva*, but it is noteworthy that a completely different engine arrangement was adopted when it came to developing the Yak-36 *Forger* for extensive operational trials from the *Kiev* class.

To recap, the Bell X-14 was of historical importance as the world's first practical jet-powered vectored-thrust aircraft for research purposes, but its system of vectoring required the use of two engines, and the forward location of the engines ruled out the development of a high-speed combat aircraft on this basis. The X-14 nonetheless encouraged designers to concentrate on vectored thrust at a time when there was widespread doubt over the feasibility of V/STOL for high performance aircraft. However, it left unsolved the riddle of how to produce a vectored-thrust powerplant for a single-engined fighter.

Wibault Gyroptère

The key to the solution of this riddle came from a distinguished French engineer, Michel Wibault, a man with many years of experience in aircraft design, having produced his first fighter in 1917. In the 1920s he had been a pioneer in the use of metal primary structure, then in monoplanes, and later in metal skins. Although he also produced successful commercial aircraft, he is possibly best remembered for his fighters, notably the Wibault 7 parasol-wing of 1925, and the Wibault 72, which made its debut in the following year. The latter remained in service for 10 years, an unusually long time for an aircraft of the period. The Wibault 74 and 75 naval fighters were operated from the carrier *Béarne* until 1934, a number of his fighters were exported to Bolivia and Brazil, and licence production took place in Poland and Britain (for export to Chile, in the latter case).

Wibault spent the war years in the United States, and, following his return to France, established a company in America to exploit his various patents. Precisely how he became interested in vectored-thrust is not known for certain. However, according to one of the several legends concerning the origins of the Harrier programme, Mme Wibault met and talked with Nelson Rockefeller, who advised that, rather than wasting his time promoting a whole raft of inventions that had no great potential, Wibault should try to achieve a major breakthrough in an area where a considerable demand already existed, such as V/STOL aircraft. Those who have been concerned with attempts to market the Harrier tend not to place great credence on this story!

Whether or not this particular legend is true, Wibault conceived the idea of a turboshaft (such as the 8,000 shp Bristol Orion) driving four vectored-thrust centrifugal compressors in the sides of the aircraft fuselage. Vectoring through 90 degrees was achieved simply by turning the casing surrounding each blower. This concept had the advantage that the engine itself could be placed behind the aircraft CG, and that the four jets could produce a ground cushion between them. In such an arrangement the jets spread out on the ground and rise in high energy sheets between the engine nozzles, producing an increase in pressure on the fuselage centre line and spanwise across the wing.

The main disadvantage of the Wibault proposal was that the long shafts and the two gearboxes that took the drive from the engine to the compressors would have been heavy, perhaps unacceptably so. Nonetheless, this was the first-ever concept of a single-engined vectored-thrust V/STOL aircraft. Wibault sketched a combat aircraft around the

powerplant, named it the '*Gyroptère*', and started looking for official support for what would clearly be an expensive development effort.

The *Gyroptère* was rejected by the French authorities and then by those in the US, so in 1956 Wibault took the proposal to the Paris office of MWDP (Mutual Weapons Development Program), a NATO agency that in essence used US Government money to fund new developments in European military equipment for the common good. There the Gyroptère met with some scepticism – it is said to have been named somewhat irreverently 'The Sex Machine' by some US Army representatives – but the head of the Paris office, Colonel (later General) 'Bill' Chapman, thought it might have potential. He accordingly arranged a meeting in Paris in July 1956 between Wibault and Dr Stanley (later Sir Stanley) Hooker, Bristol Aero Engines' technical director, whom Chapman knew through MWDP having funded 75 per cent of the company's Orpheus engine for the Fiat G.91 lightweight close support aircraft. Hooker liked the idea of a single vectored-thrust engine, but was unimpressed by the shaft drive to the four compressors. He returned to the UK, where he tasked his project office with producing a more practical arrangement.

The job of transforming the basic Wibault concept into a practical aero-engine was given to project engineer Gordon Lewis, who is now engineering director (new business) of Rolls-Royce Ltd. Instead of four remotely-driven centrifugal compressors, he proposed a single multi-stage axial-flow fan, mounted directly ahead

Sir Stanley Hooker, as Bristol Aero Engine's technical director, was a key figure in the successful development of the Pegasus. Though now retired, he still works as a consultant to Rolls-Royce Ltd

of the turboshaft, and driven through a reduction gearbox. This arrangement would not only be lighter, but also produce more thrust, due to the higher efficiency of the axial compressor.

As originally conceived, the fan and the turboshaft engine were to have had separate intakes, and the efflux from the fan was to be taken to two rotatable curved ducts in the sides of the aircraft. The hot gases from the turboshaft would simply be discharged aft, as in a conventional turbojet, producing a horizontal thrust component.

As it stood, Lewis' proposal was a comparatively simple three-nozzle powerplant with merely a limited STOL potential, since only the thrust from the fan flow could be vectored. In STO, all the thrust was available for acceleration along the ground, but only the fan flow could produce jet lift and thus reduce unstick speed. Likewise, in landing the jet lift of the fan flow could reduce touchdown speed, but there was little prospect of vertical operation.

Despite the limitations of the revised scheme, a provisional patent application was filed in January 1957, naming Wibault and Lewis as joint inventors. With an eye to minimizing the risks and cost of development, Lewis proposed to use existing engine components wherever possible, basing the initial BE.48 project on an Orion turboprop engine, driving a two-stage fan through the reduction gearbox originally designed to drive a propeller.

However, the reduction gearbox still represented a considerable weight penalty, and it was therefore decided to drive the fan directly by means of a separate power turbine designed to run at a speed that matched the requirements of the fan. It was physically impossible to add a new shaft within the two existing shafts of the Orion, so attention turned to the Orpheus turbojet, which had a single hollow shaft of large diameter. This made it possible to add a new two-stage free turbine at the rear, mounted on a shaft that passed through the middle of the existing Orpheus to drive a front-mounted fan. This fan consisted of three stages of low-pressure compressor taken from the Olympus

Gordon Lewis was responsible for the conception and early development of the BE.53/Pegasus, and was named as joint inventor with Wibault. He is now Rolls-Royce's engineering director (new business)

engine (the engine used in the Vulcan bomber, and in developed form in the Concorde supersonic transport).

The resulting BE.52 was still essentially a STOL engine, with separate intakes for the fan and the Orpheus gas generator, and three nozzles with vectoring only on two. Nonetheless, it offered the prospect of straightforward development and comparatively high T/W.

In the normal course of design refinement, the BE.52 became the BE.53, and then the BE.53/2, which was redesignated Pegasus. However, before discussing how these changes came about, it is necessary to introduce Hawker Aircraft, since the evolution of the engine represented a combined effort by the engine and airframe designers.

Chapter 2
Hawker P.1127
to Harrier

The corridor that linked the various offices of the Hawker design department was lined with photographs of the company's aircraft – invariably successful – dating back to the pre-WWI Sopwith Bat-Boat. In the minds of those who worked there, the distinction between Hawker Aircraft and Sopwith Aviation was purely a matter of financial flute-music: the product line could be traced straight back to the first fighting scout ever conceived, and beyond.

In reality, in 1920 a nimble-footed Sir 'Tom' Sopwith had simply dissolved one company, which was clearly too large to have survived the lean years of peace, and created another of more sensible proportions to take its place. The new company used the principal Kingston premises of the old one (the one-time skating rink in which Sopwith had begun was by the 1950s merely the tool-room for Hawker Aircraft). It was named after its well-known chief test pilot, an Australian called Harry Hawker.

At least for those who worked in the Canbury Park Road offices, the name Hawker was synonymous with fighters, in precisely the same way that the name of Zeppelin was with airships, and the name Ford with cars. Other British companies *dabbled* in fighters from time to time, occasionally with success (eg, the Bristol Beaufighter, de Havilland Mosquito, and Gloster Meteor), but none could rival Hawker's record. Supermarine, after achieving distinction with flying boats and racing seaplanes, had produced the Spitfire, which performed and handled well enough, but was a production engineer's nightmare in comparison with the Hurricane. However successful, the Spitfire had been only a flash-in-the-pan: that company's postwar Attacker had been a nonentity, and the Swift had been a disaster. No other British fighter manufacturer was in the same league as Hawker Aircraft.

Messerschmitt and Focke-Wulf had been worthy adversaries for a time, but they had been on the wrong side, and in consequence had lost their continuity, which was of vital importance in the

fighter game. North American had produced two milestones in fighter development with the P-51 Mustang and F-86 Sabre, but only time would tell whether this young upstart of a company had staying power. In the meantime, Hawker had produced the Hunter, advertised in its day 'The Finest Fighter Aircraft In The World', and was intent in the mid-1950s on designing the next fighter generation for the RAF.

Although the chief designer in the early years of the P.1127 was Roy Chaplin, the technical head of the company was the chief engineer, the late Sir Sydney Camm. In a very real sense, Camm *was* Hawker Aircraft. Born on 5 August 1893, he began his aviation career as a carpenter with Martinsyde in 1914, became a draughtsman with the same company, transferred to Hawker in 1923, and was promoted to chief designer two years later. Combining a natural talent with rapidly growing experience, Camm (and Hawker) went from success to success.

Conservative by nature, his aircraft were products of good, sound design, rather than technological breakthroughs. However, they were also routinely successful, and Hawker Aircraft established a reputation for having been in continuous production with aircraft of its own design for longer than any other manufacturer. Other companies came and went: Hawker Aircraft simply produced extremely good fighters year after year, aircraft renowned for their good looks and excellent handling qualities. In a highly unstable industry, Hawker Aircraft appeared to enjoy a charmed existence, thanks to the magic touch of

TOP RIGHT
One of the greatest fighters of WWI, the Sopwith Triplane could outclimb all its German contemporaries. It was designed to combine manoeuvrability with improved field of view, due to reduced wing chord.

The Bat-Boat was one of the earliest Sopwith aircraft, preceding the Tabloid floatplane that won the Schneider Trophy contest in Monaco in 1914. The link with naval flying continues with today's Sea Harrier

part. Another useful factor was his friendship with succeeding RAF Chiefs of Air Staff, which gave him a deep perception of his launch customer's requirements.

In addition, Sir Sydney had a shrewd appreciation of what it took to have a design organization of hundreds of men constantly striving for perfection, each man convinced that the Hawker team was the best in the world. Part of this group psychology involved having a specially gifted leader who stood apart from the crowd. Although shy and retiring by nature, Camm was willing to ham it up as the eccentric genius, if this was what it took to inspire his draughtsmen to ever greater achievements.

Over the years, the in-house legend grew of Camm being not simply a great designer, but some kind of all-seeing monster, who strode through the design offices, tearing up drawings that displeased him, and demolishing their perpetrators with his acid sarcasm, more especially at the time of the full moon. In reality, it took a great deal of research to find anyone who had actually seen Camm tear up anything, and the legend of his infallibility in turn produced a whole series of stories to the contrary.

It was, for example, commonly held that he had been away on sick leave at the start of the

As a young man, Camm was a leading exponent of aeromodelling in the Windsor area. He is seen here with a canard model, an arrangement that was quite conventional in the pre-WWI period

RIGHT
Sir Sydney in jovial mood at the SBAC Show. Although his constant struggle for perfection made him a demanding leader, he inspired respect and affection among those privileged to work for him

Sir Sydney Camm. From 1925 to the time of his death (12 March 1966), he was responsible to the Hawker board for 52 different aircraft types, of which around 26,000 examples were built. Taking in combination the quality, quantity, and time-span of his products, Sir Sydney was probably the greatest fighter designer of all time. Since the interval between succeeding generations of combat aircraft has now increased to 20–25 years, it is unlikely that his place in aviation history will ever be challenged.

The long-running success story of Hawker Aircraft was undoubtedly due in part to good luck. For example, Sir Sydney would readily admit that the company had private-ventured the Hurricane simply because the design office had nothing else to do at the time. However, there was far more to 40 years of repetitive success than luck alone. Perhaps the most important factor of all was Camm's highly developed ability to recognize good design, whether in the general arrangement drawing of a new project or in the smallest detail

Typical of Camm's elegant designs, the prewar Fury I was the finest biplane fighter of its day. The link with the Hurricane, which began life as the Fury Monoplane of 1933, is evident

BELOW
The Hawker Hurricane (illustrated by a Mk IIB) shot down more enemy aircraft during the Battle of Britain than all other defences combined

Aesthetically one of the finest of Hawker aircraft, the Sea Hawk had serious teething troubles, and was dumped on Armstrong-Whitworth. Indian Navy Sea Hawks are only now being replaced by Sea Harriers.

LEFT
The Hawker Typhoon IB gained an outstanding reputation in the ground attack role, using rockets and cannon in attacks on German armour following the Normandy landings, but initially suffered structural problems.

To some observers the Hunter was the most beautiful and last of the true Hawker fighters. Although designed for the air defence role, it achieved its greatest success in ground attack

Hurricane, the aircraft for which he was best known to the general public. Likewise, the more senior members of the design office took great pleasure in recalling a discarded Camm scheme for the inboard main spar of the Hunter, a massive pin-jointed structure that looked like part of the Forth Bridge, and was basically a manifestation of his limited faith in the stress office's ability to deal with kink loads in bent spar booms.

Perhaps the biggest in-joke within the design department was that *nobody had ever seen 'The Old Man' draw anything!* The one exception to this rule was a scrap of paper that was taped to the wall behind one of the photographs in the project office, and depicted two concentric circles with two kidney shapes between them. This was Camm's scheme for adding extra fuel in the rear fuselage of the Hunter. Those safeguarding this unique product of the master's hand used to emphasize to new members of the office that Camm had not

specified whether the kidney-shaped tanks shown in this fuselage cross-section were to be above and below the jetpipe (represented by the inner circle), or on either side!

Despite the iconoclastic humour, which was invariably directed against the legend and not the man, Camm was probably the best-loved leader in the British aircraft industry, a fact that was borne out by the hundreds of Hawker employees who attended his memorial service on 29 March 1966 at St Clement Danes, appropriately the church of the RAF. He may not have been the man that the public visualized, beavering away at his drawing board to produce the initial designs of the Hurricane, Hunter, and P.1127, but he was a man who successfully guided the company through more than 40 difficult years, staking his reputation on each new project, a man of tremendous natural talent, respected and loved by those privileged to work for him.

Design Organisation

In the mid-1950s Hawker Aircraft's design department had two completely separate drawing offices, one for experimental work and one for production aircraft. This organization had been set up specifically to produce prototypes quickly, the experimental drawing office designing all the details so that they could be made by hand, and the production drawing office then following up (in the case of a successful project) by redesigning all the details for manufacture on proper tooling.

This system had been well suited to the demands of the 1930s and '40s, when the company produced a new project almost every year (and sometimes more frequently), but by the 1950s it was reaching the limit of its usefulness, since the time interval between new projects was rapidly growing. The advantage in quickly producing prototypes was then beginning to be outweighed by the delay in achieving series manufacture. The rigid divorce between the two drawing offices also had the disadvantage that those working in 'experimental' tended to be ignorant of the demands of service operation.

In addition to these two main offices and a drawing office that dealt purely with modifications for in-service aircraft, there was a stress office, and a project office that also covered all aerodynamic work. Although the project office had its own department head, it also had special links with Sir Sydney, who treated 'the young gentlemen of the project office' as his proteges, on whom the future success of the company depended.

Within the secret confines of the project office, the chief engineer fostered a sense of a closed brotherhood of designers. All that mattered was designing fighters: if you had talent, then shortcomings in other areas were of no great consequence. Prime Ministers were only temporary nuisances, and Chiefs of Air Staff were to be pitied for their boring clerical jobs, but anyone who designed fighters for Sir Sydney Camm was a prince among men!

In 1957 there were around half-a-dozen project engineers looking after Hunter development and future designs. All were brash young men, out to make their reputations in fighter design; what they lacked in experience they made up for in self-confidence. In due course, all of them were to make significant contributions to V/STOL development.

At that time three members of the office were concerned with originating projects. Of these, Ron Williams was the best preliminary design man, with an encyclopaedic knowledge of aircraft. John Fozard had a reputation for somewhat complicated multi-engined projects, but was probably the only one of the trio equipped with the indestructible constitution needed for long-term survival in the role of a modern chief designer. Conversely, Ralph Hooper may well have been the one best equipped to supersede Sir Sydney in terms of a talent for good detail design. At that stage Hooper had the reputation of being the bachelor playboy of the office, indulging in such exotic pastimes as gliding, ski-ing and fast cars. In addition to these three, the long-term members of the office were Robin Balmer, the stability and control expert, and Trevor Jordan, his opposite number in the field of performance analysis.

To understand the Hawker design environment of the 1950s, it is necessary to know something of the company's past problems. During the war years the team had suffered a technical blow, when the rear fuselage of the Typhoon was found to be prone to failure at high speed, a fault eventually traced to an unfortunately placed elevator mass balance weight, causing flutter. Since that time the stress office had gone to great lengths to ensure that never again would a Hawker airframe fail. The consequences of this policy were to be seen in the Hunter structure, which weighed around 33 per cent of clean gross weight. (The corresponding figure for the P.1127 was approximately 25 per cent, which was no mean achievement.)

Typical of Camm's conservative approach was the company's long delay in the 1940s in moving from propeller-driven aircraft to jets, leaving Gloster and de Havilland to produce the RAF's first turbojet-powered fighters in the form of the Meteor and Vampire. Meantime, Hawker manufactured the outstanding Sea Fury for RN carrier operation, and exported it to Australia, Burma, Canada, Cuba, Egypt, West Germany, the Netherlands and Pakistan.

To replace the Sea Fury, the RN issued specification N.7/46, to which Hawker responded with the P.1040, which became the Sea Hawk. Aesthetically speaking, this was one of the best of Hawker fighters, and it was innovative in having a bifurcated jetpipe that allowed the maximum

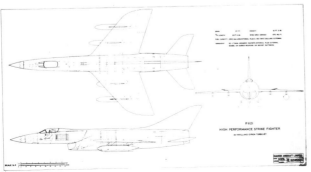

General arrangement drawing of the P.1121 strike fighter. Preliminary design by John Fozard

The Hunter was to have been followed by the P.1121 strike fighter, shown here in mockup form. Powered by a de Havilland Gyron turbojet, it would have been roughly equivalent to the Republic F-105

Airbrush painting of the P.1121

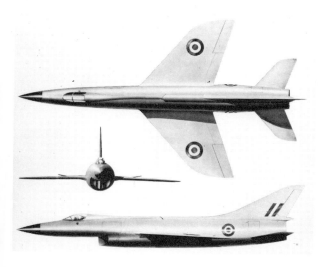

possible fuel volume in the fuselage. However, as a practical service aircraft it brought out the limitations of Hawker's experimental drawing office, a situation exacerbated by the fact that this was the company's first jet aircraft.

By 1948 Hawker had started serious work on the swept-wing Hunter (specification F.3/48) for the RAF, but was soon to be enmeshed with development problems on the Sea Hawk. One example quoted to this writer during his apprenticeship arose from the cannons in the lower front fuselage being fed from shell boxes in the top via chutes rivetted to the structure: any stoppage required major surgery on the airframe. Due to the excess workload generated by these overlapping programmes, Hawker dumped the Sea Hawk on Armstrong-Whitworth (another member of the Hawker Siddeley Group) after building only 35 at Kingston. Though solving the short-term problem, this deprived Hawker of some valuable development experience (a deprivation that probably later accentuated the Hunter problems), and created a precedent for unloading less rewarding projects on to associate companies.

Those who worked for Hawker Aircraft in the mid-1950s remember the Hunter's early days in terms of a thousand screaming agonies. It was the

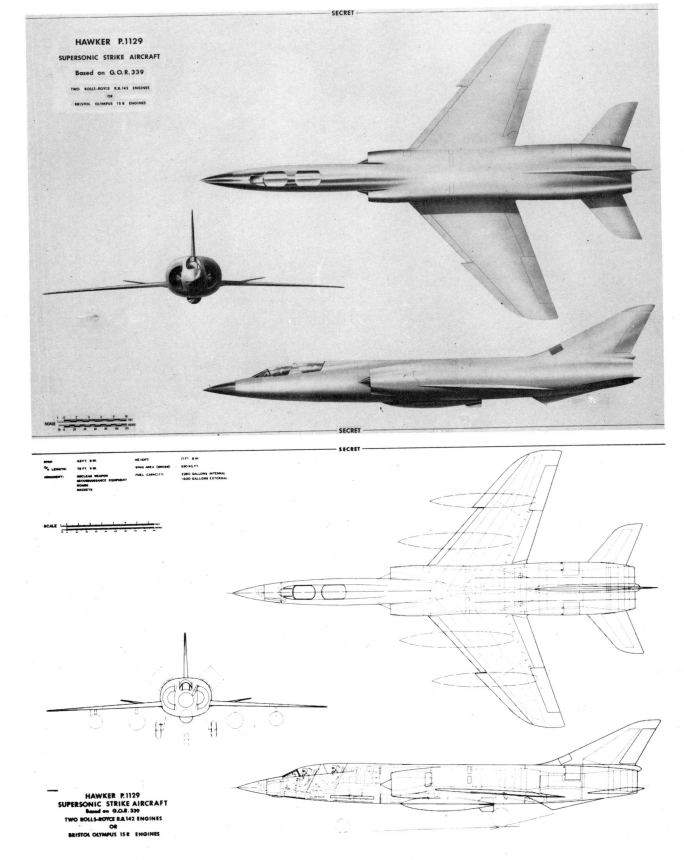

HAWKER P.1129

SUPERSONIC STRIKE AIRCRAFT

Based on G.O.R.339

TWO ROLLS-ROYCE R.B.142 ENGINES
OR
BRISTOL OLYMPUS 15 R ENGINES

Ralph Hooper was in charge of P.1127 activities from its inception in 1957 to 1965, when the P.1127(RAF) was ordered into production. He is now technical director of BAe's Kingston-Brough division

company's first experience of fully developing a jet aircraft, of a surge-prone axial-flow engine, of powered flying controls, and of the new and extremely powerful 30 mm Aden cannon. The result was a two-year delay in the type's entry into service, and a bitter hostility toward Rolls-Royce at Derby, which was held to have let the company down with the early 100-series Avon.

As the Hunter finally entered service, Hawker began design work on its first supersonic project, the P.1103 all-weather interceptor to meet RAF Operational Requirement 329. Armed with two massive wingtip-mounted Red Hebe (later Red Dean) missiles, the P.1103 followed the classic Hawker line of small, single-engined fighters, which put it at a performance disadvantage relative to larger twin-engined projects, due to the weight and drag penalties of the missiles. In any event, Fairey had supersonic hardware in the form of the record-breaking FD.2 delta-wing design, and is believed to have won the OR.329 contest with a scaled-up derivative of this aircraft. However, in 1957 the Sandys Defence White Paper heralded the end of the manned fighter for the RAF, and the expensive OR.329 interceptor was replaced by a low-cost, Firestreak-armed development of the English Electric P.1A research aircraft, which became the Lightning.

Encouraged by the issuing of OR.339 for a Canberra replacement in 1957, and by the availability of de Havilland Gyron engines from the defunct Avro 730 delta-wing fighter programme, Hawker continued to develop the P.1103 theme, firstly with the P.1121 (a John Fozard design), then the twin-engined P.1125, and finally the much larger P.1129 (by Ron Williams), which eventually lost to the ill-fated TSR.2.

Enter The BE.53

The position in 1957 was thus that Hawker Aircraft was fighting hard to maintain its position as one of the RAF's principal suppliers of high performance combat aircraft. In a rapidly-changing world the interceptor appeared to be vanishing down the tubes, but anyone could see that the job of dropping bombs and firing rockets was not about to be taken over by some guided missile. The need to replace the Canberra was well established, and – if the RAF order somehow went elsewhere – there was arguably scope in the overseas market for a less expensive but well-

OPPOSITE
Airbrush painting and general arrangement drawing of the P.1129. Preliminary design by Ron Williams

designed strike fighter that Hawker might private-venture on the strength of the profits from the Hunter programme. In time the RAF might even change its mind and adopt the Hawker approach.

In parallel with the work on supersonic strike fighters, studies continued on possible Hunter derivatives and a target drone project. Some thought was also given to the idea of V/STOL, which was largely being promoted by the late Dr A A Griffith of Rolls-Royce. Fozard and Williams visited Derby and talked with Griffith regarding lift engines. This resulted in various project designs based on the Rolls-Royce concept, including Williams' P.1126, with ten RB.108 lift engines and two Bristol Orpheus for propulsion. However, there was no great enthusiasm for such aircraft at Kingston, and Sir Sydney continued to insist that there had to be a simpler way to achieve the same result, if Hawker Aircraft was to become involved in V/STOL.

It is against this background that the arrival at Kingston of the BE.53 engine proposal has to be seen. Hawker Aircraft became associated with the project as a result of a visit by Sir Sydney to the Paris Air Show at Le Bourget in early June 1957. At the show, VTOL was demonstrated by the SNECMA 'Flying Atar', the French equivalent of the R-R 'Flying Bedstead', ie a crude VTOL platform that could take-off, hover, translate over

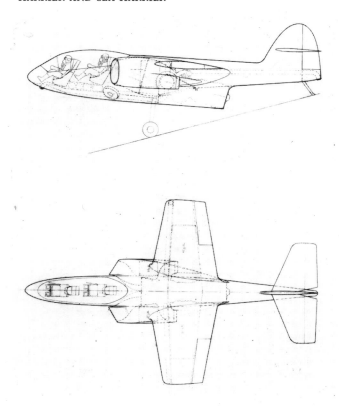

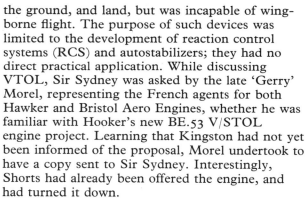

Hooper's general arrangement drawing of the P.1127 Mk 2, dated 5 July 1957. At this stage the hot engine gases still exhausted through a single fixed nozzle; only the two cold nozzles rotated

the ground, and land, but was incapable of wing-borne flight. The purpose of such devices was limited to the development of reaction control systems (RCS) and autostabilizers; they had no direct practical application. While discussing VTOL, Sir Sydney was asked by the late 'Gerry' Morel, representing the French agents for both Hawker and Bristol Aero Engines, whether he was familiar with Hooker's new BE.53 V/STOL engine project. Learning that Kingston had not yet been informed of the proposal, Morel undertook to have a copy sent to Sir Sydney. Interestingly, Shorts had already been offered the engine, and had turned it down.

According to some authors' accounts of the momentous arrival of this document, Sir Sydney took the brochure downstairs to the project office and dumped it on Hooper's desk. In reality, the two offices were on the same floor, and the brochure was simply passed on by Sir Sydney to the project office for circulation and comment. Nobody in the office was impressed by what was clearly an engine of low thrust, with only a limited STOL potential. Nonetheless, Hooper, who was getting bored designing a flying controls test rig for the P.1121, picked up the discarded brochure and decided to see what sort of aircraft could be designed around this new engine.

He was immediately attracted by its simplicity in comparison with the multi-engined VTOL projects of Williams and Fozard. However, even at first glance it was clear that a fighter in the

traditional Hawker mould was not to be produced around a front-fan derivative of the Orpheus, with an anticipated maximum testbed thrust of 11,300 lb (5,125 kg). At this time the engine still had a three-nozzle arrangement with vectoring only on the two fan ducts, which were crude bent pipes. The fan and the Orpheus had separate intakes, and the two engine spools rotated in the same sense, with undesirable implications in regard to gyroscopic effects.

With jet lift available from only half the testbed thrust, it was blindingly obvious that the normal form of take-off would be STO, not VTO. However, it was just conceivable that by the end of the mission, with most of the fuel burned off, the weight would be reduced sufficiently for a vertical landing to be carried out. If the thrust from the three nozzles was to give a purely vertical force, then the aircraft would have to be landed in a pronounced nose-high attitude, with the two rotatable nozzles pointing somewhat ahead of the vertical in order to balance the horizontal thrust component of the rear nozzle.

Such an aircraft would certainly be a far cry from the normal Hawker product line. The best that Hooper could foresee for it was a role as a lightweight reconnaissance/liaison aircraft, which

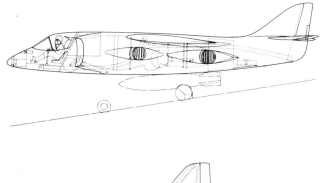

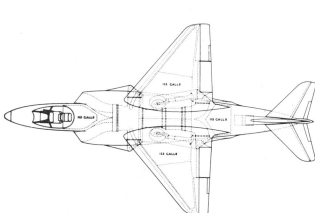

V/s. T.O.L. STRIKE AIRCRAFT

SPAN–26 FT.   WING AREA (GROSS) 184 SQ. FT.
°/A LENGTH–37 FT. 9 INS.   WING L.E. SWEEP – 40°
INTERNAL FUEL CAPACITY – 500 GALLONS
BRISTOL B.E. 53 ENGINE
(WITH WATER METHANOL INJECTION)

might conceivably find a market by virtue of its suitability for front-line basing. In effect it would perform the functions of a light observation helicopter (LOH), but carrying more comprehensive surveillance equipment at far higher flight speeds, enabling it to operate over enemy forces with a reasonable degree of immunity from ground fire. Like the LOH, it would also be suitable for liaison duties, but again with far higher transit speeds.

Hooper's first drawing was of a three-seat aircraft that was mainly remarkable for its 30-degree nose-in-the-air ground attitude. It was referred to as the P.1127 Mk I or High-Speed Helicopter, (HSH). However, weight estimates immediately showed that the HSH was too heavy for the thrust envisaged, so the design was rehashed as a two-seater, redesignated P.1127 Mk II. Dr Hooker visited Kingston on 25 June 1957, when he had his first sight of the Hawker project. He quoted a date for availability of the first flight engine as mid-1959, assuming that financial support for engine development would be forthcoming.

Further study showed that hover capability was still marginal, despite the one-third reduction in payload. Eventually (in Hooper's own words) 'the blinding flash of the obvious occurred', and the aircraft was redesigned around a Hawker-modified BE.53 in which the rear jet was split in two (as on the Sea Hawk) and exhausted through a second pair of rotatable nozzles in the fuselage sides. This

Some way from the P.1127 that flew in 1960, the aircraft is shown here with two fuselage-mounted main undercarriage units (rather than the centreline gear actually used) and undrooped wing

was clearly a more promising concept from a performance viewpoint, although it moved the engine CG forward relative to that of the aircraft. The result was an aircraft that could just be made to balance by placing as much avionics as possible in the rear fuselage, although the situation was later to become critical with the introduction of nose radar in the case of the Sea Harrier.

As with many of the most important engineering concepts, the 'four-poster' arrangement of jets was both simple and obvious. In fact it was so obvious that Bristol's patent agent had included it in the patent specification (No 881662, dated 29 January 1957) as one of the possible forms of the invention, in order to make its legal coverage as comprehensive as possible. However, the drawings showed two hot nozzles at the rear of the aircraft, a clearly impractical scheme.

Dr Hooker and Gordon Lewis must both have been aware of this feature of the patent specification, but evidently attached no practical significance to it, at least in the context of the BE.53. At an engineering level, there is no doubt that the close-coupled four-poster arrangement originated at Kingston. By late July that year, Bristol had nonetheless approved the concept, albeit with reservations to the effect that some

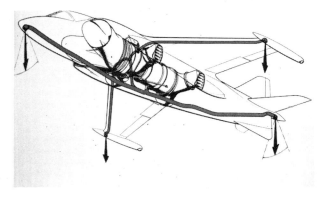

As originally developed, the P.1127's reaction controls operated on a constant-bleed system, and yaw control was obtained by rotation of the pitch puffers in the nose and tail

mixing length might be needed for the gases emerging from the turbine, before the two-way split.

Since the aircraft's aerodynamic controls (ie, tailplane, ailerons and rudder) would be ineffective at low airspeeds, it was planned to have reaction controls in the nose, tail, and wingtips, with the constant flow of compressed air to these attitude control jets divided between the four according to the positions of the control column and rudder bar. In order to minimize the number of control jets, it was decided that yaw control would be provided by lateral rotation of the pitch nozzles in nose and tail. To avoid temperature problems in the RCS, the original scheme was that the compressed air would be bled from the low pressure compressor and taken to the control nozzles through aluminium ducts. However, when it came to designing the system, it was soon found that the large diameter ducts could not be

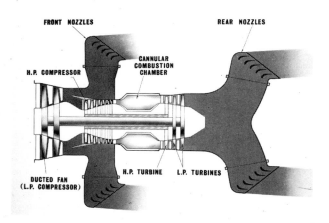

This sectional view of the Pegasus shows the flow of the fan efflux to the front nozzles, and the hot turbine exhaust to the rear nozzles. The shafts contra-rotate to avoid gyroscopic effects

accommodated, hence the change was made to high-pressure air bleed and special high temperature (Nimonic) materials for the system. As indicated above, in their original form the reaction controls in combination used a constant bleed flow from the engine (this was clearly necessary if the pitch 'puffers' were also to provide yaw control), though the flow was progressively reduced to zero as the engine nozzles rotated back to the horizontal during transition to wingborne flight.

Now that the thrust of both the bypass air and the turbine exhaust was available for vectoring (over a 100-degree angle), Hooper began thinking in terms of a modest ground attack and reconnaissance aircraft, rather than an unarmed HSH. The resulting design retained the project office designation P.1127 and the first brochure was produced in August 1957. The aircraft was estimated to take off vertically at a clean gross weight of 8,500 lb (3,855 kg), ie, at a relatively conservative T/W of 1.33. With an external load of 2,000 lb (907 kg), it was calculated to require a take-off ground roll of 600 ft (185 m).

In the same month Hooper proposed to Bristol that the two spools of the engine should be designed to counter-rotate, in order to minimize gyroscopic effects that would seriously complicate the pilot's task. Although previous British experience with the R-R 'Flying Bedstead' and Shorts SC.1 had indicated that autostabilization was essential, the Hawker philosophy was to aim for an aircraft that could (at least in emergency) be flown manually, even if autostabilizer was normally used at low speeds. The first brochure actually claimed that no autostabilizer was required, based on tests with a simple simulator.

Despite the fact that contra-rotation was included in the engine manufacturer's patent, Bristol objected that in practice this would mean reblading the Olympus fan stages used, and foresaw trouble in regard to the intershaft bearings. The airframe manufacturer was thus thwarted in efforts to produce the simplest possible aircraft, but only temporarily.

At this stage Hawker Aircraft began drafting its own provisional patent specification for a single-engined V/STOL aircraft with four rotatable nozzles, contra-rotating spools, and much more efficient nozzles with internal turning vanes. To a large extent this undoubtedly overlapped with the slightly earlier Bristol patent, and it will never be known whether either would have stood up in court, bearing in mind earlier publications dealing with thrust vectoring, and the fact that both the split rear duct and contra-rotation (an idea dating back to a German WWII development) might both have been argued to be obvious features.

Nonetheless, at a time when the first turbofans (then known in the UK as 'bypass engines') were just appearing, and in America General Electric was promoting the idea of single-shaft, aft-fan engines that bore no resemblance whatever to the BE.53, the British concept was genuinely innovative. Within five years, both Pratt & Whitney and R-R were manufacturing front-fan two-spool engines, for both civil and military applications, and the Pegasus no longer appeared to be much of an innovation. Nonetheless, their patents provided both Hawker and Bristol with useful negotiating material, and helped ensure a virtual monopoly of this type of aircraft and engine until the early 1980s. It may be noted that, in the case of the VFW 1262, Hawker Aircraft ceded its rights to Bristol.

In September Col Chapman of MWDP was shown the P.1127 brochure, while visiting the Hawker chalet at the SBAC Show at Farnborough. He is reported to have been generally favourable in his comments, but suggested that double the range was necessary if the aircraft was to have a useful military potential. More range implied more fuel, and thus an increase in take-off weight. For a fixed take-off distance, the dramatic improvement suggested by Col Chapman undoubtedly demanded a significant thrust increase.

Short of a major redesign of the engine, Hooper could visualise this thrust increase only by virtue of water injection. Bristol agreed, and estimated a thrust of 13,300 lb (6,032 kg). The P.1127 was redesigned around this uprated version, mainly to provide extra range by virtue of integral fuel tanks in the fuselage, increasing capacity from 270 to 500 Imp gal (ie, from 1,227 to 2,273 litres). Water injection was added to the Hawker patent, although it had already been used in the D.H. Ghost engine.

Hooper had spent less than six months on the project, but felt that the P.1127 could now offer an acceptable performance, so studies turned to the matter of equipment fit. However, despite the much better technical prospects, there was still no hint of support from the UK Government. In fact, during November Sir Sydney was formally notified by the Controller (Aircraft) that no support for the P.1127 or BE.53 would be forthcoming from HMG, which already had the Shorts SC.1 with its R-R lift engines to provide all the V/STOL know-how required.

Work that had been in progress on the P.1127 by literally two or three people stopped during the last two months of 1957, while Hawker Aircraft concentrated its meagre project resources on the official submission of Ron Williams' P.1129, then being promoted in collaboration with Avro in the OR.339 competition for an RAF Canberra replacement. As Hooper freely admits, if the P.1129 had won that contest, Hawker Aircraft would gladly have abandoned the P.1127 and gone back to the mainstream of high performance

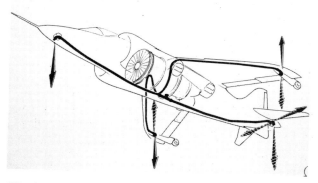

The definitive reaction control system functioned only when the control column or rudder bar was moved from the central position. It had separate yaw puffers, and the roll puffers blew down or upwards

combat aircraft. Aside from the fact that the Canberra replacement appeared to have an assured future, the company was deeply conscious of its loss of supersonic fighter experience resulting from the Lightning order, and was anxious to rectify the situation.

In the event, BAC's TSR.2 won the OR.339 contest (only to be cancelled in 1965), and in January 1958 work therefore resumed at Kingston on the P.1127. During a visit to MWDP in Paris that month, it was learned that there were good prospects for US funding for the engine, but the Americans were suddenly placing increased emphasis on the aircraft having good VTO performance. Since little extra thrust appeared to be on the cards, Hawker attention turned to weight saving, and the aircraft was once again redesigned to be smaller, being redesignated P.1127B.

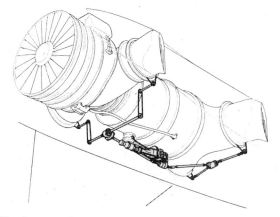

The four nozzles of the Pegasus are rotated together by duplicated air motors powered by engine bleed air, the drive being taken through a system of shafts, bevel gears, chains and sprockets

Unknown to Hooper and his colleagues, the decision had meantime been taken at Bristol to redesign the engine to produce 13,000 lb (5,895 kg) of thrust without recourse to water injection. This was to be done by replacing the existing Olympus stages with a new two-stage transonic fan mounted directly on the front of the Orpheus, shortening the engine and deleting the need for separate intakes. The BE.53/2 thus became a conventional front-fan high-bypass engine, though still with four rotatable nozzles. Since the fan was to be designed from scratch, the main objection to contra-rotation was removed.

Aside from providing more thrust, the new fan also reduced the specific fuel consumption (SFC) of the engine, hence internal fuel could be reduced from 500 to 430 Imp gal (ie, from 2,273 to 1,955 litres). Working through the weekend to finish the latest drawings to be presented to Col Chapman on 24 March 1958, Hooper found that the aircraft's frontal area could be reduced substantially if the engine's gearbox and accessories (ie pumps and generators) were moved from underneath to the top of the casing, where they fitted in neatly ahead of the wing structural box. This feature was later to be added to the Hawker patent specification.

An airbrush painting of the P.1127 in definitive prototype form, with cropped-delta wing, sharply anhedralled to tip-mounted outriggers. The wing and the small, flat tailplane had to be redesigned

By now the project was becoming more serious, and it had to be accepted that a conventional undercarriage was out of the question, since the hot jets of the rear nozzles would strike the tyres of the main gear. The decision was therefore taken to adopt a centre-line undercarriage with outriggers on the wingtips, a novel arrangement for a small combat aircraft. Heavy bombers such as the Boeing B-47 and B-52 had used 'bicycle' undercarriages, in which the aircraft's weight was distributed equally between front and rear, making it impossible to rotate the aircraft for take-off. The P.1127 undercarriage initially had two-thirds of the weight on the main (rear) leg and roughly one third on the noseleg. This was later to be described by company salesmen as a 'zero-track tricycle' to make the distinction from a bicycle gear, but the fact remained that the aircraft could not be rotated in STO (ie, the tailplane did not have the power to pull the nosewheel off the ground for unstick), hence it had to have a nose-high ground attitude.

Aside from its bulbous appearance, which arose from the large diameter of the BE.53 and the need for a short fuselage to reduce weight, and its outrigger undercarriage, the other unusual feature of the P.1127 was its cropped delta wing planform. Like the short fuselage, this was dictated by the need to minimize structure weight. A highly-tapered wing naturally gives the greatest depth where strength is needed most, ie toward the wing

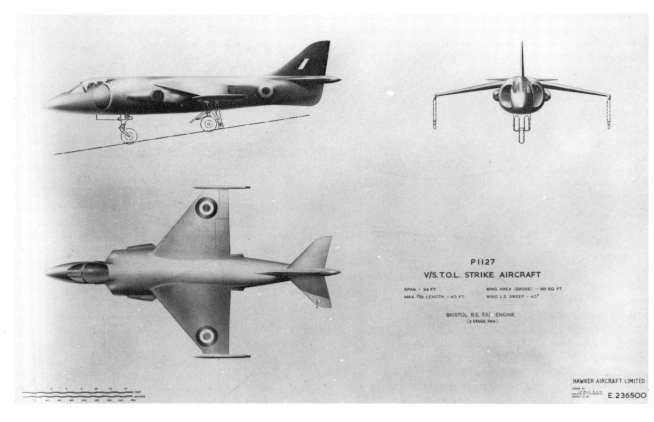

P 1127
V/S.T.O.L. STRIKE AIRCRAFT

SPAN - 24 FT.   WING AREA (GROSS) - 185 SQ. FT.
MAX O/A LENGTH - 40 FT.   WING L.E. SWEEP - 40°

BRISTOL B.E. 53/ ENGINE
(2 STAGE FAN)

HAWKER AIRCRAFT LIMITED

E.236500

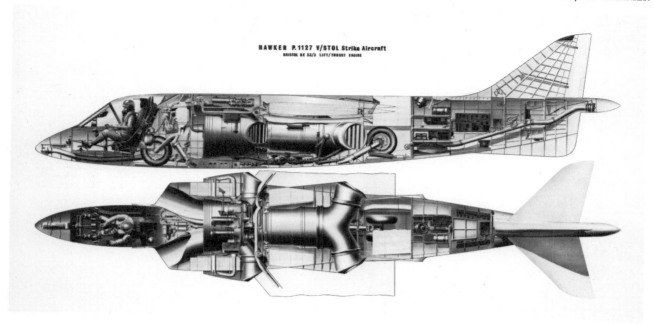

HAWKER P.1127 V/STOL Strike Aircraft
BRISTOL BE 53/3 LIFT/THRUST ENGINE

Inboard profile of the P.1127, showing the reaction control ducting, the undercarriage retracting in front of and behind the engine, the rear fuselage avionics bay, and the engine accessories ahead of the wing box

root, hence weight is minimized. No-one questioned the weight-saving properties of a cropped delta, but everyone in the project office recognised the aerodynamic risks associated with high taper. Short outboard chords implied high local lift coefficients, and hence a tendency to tip-stall.

To such criticism Hooper replied that 'If *Douglas* can get away with it' (referring to the A-4 Skyhawk, which had first flown in 1954), '*we* can get away with it'. Most designers of combat aircraft in the mid/late 1950s had been influenced by 'Ed Heinemann's Hot-Rod', which was a remarkable example of weight saving, resulting in a warload-radius performance that the US Navy had anticipated would call for a much larger aircraft. However, Hooper had glossed over the fact that the A-4 had no outrigger fairings on the wingtips, and relied on leading edge slats (not used on the P.1127) to achieve acceptable lift characteristics. Only many years later was the Hawker project office to see data on A-4 maximum lift coefficient. It was immediately clear that the A-4 also relied for its flying qualities on a relatively low wing loading, something else that the P.1127 did not have. The cropped delta wing of the P.1127 was to prove completely unacceptable.

One useful function performed by this wing was to support the outriggers. The pronounced anhedral of the original wing was motivated by the desire to limit outrigger length, but the need for

this droop was later confirmed by wind tunnel tests. It was, in fact, increased by two degrees in the design of the Kestrel of 1965.

Intensely conservative by nature, Sir Sydney voiced fears about the strength of the outriggers: '*They'll break off like ruddy carrots, I tell you*'. In the event, although designed to withstand purely empirical loads, the outriggers have performed quite well. One was lost due to shimmy in a P.1127 taxiing run, and they are occasionally broken in rough vertical landings, but they have been far less of a problem than he feared.

With its revised engine, centre-line undercarriage with outriggers, and cropped delta wing the project became the P.1127C, presentations on which were given to MWDP in Paris in the spring of 1958. Back at Kingston, a simple model was constructed, and supplied with high pressure air to investigate ground effects in VTOL. This led to experiments with underfuselage strakes to produce a positive ground cushion, an effect that was later to be achieved on the production Harrier by means of the Aden gunpods, and to be considerably amplified for the AV-8B.

It was to be a year of mixed fortunes for the programme. The good news was that the engine was to go ahead, with Bristol funding 25 per cent of development, and MWDP the remainder. Four flight test and two bench test engines were to be produced. The bad news was that Air Ministry persisted in the view that the P.1127 was of no interest to the RAF, unless a supersonic interceptor derivative could be developed. Some encouragement should have come from the fact that the vectored-thrust Bell X-14 made its first successful transitions in June, but Kingston was

An early blowing model, used to investigate ground proximity effects. Such models were employed to assist in the design of underfuselage strakes to improve ground cushion and reduce hot gas reingestion

not to hear of this for some time. More significant was the fact that Air Ministry persuaded Hawker to drop the P.1121, which threatened to become a low-cost alternative to the TSR.2. With nothing else to do, the experimental drawing office began work on the P.1127 under company funding. Although there was no British requirement for the aircraft, the Ministry of Supply indicated that Hawker models could be tested in the wind tunnels of the Royal Aircraft Establishment, Farnborough. For better or worse, the P.1127 had been launched!

In early 1959 came the first hint of possible government support for two prototype P.1127s, and in March the Hawker Siddeley board committed the company to build these aircraft, in expectation of contractual cover from the Aircraft Research branch of the Ministry of Supply. In the same month the first issue was produced of GOR.345 for an aircraft to replace the Hunter in the ground attack and reconnaissance roles from 1965 onwards, although this was not to reach Kingston until April.

In July Hooper and Marsh visited NASA Langley (Virginia), inspected the Bell X-14, and were assured that transitions were feasible without autostabiliser. Even more helpful to the Hawker cause was an offer by the late John Stack, a director of the establishment, to build and test a one-sixth scale free-flight model of the P.1127, and a transonic model with jets represented by steam produced from hydrogen peroxide. In view of the important role that the free-flight model was to play in the programme, it is perhaps worth emphasising that this work at NASA was funded by the USAF, not to advance the P.1127, but to keep the US abreast of V/STOL developments and to strengthen correlation between NASA model tests and successful V/STOL aircraft, which in 1959 were in short supply.

While work on these models proceeded at a staggering pace (Stack having ordered round-the-clock three-shift working), the construction of the two prototype P.1127 airframes continued at Kingston, and engine development went ahead at Bristol. The BE.53/2 or Pegasus 1 of 9,000 lb (4,082 kg) thrust had its first run on the testbed in September 1959. In the following month the Ministry of Aviation awarded Hawker a holding contract to cover airframe design work then in progress, to the extent of £75,000! After more than two years of work, government money was dribbling in.

Late in 1959 the first wind tunnel test results became available from RAE Farnborough, showing measurements of stability in partially-jetborne flight, ie with the jets deflected below the longitudinal fuselage datum. Having seen the majority of V/STOL projects fail, it now appeared that the P.1127 (then less than a year from first lift-off) was doomed to the same fate. It was obvious that the aircraft was highly unstable in pitch due to the downwash produced at the tailplane by the inclined jets emerging from the sides of the centre fuselage. Everyone in the project office had seen pitch-up characteristics, but nobody had seen anything remotely resembling this. At the end of 1959 the future for the programme appeared very bleak indeed. If the NASA free-flight tests bore out what the Farnborough tests appeared to suggest, then someone would have to think very hard before risking a test pilot in the P.1127.

The Full-Scale Tunnel (FST) at Langley had been built in the 1930s to carry out aerodynamic measurements, not on models, but on real aeroplanes. These were mounted on streamlined pylons in an open working section 30 ft (9.15 m) high and 60 ft (18.30 m) wide. Air was sucked past the specimen by propellors, and recirculated around return passages on either side of the working section. By 1960 the FST was rarely used for such tests: aircraft had grown too big, and its maximum airspeed of 56 mph (90 km/hr) made its results non-representative.

Instead, NASA had found a new use for the FST's massive open working section. Here was a means to assess directly the handling qualities of unusual aircraft, without the lengthy analyses based on conventional measurements from a fixed model. A scale model could be provided with propulsion and controls, and its handling characteristics assessed without risking a single life. Operationally, the FST staff was divided into two teams: the 'space' element (testing re-entry vehicles), and the V/STOL element under Marion McKinney.

For this crucial test a one-sixth scale model of the P.1127 had been made in balsa wood, powered by contra-rotating fans in the centre fuselage, the fans being tip-driven by jets of air supplied down a flexible hose at 300 psi (21 kg/cm²) which also powered the reaction controls. The original plan was to ballast the model to reproduce the aircraft's moments of inertia to an appropriate scale, and to equip it with proportional controls. In the event, the model engine was just barely powerful enough to sustain the 43 lb (19.5 kg) model at the hover, hence ballast plans were abandoned, the undercarriage removed, and the electrically-controlled proportional actuators replaced by simple pneumatic 'flicker' controls.

McKinney had been shown the results of the British static wind tunnel tests, but (being at that stage far more experienced in V/STOL

Marion ('Mac') McKinney was in 1960 responsible for the tests at NASA Langley that proved that the P.1127 could be flown successfully through transition without the use of autostabilizer

Artist's impression of the transition tests of the P.1127 model in the NASA (Langley) Full-Scale Tunnel. As tunnel speed increased, the model was flown through an accelerating transition, while remaining roughly stationary

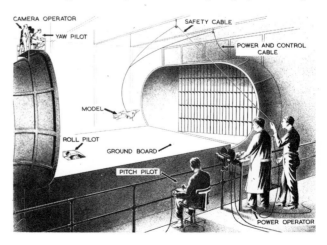

'Bill' Bedford, then chief test pilot of Hawker Aircraft, was responsible for flight trials of the series until 1967, being succeeded in turn by Hugh Merewether, Duncan Simpson, John Farley and 'Andy' Jones

The first prototype P.1127 on the grid that ducted engine gases away from the aircraft, reducing hot gas reingestion and induced downwash, thus increasing the weight at which it could be hovered

characteristics than anyone at Kingston) attached little significance to them. Attempts at accelerating transitions began on 1 February 1960, the aim being to hold the model in a roughly fixed position as the tunnel speed was increased from zero to maximum. One man controlled tunnel speed, another jet angle, and three 'pilots' flew the aircraft in roll, pitch, and yaw.

In the words of the subsequent report, 'transitions were immediately successful. The practicality of slow transitions from hovering to wingborne flight was demonstrated over a wide range of angles of attack and flap settings'. In essence, the pitch instability in transition could be overcome by means of powerful controls for the short period of time needed to attain flying speed. The NASA findings nonetheless called attention to poor directional stability at high angle of attack (AOA). The emphasis in the report on slow

transitions underlined the fact that the air in the FST takes time to accelerate: a more accurate representation of quick transitions was obtained in the summer using an outdoor rotating crane rig, but with the same model.

Thus encouraged, Hawker chief test pilot A W 'Bill' Bedford and his deputy Hugh Merewether visited the States in March 1960 to gain some background experience for the V/STOL testing that was to commence later in the year. The first BE.53/3 or Pegasus 2 of 11,000 lb (4,989 kg) had run on the testbed in February, and prospects were improving, although thrust would clearly be marginal.

Both pilots had done some preliminary helicopter training on a Hiller UH-12C at Luton during February. Before reaching the X-14 (on which they were both scheduled to fly), they gained experience on a variable-stability Sikorsky

S-51 helicopter at Langley, and on a V/STOL simulator at Moffett Field (NASA Ames, California). This gave them a proper appreciation of the control sensitivities needed in V/STOL, although the immediate result at Kingston was limited to making provisions to change the control gearing of the P.1127. Bedford now looks back on this experience as 'a pearl of great price', an invaluable opportunity to get 'mentally calibrated' in terms of aircraft response per unit of stick movement.

Merewether had done very well on the simulator, and it may be suspected that NASA was also influenced by the fact that he was the younger of the two, and presumably quicker in his responses. In any event, he was given first flight on the X-14, got into a pilot-induced oscillation (PIO) close to the ground, and broke the undercarriage. Luckily, the X-14 was due to be

grounded for an engine change, and NASA took the accident very well. In Bedford's eyes, it taught both of them the importance of high control sensitivity in unautostabilized flight, especially in roll. It also reinforced the correctness of the Hawker philosophy, ie a single-channel, limited authority auto-stabilizer, but an aircraft that in emergency could be flown manually. This went directly against British experience with the Flying Bedstead and SC.1, which suggested that the only approach was to have a full-authority, triple-channel autostabilizer.

Meanwhile, the company was invited to tender for the manufacture of four development batch (DB) aircraft, although the two prototypes were not funded until 22 June 1960. On July 15th the first prototype was delivered from Kingston to the Hawker airfield at Dunsfold, where the first flight engine arrived in September. The first tethered hover took place on 21 October 1960. The P.1127 was off the ground at last.

Into The Air

It had not been a case of love at first sight. Bedford recalls thinking 'What an ugly brute!' and 'Fancy trying to make friends with a thing like that!' Ironically, the company almost lost XP831 before it ever left the ground, when a fire started from a fuel leak after an engine run in an enclosed pen on the airfield. Following that incident, engine runs were done in the open, so that there was better access to and from the test site.

For the first tests the Pegasus 2 was still producing only 11,300 lb (5,125 kg), so the aircraft was stripped of its pitot head, undercarriage doors, outrigger leg fairings, radios, ram air turbine (RAT), braking parachute, airbrake, and air conditioning equipment. Thus lightened, it weighed 9,243 lb (4,192 kg), ie basic weight plus pilot. It was given 400 lb (180 kg) of fuel per side, which was just enough for three minutes at maximum thrust.

On the historic occasion of the first tethered hover, the chief test pilot had his right leg in plaster as a result of a motoring accident. Bedford happens to be an extremely fast driver, but it has been as a passenger that he has sustained both his serious accidents: one in India, and this one in Germany. However, in view of the importance of the event, he had been given special clearance on the basis of 'Fit, civil test pilot, tethered hovering only'. This was soon to be amended to 'Free hover, but not more than four feet (1.22 m) off the ground', or such is Bedford's recollection.

He also remembers 'a tiny cockpit – like putting a glove on', with the centre instrument panel strangely occupied with the vital engine and fuel gauges, ie jetpipe temperature (JPT), fan RPM, oil pressure, and port and starboard fuel contents. He recalls the smell of oil and of the hot metal of the RCS, an odour 'rather like some WWII German aircraft'. The cockpit was noisy, with a high frequency whine from the engine, but there were no jet disturbance effects in hovering over the grid (a device that channelled the hot exhaust gases away, rather than allowing them to spread over the ground, and thus simulated conditions in free air).

The tethers were frustrating: it was impossible to control the aircraft properly, and there was little chance to refine techniques in the three minutes available. After 21 tethered hops (some without autostabilizer), untethered hovering began on 19 November 1960, just after the contract for the four DB aircraft had been signed. Despite all the constraints, Bedford and Merewether were learning. For example, they learned the importance of lifting off in a level attitude (at one stage XP831 was 'cavorting round the nosewheel like a drunken cow'), and the need for non-linear throttle gearing, to vary the sensitivity between hover and conventional flight.

They had no radio altimeter, no low-speed ASI, no sensitive VSI. For height information they

An early tethered hover by XP831, the first historic lift-off apparently having gone unrecorded by the official company photographer. Note the bellmouth intake, and the absence of undercarriage doors

Another early hover, in this case untethered, the cable at left being for communication purposes. The 'Meccano' extensions to the outriggers were to ensure a level liftoff, minimizing the lateral drift

relied on visual cues, and therefore they stayed low. Thrust was marginal in the extreme: VTO was possible only from the grid, not from a solid surface, which would have allowed hot air to recirculate to the intakes, and produced more downwash over the airframe due to the entrainment effect of the jets spreading over the ground. As Bedford recalls, 'If you were at the hover and were harsh with the rudder, it would settle back on the grid; you had to have height, even for a gentle turn. We would have liked much more RCS power, but (with more engine bleed) couldn't have got off'. Take-off performance improved slightly when the RCS was changed to a demand system, so that air was bled from the engine only if the stick or rudder bar was moved from the neutral position.

The first conventional flight was made on 13 March 1961, with normal intake lips in place of the bell-mouth used to improve engine performance at the hover. Without reference to Bedford, someone wrote a press release quoting him as saying that XP831 had 'handled beautifully and has great potential'. He actually felt that 'it was ideal for a test pilots' school: a lot of vibration and buffet. It had wing drop, engine restrictions, was short of stability, and had a nose-down pitch due to flap deflection. Its only good points were that it handled beautifully in roll, and had good

acceleration.' So much for press releases!

In fairness to the public relations (PR) manager, it must be added that in 1960 the company hoped to sell a production form of the P.1127 to meet the RAF's OR.345. Presentations emphasized that the prototype was been 'designed from the outset as a combat aircraft'. In reality this only meant that it had been stressed to 8G: it had no armament provisions, and was a servicing nightmare.

The second prototype (XP836) made its first flight on 7 July 1961, using CTOL. There followed three months of tests, in which XP831 was gradually accelerated from VTO to speeds up to 95 knots (176 km/hr), while XP836 was flown progressively slower from conventional flight speeds down to partially jetborne flight. In time the aircraft had been evaluated throughout the transition speed range without encountering any serious problems, and on 12 September 1961 the first complete transitions from jetborne to wingborne flight and back again were made on XP831 by Bedford, with Merewether duplicating each sortie in turn. In Bedford's words, 'We felt that at last we were getting somewhere'.

Despite the NASA free-flight model tests and the relative ease of transition flying, this phase of the trials undoubtedly contained a large element of risk. The Ministry of Aviation wanted the exploratory tests on the two aircraft analysed before any attempt at a complete transition was made, but Hawker went ahead regardless, later excusing the action on the grounds that Bedford had found himself accelerating so fast that it seemed safer to continue the transition than to slow down! It is relevant to note that the zero-zero ejection seats that we now take for granted were not to appear for several years. The initial trials were done with a seat that would save the pilot from a zero-height ejection, but only if the wings were level and the aircraft was doing at least 90 knots (167 km/hr). As Bedford says, 'It didn't do to have too much imagination'.

Developing The Breed

The first transitions were followed by STO tests (the first on 28 October 1961), which demonstrated that a relatively short ground run made it possible to lift far heavier disposable loads than in VTO, due to the combination of wing lift and jet lift. It was probably in this period that journalists began writing that the P.1127 could achieve very little from VTO because of the high fuel consumption in this mode of operation, a story that dogs the Harrier to this day. The truth is that the fuel consumed in VTO is a very small amount; what limits VTO payload and radius is simply the fact that VTO weight does not benefit from wing lift, relying purely on jet lift provided by the engine.

By late 1961 it was clear that Hawker had the basis for a modest, practical V/STOL military aircraft, although the prototypes were short of thrust and RCS power, and for conventional flight had an unsatisfactory wing and suffered from pitch-up. In due course the pitch-up was cured by drooping the tailplane, partly to reach a more favourable downwash region, but also to benefit from a sidewash found in tunnel tests. The wing was improved by the addition of vortex generators, and then went through a multi-stage redesign programme, leading to a completely new wing for the Kestrel and a far more advanced one for the Harrier.

In late 1961 OR.345 was withdrawn, the RAF supporting instead the draft NATO NBMR-3 requirement for a supersonic V/STOL strike fighter. The P.1127 was therefore pushed into the background, while for the next three years Hawker design efforts were concentrated on more advanced forms of V/STOL. However, while the designers were working on new projects, the factory was working on the DB aircraft (and later the Kestrels), and the fundamentals of V/STOL flying

The second prototype carried out conventional flight trials and approached jetborne flight from the high-speed end. It was lost in December 1961 following in-flight separation of a 'cold' nozzle

RIGHT
This photograph of the second aircraft illustrates the cropped-delta wing planform and outrigger fairings, which combined to produce severe buffeting at comparatively small lift coefficients

were being explored in greater depth.

Rather than attempt a comprehensive record of all the modifications that were made to the aircraft in the early 1960s, the following account discusses only the main events of the flying programme, and how the principal technical problems were overcome in the course of developing the breed.

The first crash came on 14 December 1961, when Bedford was making flutter checks near Yeovilton in XP836 with Merewether flying chase. The first aircraft had done the backbone of the work, and was regarded with some affection, but XP836 was felt by the pilots to be 'hostile – never a very friendly aeroplane', hence its loss was less of a blow than if it had been XP831. Bedford had been flying at 1,000 ft (300 m) and 550 knots (1,020 km/hr), and was climbing through 8,000 ft (2,400 km) when he heard a sudden roaring noise and felt some tendency to roll. The aircraft decelerated and got extremely rough, so he decided to make a precautionary landing at Yeovilton.

At 170 knots (315 km/hr) and 200 ft (60 m), full aileron would not hold the wings level, so Bedford applied power to regain speed, but this worsened it, and he ejected with the aircraft in a 30 degree roll attitude. At the time it seemed as though something drastic had happened inside the engine (eg, some form of bearing failure), but a few days later a farmer found the front left-hand nozzle remote from the accident, and the affair was explained. This fibreglass nozzle had evidently failed in flight, reducing thrust significantly and allowing the fan flow to blow on the deflected wing flap, giving a strong rolling moment. Bristol promptly began making new nozzles in stainless steel.

If there was any criticism of Merewether, who might conceivably have saved XP836 by examining the port side of the aircraft from his Hunter, his reputation was re-established by a remarkable forced landing that he made at Tangmere on 30 October 1962. The aircraft (XP972) was the first of the DB, and had its maiden flight on April 5th of that year. On entering a hard turn, the engine had suddenly lost power and caught fire. All aircraft of the P.1127 series (like the F-104 Starfighter) glide like bricks, but Merewether managed to reach the runway. The undercarriage had been blown down by the emergency air system but failed to lock, so it collapsed on touchdown and the aircraft was severely damaged. However, the pilot's brave and skilful action had saved the engine for examination. It transpired that, under gas and 'g' loads the titanium HP stator and rotor blades had come into contact and started a fire, which left a gaping hole in the casing. The Pegasus stators were subsequently cut back to avoid any repeat.

Bedford carried out the world's first high performance V/STOL trials from an aircraft carrier on 8 February 1963, the ship being HMS *Ark Royal* and the aircraft XP831. In these preliminary tests no serious problems were encountered, and it was found that height could be judged more accurately than over land, due to the proximity of the ship's island.

Bedford and XP831 were in the news again on 16 June 1963, when they made an extremely heavy vertical landing at the Paris Air Show. It was later concluded that a piece of grit had jammed a valve in the pneumatic system that controlled the angle of the engine nozzles, causing the nozzles to rotate aft and thus reduce jet lift. The aircraft was repaired (XP831 now rests in the Camm Hall of the RAF Museum at Hendon), but the crash – like another one that occurred many years later during a Middle East sales tour – did nothing to help market prospects.

The Pegasus 3 of 13,500 lb (6,122 kg) was fitted to the last three DB aircraft (XP976, 980, and 984), although XP984 which first flew on 13 February 1964, was soon to have the 15,500 lb (7,030 kg) Pegasus 5 developed for the Kestrel. Whereas the step from the Pegasus 2 to 3 had been achieved by an additional stage for the HP compressor and turbine, the Pegasus 5 was a redesigned engine with a new three-stage fan, air-cooled blades for the first turbine stage, an annular combustion chamber, inlet guide vanes (IGV) deleted from the fan, and variable-angle IGV added to the compressor. It first ran in June 1962, and by 1965 (when the Kestrel trials were held) it had a life of 50 hours, compared to 30 for the Pegasus 3.

A pair of Pegasus 5s was used in the prototype of the Dornier Do 31 V/STOL transport, in combination with R-R lift engines in wingtip pods, although the production aircraft was to have had a vectored thrust version of the more economical R-R Spey. The Do 31 was the world's first technology demonstrator for a high-speed V/STOL transport aircraft.

The Pegasus 5 highlighted two points. Firstly, the design of the Pegasus had emphasized high T/W at the expense of fuel economy, hence there was no other application for the engine, and the Harrier programme had to bear the full cost of Pegasus development. Secondly, it illustrated the never-ending struggle for sufficient thrust, the performance gain from each stage of Pegasus development soon being lost in weight growth of the aircraft. This had no serious consequences in the 1960s, since the Pegasus roughly doubled in thrust over a period of ten years, but the sudden ending of thrust development with the advent of the Pegasus 11 was later to become the cause of some concern.

Kestrel Evaluation

Returning to the subject of the last DB aircraft, XP984 in effect became a prototype for the nine Kestrel operational evaluation aircraft, the go-ahead for which had been received in May 1962. In addition to the Pegasus 5, XP984 had a new swept wing with integral-machined skins and far better lifting characteristics, a drooped tailplane, modified RCS (the tip puffers could now blow either up or down), and a 9-inch (23 cm) extension spliced into the rear fuselage, which was later to provide space for a water tank on the Harrier. In

TOP RIGHT
The P.1127 needed several major wing modifications to achieve satisfactory handling in conventional flight, whereas V/STOL development was straightforward. The third aircraft is seen with the 'poor-man's streamwise tip' (PMST)

This cutaway view of the Dornier Do 31 V/STOL transport shows the complexity involved in the use of separate lift engines. In the event, V/STOL fighters at dispersal are supplied by ground vehicles

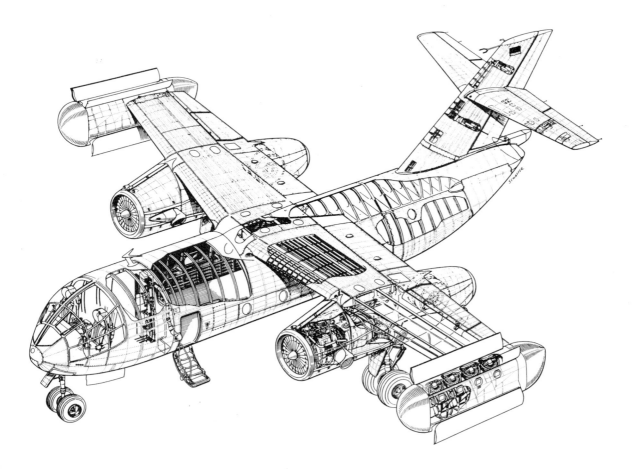

addition to these changes, the Kestrel had a forward-oblique camera in the nose, two wing pylons with provisions for drop tanks, a simple gunsight, an extended span tailplane, and inflatable intake lips to improve vertical performance. However, these rubber lips tended to tear in high-speed flight, and were soon phased out. The Kestrel had no autostabiliser and no weapons provisions.

The Tripartite Agreement between the UK, US, and West Germany to fund the Kestrel squadron was signed in Paris on 16 January 1963. The unit was formed in 1964 under the command of Wg Cdr (now Air Commodore) David Scrimgeour, with three other RAF pilots, two from the *Luftwaffe*, one USN, two US Army, and one from the USAF. Following an introductory course on Hunters and helicopters, the pilots converted to the Kestrel early in 1965 at Dunsfold, and began operations at RAF West Raynham in Norfolk on April 1st.

Although one Kestrel (XS 696) was written off that same day, when a US Army pilot ground-looped in an attempted take-off with brakes applied, the trials were generally successful. They lasted nine months, in which time 938 sorties were flown, mainly to test the feasibility of dispersed operations from grass fields, with various types of surface protection evaluated for the first time. These included metal planking and a shocking pink fibreglass concoction that was sprayed over the grass. Among many other practical lessons, the Kestrel trials showed that the roughness of grass fields was best assessed by driving a Land Rover across them at 40 mph (64 km/hr), and that ground erosion problems could largely be avoided by 'rolling vertical' operations, eg landing with a forward speed of around 40 knots (74 km/hr). Since the standard form of operation was STO and VL (more recently abbreviated to STOVL), the landing phase clearly had more potential hazards to to both surface and aircraft, and this technique was an important step in validating the P.1127 concept.

On the completion of the trials, Britain retained two Kestrels, but Germany declined the opportunity to use its three aircraft in further tests, selling them to the US, which consequently acquired a total of six. Designated XV-6A, they were used for miscellaneous V/STOL tests, and over a period of several years were mostly grounded following minor accidents.

Technical Problems

The Kestrel trials of 1965 undoubtedly strengthened the case for the RAF having an operational derivative of the P.1127, but they had little impact on the overseas market. It was still an aircraft of very limited capability (the nose camera and the two pylons said it all), and it was still extremely expensive, if only due to its disproportionately powerful engine. Moreover, by 1965 the prospect of a nuclear war in Europe had largely given way to the concept of a 'graduated response' in which all-out war would only follow a period of escalating conventional warfare.

Nonetheless, the year of these trials was also the year in which the P.1127 (RAF) was given the go-ahead, two years later being renamed the Harrier (a name originally planned for the P.1154). Before proceeding with the story of how the RAF came to order this aircraft, it may be worthwile to review the main V/STOL problems that had been encountered in the early days of the P.1127 programme, and how these were eventually overcome.

To put these problems into perspective, the initial feeling at Hawker following the successful transitions of 1961 was that the difficulties envisaged for V/STOL had been exaggerated, and that the problems of the P.1127 were really in conventional flight, where it started out as appalling. Nevertheless, there were important lessons to be learned both in regard to vertical operations and handling characteristics in transition.

As Bedford and Merewether had found in their 1960 visits to NASA establishments, control at the hover demanded high control sensitivity (ie, large-scale responses to small movements of the controls in the cockpit), especially in roll. The company had ignored these recommendations, and as a result the P.1127 could initially be flown only with (Sperry) autostabilizer on the pitch and roll channels. Since the rudder was unpowered, there was no autostabilizer input in yaw. Roll control sensitivity had to be increased by a factor of 8.75, and yaw control by a factor of 3.2 (the increase in the pitch channel was relatively modest) before satisfactory hovering control was achieved.

The other 'vertical' problem was an occasional undemanded roll during VTO, which was so rare that it became a serious matter only when the aircraft entered squadron service. It was particularly difficult to explain, since approximately 90 per cent of occurences were to the right, yet it became important that it was cured, since outriggers are expensive. It was known that the aircraft was strongly unstable in

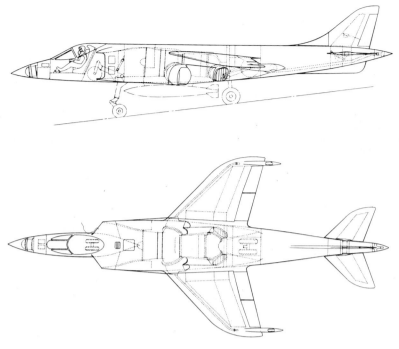

P.1150
SUPERSONIC V.T.O.L. STRIKE AIRCRAFT

SPAN 24 FT. 3 INS.	WING AREA 220 SQ.FT.	WING L.E. SWEEP 42·5 DEG.
B/SIDD PEGASUS 5 ENGINE WITH 1200°K P.C.B.		B/SIDD. PEGASUS 6 ENGINE WITH 1200°K P.C.B.
O/A LENGTH 50 FT.		O/A LENGTH 52 FT
INTERNAL FUEL CAPACITY 850 GALLONS		INTERNAL FUEL CAPACITY 1000 GALLONS

PEGASUS 5 VERSION DRAWN
FRONT AND REAR TANK SECTIONS
EXTENDED FOR PEGASUS 6 VERSION

General arrangement drawing of the P.1150 strike fighter with PCB Pegasus engine. Preliminary design by Ralph Hooper

BELOW
Forerunner of the P.1154, this later, heavier P.1150/3 had a more powerful BS.100 engine, and was aimed at NBMR-3. Preliminary design by Ralph Hooper

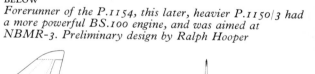

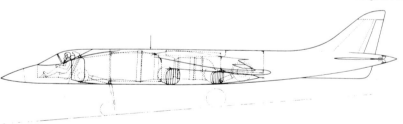

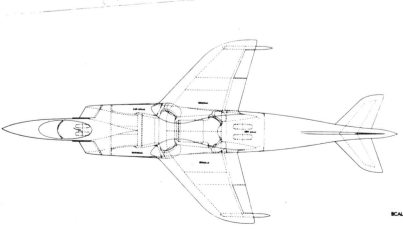

HAWKER P.1150/3
SUPERSONIC V.T.O.L. STRIKE AIRCRAFT
SCALED BRISTOL SIDDELEY BS.100 ENGINE WITH 1200°K PLENUM CHAMBER BURNING.

SPAN 26 FT.	WING AREA (GROSS) 344 SQ. FT.
O/A LENGTH 58 FT. 4 IN.	WING L.E. SWEEP 42·9°
INTERNAL FUEL CAPACITY 1,300 GALLS.	

roll (ie, it had an unstable rolling moment due to bank angle when in ground effect), but there was no obvious reason why it should roll to starboard. In the end it was conjectured (and not everyone concerned believes this) that, since the aircraft unsticks trimmed nose down in order to keep the nose puffer closed and its hot gas out of the intake, the pilot has to pull back the stick immediately after take-off and in so doing tends to pull to the right. Whether or not this is correct, the problem was solved by a change in longitudinal trim and by making pilots aware of this tendency.

In transition, with the aircraft partially jetborne, its handling characteristics are unusual in several respects. The basic longitudinal instability has been present from the outset, but the aerodynamic forces are low, hence the aircraft is controllable, and the situation is helped by autostabilisation. More serious are the effects associated with intake momentum drag, ie the force on the intakes due to the engine mass flow, acting in the direction of the relative airflow.

This first manifested itself during an early P.1127 demonstration by Bill Bedford for Air Marshal McGregor, then C-in-C Fighter Command. Having taken off vertically and accelerated to 40 knots (74 km/hr), Bedford tried to do a smart turn, but found the aircraft pirouetting, virtually out of control. The 'McGregor Turn' (as it became known) was simply a case of intake momentum drag decreasing the aircraft's natural damping in yaw, but subsequent investigations showed that intake drag also decreased weathercock stability. This was potentially dangerous, because if sideslip angle was allowed to build up, the aircraft would roll, due to an induced dihedral effect in partially jetborne flight. This led to the installation of a yaw vane directly ahead of the windscreen, and an instruction to pilots to minimize sideslip during transition.

The Kestrels experienced no sideslip problems, but on 27 January 1969 there was a fatal accident at Dunsfold, when Major C R Rosburg of the USAF got into sideslip while taking off in Harrier XV743. An uncontrollable roll developed, and the pilot ejected into the ground. How an experienced V/STOL pilot such as Rosburg could allow sideslip to develop can only be conjectured, but there is a theory that in taking off into the sun he was unable to see the yaw vane. As a direct result of that accident, the Harrier was given yaw autostabilizer (on the RCS), a head-up indication of lateral acceleration (showing a 0.06G limit), and rudder pedal-shakers activated at 0.06G. These worked in such a way that the pilot had only to 'stamp out the vibration'.

Advanced V/STOL Projects

As mentioned earlier, the RAF had withdrawn OR.345 late in 1961, in favour of joining with other NATO air forces in the NBMR-3 programme for a supersonic strike fighter. Ralph Hooper had drawn the first supersonic derivative of the P.1127 early in 1961, a larger and more handsome aircraft, powered by a BE.53/6 engine with combustion in the fan flow (ie, plenum chamber burning, or PCB). However, when NBMR-3 arrived at Kingston in April, it was found to demand a 250 nm (465 km) LO-LO radius with a 2,000 lb (907 kg) warload, from a take-off distance of 500 ft to 50 ft (150 m to 15 m).

The P.1150/1 was clearly too small for this task, so it was superseded by the P.1150/3 with a BS.100/9 engine of 33,000 lb (14,965 kg) thrust. Redesignated P.1154, this was submitted to NATO in January 1962. The P.1154 and Dassault Mirage IIIV were declared joint winners of the contest, but, since NATO *per se* does not buy aircraft, it was left to the two countries to develop the projects on a national basis and offer them for sale.

Kingston now had two active projects, so the responsibilities were split between Hooper, who retained the P.1127 programme, and John Fozard, who took over development of the P.1154. The RAF was strongly behind the P.1154, but commonality was the buzz-word of the early 1960s, and HMG insisted that the P.1154 should also fulfil RN needs for a Sea Vixen replacement, although the Navy was intent on having the F-4 Phantom.

This led to extensive redesign, and consideration of a twin-Spey powerplant, although this would only have allowed the aircraft to return to the carrier in the event of an engine failure. Stall speed with one Spey operating was too high for an arrested landing. The result of attempted commonality was a two-year delay, leading to cancellation of the P.1154 programme in February 1965 on cost and timescale grounds. The only consolation was an order for the P.1127(RAF) or Harrier.

Sir Sydney Camm had predicted that 'V/STOL will never amount to anything until we can offer the same performance as a Phantom', and many at Kingston felt cancellation of the P.1154 was a mistake. On the other hand there were many problems in the way of its practical application. The RAF planned to use it from sand strips in the Middle East and grass airfields in the Far East,

OVERLEAF
Line-up of three VFW 1262 prototypes, designed to meet Luftwaffe requirement VAK 191B, and constructed by VFW-Fokker and Fiat. The diminutive wing reflects the fact that no turning performance was specified

The P.1154 (uncharacteristically, at medium level), as it might have eventuated. This programme was cancelled in 1965 due to timescale and funding problems, its place taken by the F-4, Jaguar and Harrier

The British contender for the VAK 191 contest, as it might have appeared in RAF form. Preliminary design by Roy Braybrook. Airbrush painting by 'Ted' Freeman

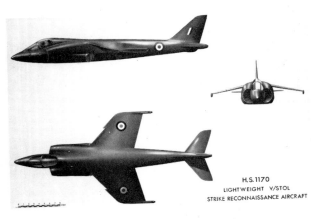

H.S. 1170
LIGHTWEIGHT V/STOL
STRIKE RECONNAISSANCE AIRCRAFT

operational concepts that were completely unrealistic. Logistic support at dispersed sites was linked to the development of the highly expensive Armstrong-Whitworth AW.681 V/STOL transport. The storage and activation of nuclear weapons at dispersed sites posed all kinds of problems. The crucial problem of ground erosion from the four high-energy jets could only be assessed by building the aircraft and testing it. Whereas the P.1127 with its comparatively gentle Pegasus could operate anywhere in the world with the minimum of surface preparation, the P.1154 would have been far more of a problem.

Another advanced V/STOL project that failed to see the light of day was the P.1163, which was redesignated HS.1170 when Hawker Aircraft became part of Hawker Siddeley Aviation (HSA). This design arose from a *Luftwaffe* requirement for a seven-ton VTOL nuclear strike fighter to replace the Fiat G.91, designated VAK 191 (*Vertikal Aufklärungs und Kampfflugzeug* = VTO reconnaissance and combat aircraft). It called for a 180 nm (333 km) LO-LO radius from VTO, cruising at Mach 0.92 and carrying a 2,000 lb (907 kg) weapon. It was written around the estimated performance of the Focke-Wulf Fw 1262, which had a small RB.153-75 vectored-thrust engine in the centre fuselage, and two RB.162-3 lift engines. In January 1961, without consulting Kingston, HMG representatives rubber-stamped the VAK 191 requirement as the basis for a joint Anglo-German development programme, in the misguided belief that this was all that was needed to enable Hawker to sell P.1127s to Germany.

In reality, at that stage the P.1127 would have been hard-pressed to achieve one tenth of the VTO radius required, and the most promising development that could be forseen, with the 21,000 lb (9,525 kg) Pegasus 5-6A, would have reached only 125 nm (232 km), would have been a ton above the weight limit, and would have needed relaxation of the cruise speed requirement. Bearing in mind that the Germans had signed the agreement to gain design experience, the P.1127 was obviously a non-starter.

It was therefore decided at Kingston to design a completely new airframe-engine combination, optimized around the VAK 191 requirement, to demonstrate to the Germans that their needs could be met by a safe (single-engined) aircraft. The hope was that they would agree to a joint development on the lines of the Hawker project, possibly accepting the P.1127 as an interim step. This was a once-in-a-lifetime opportunity for any young Hawker project engineer: to be designing in direct competition with the best men from Focke-Wulf (Prof Rolf Riccius, now marketing director for Panavia) and Messerschmitt (Prof Gero Madelung, later to become chairman of MBB). However, the operational requirement was an extremely difficult one to meet.

The Pegasus and BS.100 had both been engines that were convenient and relatively inexpensive for Bristol to develop, being based on existing rotating machinery. In contrast, the success of the new aircraft depended on having an engine optimized for the role, with a far higher thrust/weight ratio and lower specific fuel consumption (SFC) than any vectored thrust engine so far proposed. The Hawker project engineers therefore went to Derby and Bristol with detailed specifications for refanned PCB developments of the RB.153 and BS.94 respectively, demanding more than twice the estimated thrust of these basic engines.

Before the financial collapse of the company, Rolls-Royce engineers had a reputation for being somewhat stuffy, and the idea of being told how to design engines by mere tin-bashers was greeted with something short of enthusiasm. The proposal was nonetheless studied, but the conclusion reached was that the RB.153 could not be taken beyond 17,000 lb (7,710 kg) without a reduction gearbox to achieve better matching of the fan and turbine.

The Bristol project team under 'Geoff' Landamore was altogether more receptive to Kingston's proposals, and in due course came up with the BS.94/5, which was estimated to give a PCB thrust of 18,500 lb (8,390 kg) and required no reduction gearbox. Compared to the Pegasus, it reduced inlet diameter from 46.25 in (117.5 cm) to 40 in (101.6 cm), it increased T/W from 7.0 to 8.6, it gave a 15 per cent improvement in cruise SFC, it allowed a 27 per cent reduction in wetted area, and it meant that the HS.1170 could more than meet the requirement.

The key to this advance was a massive 60 per cent PCB boost in take-off thrust, permitting the use of a comparatively small engine, which was (PCB off) better matched to cruise demands, and produced less spill drag. Since PCB gave a thrust-split of 4:1 between front and rear nozzles, the engine could be moved aft, easing the balance problem and giving longer intakes, smoothing the flow to the engine. On the original plan, the HS.1170 was to have flown in 1966 and entered service in 1969, the year in which the Harrier reached the RAF.

The BS.94/5 projected for the HS.1170 is worthy of note because it was probably the most advanced V/STOL powerplant to be proposed for the next 20 years. The aircraft it was to have powered would have reached Mach 1.7 at altitude, or Mach 2.1 with two-shock intakes. Unfortunately, those responsible on the British side for the commercial negotiations destroyed this opportunity to collaborate with Germany on an advanced V/STOL aircraft, by insisting that whichever aircraft won the design contest, royalties would be paid to Hawker in acknowledgment of the company's far greater experience in the V/STOL field. Not surprisingly, the Germans refused to accept this condition, and work on the HS.1170 and the BS.94/5 engine was terminated. Germany built the Fw 1262 (later redesignated VFW 1262), but abandoned the project after flight trials. Britain settled for the P.1127(RAF), or Harrier, which (though far less advanced than the HS.1170) was a more flexible aircraft in terms of dispersed operations and overseas deployments to areas lacking in hardened runways.

Chapter 3
Production Aircraft

After several years of planning for the introduction of the P.1154, which would have made Britain the first country in the world to place a supersonic V/STOL fighter in service (the Mirage IIIV meantime having been abandoned by France), the idea of a warmed-over P.1127 was not well received in the RAF. The Harrier order was viewed purely as a consolation prize for the manufacturers, and there was quite open hostility within the service toward the programme.

It was to take several years for this attitude to change, but eventually, as more and more officers gained experience on Harrier squadrons, the operational flexibility provided by V/STOL came to be appreciated. Today, the RAF is firmly behind the idea of a strong V/STOL element in its offensive support component.

For HSA (Kingston) 1965 represented a watershed between exploratory V/STOL work and the development of the first production series. Sir Sydney Camm was now director of design for the whole of HSA, and as he became involved in the projects of other branches – including Airbus studies at de Havilland, then HSA(Hatfield) – he relaxed his control of design work at Kingston. In the ensuing reshuffle Ralph Hooper, who had carried the very considerable burden of the P.1127 since its inception in 1957, was kicked upstairs, becoming chief engineer at Kingston and later technical director for the Kingston-Brough Division of British Aerospace (BAe). Taking Hooper's place, John Fozard was made chief designer (Harrier), a position he was to hold until 1978, when Robin Balmer took over the responsibility as chief project engineer, Harrier, supported by Wilf Firth as project engineer, Sea Harrier, and Colin Wilson as project engineer, AV-8B.

Although the initial designation P.1127(RAF)

A Harrier GR.1 of No 1(F) Sqn on exercise in Norway, fitted with drop tanks, rocket pods, and centre-line practice bomb carrier. The aircraft were camouflaged with whitewash, for easy removal in return to the UK

was attractive politically in implying a relatively low-cost development programme, it was technically misleading, since a large-scale redesign was required to achieve a major advance in operational capability and handling characteristics. In the course of this redesign, the yuck-look P.1127 was transformed into a very handsome aircraft, at least until the introduction of the laser nose. Harrier salesmen tore their hair out at the sight of photographs showing its gaping intakes, but the GR.1 was an attractive beast by V/STOL standards.

The change from the Kestrel to the Harrier GR Mk 1 (to give it its full title) involved modifications not only to the airframe, but also to the engine, the aircraft systems, and its operational equipment. The principal airframe changes consisted of new air intakes with auxiliary inlets to increase the effective throat area, a 15-inch (38 cm) wingtip extension to increase area and move the aerodynamic centre (AC) aft, a redesigned leading edge with fences and vortex generators, a stronger tailplane, the introduction of an airbrake (a function having been performed by the main gear door on the Kestrel), a highly modified undercarriage with doors that closed when the gear was down to minimize dirt ingestion, and improved nosewheel steering.

The Harrier also had a new low-speed Marconi autostabilizer (initially on pitch and roll only, but

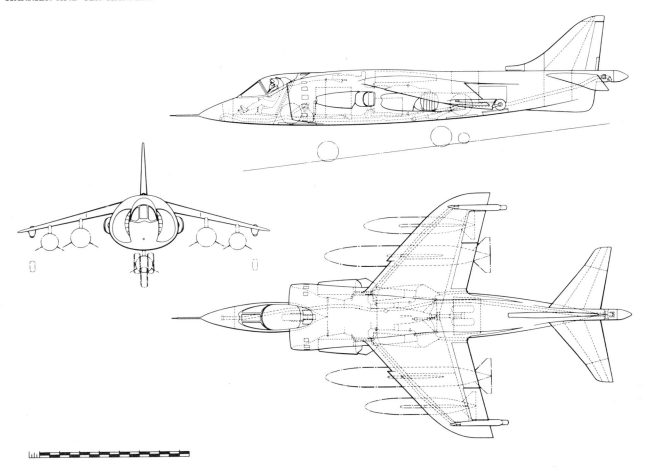

General arrangement drawing of the P.1127(RAF), which became the Harrier GR.1, a handsome aircraft by V/STOL standards. Differences from the original Kestrel include the enlarged wing and tailplane

later extended to yaw), the 'demand' RCS mentioned earlier, a zero-zero Martin-Baker Mk 9 ejection seat with miniature detonating cord (MDC) on the canopy for safe fast escape, and provisions for a flight refuelling probe to be attached to the port intake for ferry flights. Detachable long-span wingtips were later developed to improve ferry range, but these do not appear to be used. The Harrier is normally ferried with either 330 Imp gal (1,500 lit) or 100 Imp gal (454 lit) tanks, in company with a Victor tanker.

The Pegasus 6 or Mk 101 was the first production version of the engine, its take-off thrust of 19,000 lb (8,617 kg) representing a vast improvement over the 15,500 lb (7,030 kg) of the Kestrel's Pegasus 5.

It should perhaps be emphasized that in a conventional aircraft a 22.5 per cent improvement in thrust gives an 11 per cent increase in weight for a given take-off run, but a V/STOL aircraft experiences the full percentage improvement. Since it began with a very small disposable load, such a thrust increase produced a major improvement in operational effectiveness.

The Pegasus 6 differed from its predecessor in having an all-titanium fan, two stages of cooled turbine, a revised combustion system with water injection to maintain thrust to higher temperatures, a revised fuel system, and two-vane nozzles. Life was increased to a useful 300 hours. This engine first ran in March 1965, and entered service with the RAF in the Harrier GR.1 in April 1969.

The Pegasus 10 or Mk 102 (designated F402-RR-400 in US use) increased thrust to 20,500 lb (9,297 kg), the aircraft now becoming the Harrier GR.1A. The extra thrust was achieved by means of a 32 per cent increase in water flow and a 36°F (20°C) increase in turbine entry temperature (TET). The Pegasus 10 entered service in early 1971, with a life of 400 hours and hot-end replacement at half this period.

The definitive Harrier engine (associated with the GR.3) is the Pegasus 11, which has the RAF designation Mk 103, the export designation Mk

803, and is known to the USMC as the F402-RR-401. This variant produces a thrust of 21,500 lb (9,750 kg), the increase coming mainly from a rebladed fan of increased mass flow, but the engine also has a revised fuel system, improved water injection, and increased turbine cooling. Engine life is currently 800 hours, with hot-end inspection at 400 hours. All the above thrust figures are 15-second short lift wet ratings under standard atmosphere sea level conditions. At a temperature of 86°F (30°C) the thrust of the Pegasus 10 and 11 is reduced by 500 lb (227 kg).

With almost 40 per cent more thrust than the Kestrel, the Harrier can accept far heavier disposable loads (ie fuel and armament). Internal fuel capacity is increased to 632 Imp gal (2,870 lit), and there is provision for 50 Imp gal (227 lit) of water. The aircraft can take drop tanks on the inboard wing pylons, and a total of three extra pylons have been added under the fuselage and outboard wings. Two 30 mm Aden gunpods with up to 130 rounds/gun are normally mounted under the centre fuselage, these pods also acting as strakes to enhance ground cushion effect. In addition to a port oblique camera in the nose, the centre-line pylon can mount a five-camera pod with a data conversion unit that records longitude, latitude and aircraft heading on the side of the exposed film.

Because the Harrier was intended from the outset to operate at low level and achieve first-pass attacks against heavily defended targets, a comprehensive navigation and attack system was specified to guide the aircraft accurately to its objective and allow the pilot to fly safely at tree-top height. Accurate navigation is provided by a Ferranti FE541 inertial system, which gives an average error of less than 2 nm (3.7 km) per hour after a normal (12 minute) alignment, and less than 3 nm (5.6 km) after a rapid (2 minute) alignment. The aircraft's position is presented on a moving map display, the map being stored on a casette of 35 mm colour film covering an area 850 nm (1,575 km) square.

It is debatable whether the performance penalty of a large head-down map display is justified in the case of a V/STOL aircraft that is weight-critical and is intended to operate at low levels. What makes clear sense is the Smiths head-up display (HUD), which combines primary flight instrument information with navigation data and weapon aiming marks.

Other equipment includes VHF and UHF radio, UHF homing, HF radio, TACAN, and IFF. A

Rolls-Royce cutaway illustration of the Pegasus turbofan, the basis for the BAe Harrier and Sea Harrier series. Note the angled cutoff of the nozzles, the nozzle rotation system, and the accessories

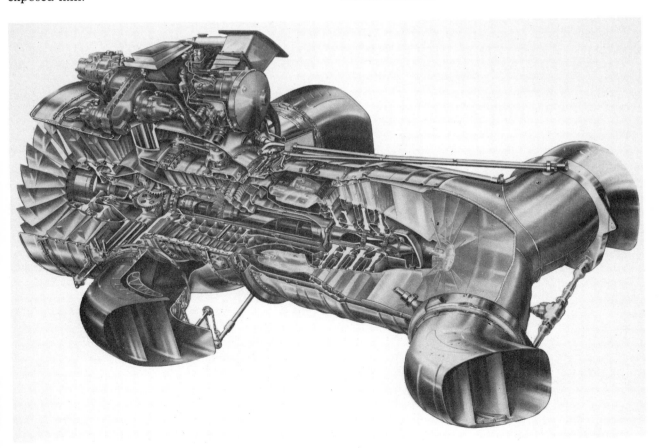

The 'thimble' nose of the Ferranti laser ranger and marked-target seeker (LRMTS) identifies the 'Snoopy' or GR.3 version of the RAF Harrier. This example is carrying a five-camera pod on the centre-line

Ferranti laser-ranger and marked target seeker (LRMTS) was added to the Harrier GR.3, as was a radar-warning receiver (RWR) with forward-looking fin antennas and aft-looking antennas in the fairing behind the tail puffers.

Into Service

The various modifications and new systems were tested on six DB aircraft (XV276-281), the first of which had its maiden flight on 31 August 1966, with Bill Bedford at the controls. The initial RAF plan was to have only two squadrons, one in the UK and one in Germany, hence the first order was limited to 60 aircraft. This number was later increased to 61 to allow replacement for an aircraft (XV743) that crashed before delivery. After lengthy negotiations, the first production order was finally signed early in 1967, and the first production Harrier (XV738) was flown by Duncan Simpson on December 28th of that year. Later batches, to provide for a total of four operational squadrons and peacetime attrition, called for 17, 12, and 24 aircraft, giving a total of 114 single-seaters for the RAF. Subsequent to the Falklands conflict, four GR.3s have been ordered to replace combat losses.

The RAF Harrier Conversion Unit began work at Dunsfold in January 1969, with instructors and groundcrew learning how to deal with their new aircraft. However, the official date for the Harrier's entry into service is normally quoted as 1 April 1969, when the operational conversion unit (No 233 OCU) was formed at Wittering.

The first squadron to be converted was No 1(F) Sqn, which was to be based at Wittering alongside the OCU. This unit is part of the Allied Command Europe Mobile Force, and in the event of war with the Soviet Union would be deployed to reinforce either NATO's flanks (ie, Norway, Denmark, Italy, Greece, or Turkey) or RAF Germany. In addition, as part of the RAF's No 38 Group, No 1(F) Sqn can be deployed virtually anywhere in the world, hence its more recent detachments to Belize and the Falklands.

The Harriers of No 1(F) Sqn first reached the attention of the general public in the Daily Mail Transatlantic Air Race of May 1969, when their unique capability to take-off and land vertically was put to dramatic use in this contest to establish the shortest possible time for the 3,030 nm (5,615 km) between the city centres of London and New York. Two Harriers (XV741 and 744) were flown between a disused railway siding near St Pancras Station and wharf on Manhattan Island, establishing a record time of 5 hr 57 min westbound, with numerous refuellings. In fairness it must be recorded that their eastbound time was shorter (5 hr 31 min), but this was beaten by the combination of helicopters and Phantoms, although the latter exceeded service restrictions on continuous afterburner operation.

Techniques were developed in early service use to minimize debris ingestion over soft ground. This Harrier is performing a 'rolling vertical' landing to keep its intakes ahead of the dust cloud

The second unit to convert to the Harrier was No 4 Sqn, based at Wildenrath with RAF Germany, where it was joined by No 20 Sqn in 1971 and No 3(F) Sqn in 1972. Since Wildenrath is set back close to the Netherlands border, it was difficult to make proper use of the aircraft's quick reaction close support capability, so in 1977 the Harrier wing was moved forward to Gütersloh, which is only 65 nm (120 km) from East Germany. Due to a shortage of administrative accommodation, it was necessary to reorganize the wing into two large squadrons, so No 20 Sqn reformed as a Jaguar unit at Brüggen, while its Harriers were divided between the two Gütersloh squadrons.

Dispersal

Germany proved an ideal testing-ground for the concept of dispersed operations, having an excellent road network for low-cost logistics and ample natural camouflage in the form of woodlands, although security on the ground would be a problem in wartime. In a non-nuclear war there could thus be a case for continuing operations from Gütersloh, making use of the Harrier's ability to fly from heavily-cratered runways, and taking advantage of main base supplies, maintenance facilities, and air defence (ie,

the Rapiers of the RAF Regiment's No 63 Sqn). Nonetheless, in a period of tension preceding the outbreak of war, the Harriers would probably be taken some distance off the base, in case it should be attacked with nuclear, biological, or chemical (NBC) weapons.

Judging by peacetime exercises, in the case of forward dispersal the 36 Harriers, together with around 400 vehicles and 440 maintenance men, would be taken to pre-selected sites in the Teutoburger Wald, although urban sites might also be used. From these sites they would be operated in the offensive support role, ie close air support (CAS), battlefield air interdiction (BAI) and tactical air reconnaissance (TAR), primarily in support of the 1st British Corps, although they could alternatively be switched to support the Germans to the north, or the Belgians to the south.

The Gütersloh wing would divide its aircraft between six forward sites, which would have a central logistics park. Each of the two squadron commanders would have charge of a primary site, the four sub-sites being run by flight commanders. Each site would have basic servicing and repair facilities, enough armament and fuel for at least two days of operations, and an RAF Regiment detachment for protection against infiltrators.

OVERLEAF
The performance of No 1(F) Sqn Harriers in the Daily Mail TransAtlantic Air Race dramatised the basing flexibility of what became known as the 'Jump-Jet', seen here approaching St Pancras station

Since the sites can be detected by enemy agents or IR reconnaissance, they would be moved frequently to minimize the danger of air attack. A dispersed site can be vacated in one hour, and a new one activated in three. The wing could generate 200 sorties per day, the pilots remaining in the cockpits during the 20-minute turnrounds.

Two-Seater

Before leaving the subject of the RAF Harrier, mention must also be made of the development of the two-seat trainer. Such an aircraft had been considered in the Hawker project office as far back as 1960, when various possible layouts had been drawn by 'Dick' Abel. However, it was clear that any two-seat variant would be difficult, since (a) even the single-seater was short of thrust, (b) the intakes would not tolerate a wider fuselage, and (c) there was a tight constraint on CG position. Whereas in a conventional aircraft there is a certain latitude between the relative positions of CG and AC, in the case of a V/STOL aircraft the CG position is rigidly fixed by the engine's thrust centre, hence major configuration changes are problematical.

Due to these difficulties and the switch in emphasis toward the P.1154, studies of a two-seat P.1127 lapsed until 1964, when the RAF became interested in the idea of a low-cost V/STOL trainer for the P.1154. The first drawing of what was to become the Harrier T.2 was actually produced by Ralph Hooper while Sir Sydney was on holiday at St Ives, where he went each year to play golf. Hooper's proposal was to have a tandem-seat cockpit, and to balance the extra weight by means of a ballasted sting at the rear.

On his return, Sir Sydney proved to be adamantly opposed to the concept, saying that the correct solution was to insert a structural plug aft of the engine bay, moving the whole rear fuselage aft. Hooper's two-seater would go ahead, said Sir Sydney, only over his dead body. Regrettably, he was proved right once again, he died without succeeding in having the design changed.

The initial contract was placed in 1966 for two DB aircraft, the requirement being to train pilots on the nav-attack system as well as to provide V/STOL conversion, and to have an aircraft that in war could fly operationally with the rear pilot and seat removed. In modifying the single-seater, the cockpit was moved forward 47 inches (119 cm) and a second cockpit installed in its place, but raised 18 inches (46 cm) to enhance forward view and allow the nosewheel to be retracted under it.

The change in nose shape associated with the Ferranti LRMTS is well illustrated by these two Harriers from No 3 Sqn, based at Gütersloh. While spoiling its lines, the LRMTS gave better attack accuracy

The Harrier T.2 (foreground) with vastly heightened fin, and emergency parachute in the rear of the tail sting, formating with a Harrier GR.1

RIGHT
This line-up of two-seat Harriers illustrates the two markedly different fin shapes still used at time of writing on RAF aircraft. Eventually all T.4s will be standardized on the shorter fin

General arrangement drawing of the Harrier T.2, showing the revised front fuselage, tail sting, raised fin and ventral strake

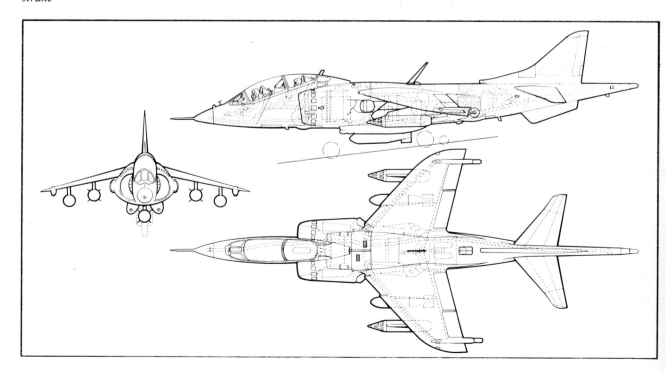

The air conditioning system was uprated and relocated aft of the canopy, while the inertial platform and F.95 camera were moved from the nose to a position below the rear cockpit, to reduce the balance problem.

To maintain weathercock stability, the fin was moved aft 33 inches (84 cm) and placed on an 11 inch (28 cm) stub, and an enlarged underfin was introduced. To bring the CG to an acceptable position, approximately 170 lb (77 kg) of ballast was added in the tail sting, this ballast being removed for operational use as a single-seater. The resulting aircraft was 1,450 lb (658 kg) heavier than the single-seater in terms of basic weight plus pilot(s), and 850 lb (386 kg) heavier in operational form with a single pilot and seat. The trainer has the full nav-attack system, but the rear cockpit lacks the moving map display.

The first prototype Harrier T.2 (XW174) flew on 22 April 1969, with Duncan Simpson at the controls. It was destroyed a few weeks later, on June 4th, following an engine run-down due to a fuel system failure, and Simpson's neck was severely damaged in the ejection. This accident was, in fact, the driving force behind the development of MDC to ensure the proper fragmentation of the hood, and a backup (manual) fuel control system to facilitate relight.

The second aircraft (XW175) flew on July 14th, and it was soon found that the two-seater lacked directional stability above 15 degrees AOA. It was conjectured that this was due to flow separations at the rear of the canopy or from the upper lip of the intake, but minor changes in this area (vortex generators, moving two small air inlets, and reshaping the intake lips) failed to produce a significant improvement, so it was decided to extend the tip of the vertical tail. This was done in three stages, of 6, 18, and 23 inches (15, 46, and 58 cm). The tallest of these extensions gave satisfactory aerodynamic results, but would have required a major strengthening programme, so the second-largest increment was re-assessed and found to be acceptable. Augmenting the original fin as an interim measure, partial airbrake extension had been used, triggered by tailplane position, and known in-house as 'Fozard's Flipping Airbrake'. It may be noted that all Harriers land with airbrake cracked open, to improve directional stability.

In service it was found that the extended fin gave excessive stability at low AOA, making weapon-aiming difficult, especially in gusts. In consequence, when the RWR was installed, adding 5 inches (12.7 cm) to the height of the fin, it was

The company aircraft (G-VTOL) over Rio, during a demonstration tour of South American countries in 1973. As was found elsewhere, this regional tour aroused considerable technical interest, but no sales

This accident to G-VTOL in Abu Dhabi in 1971 dashed HSA's hopes of sales to the Gulf States. While hovering over sand near the Ruler's residence, the pilot lost his horizon and made a heavy landing

decided to revert to the standard GR.1 fin (still mounted on the fixed stub-fin), and accept a lower AOA limit, which was tolerable for low level operations. At time of writing, there are thus two standards of fin on the two-seater, since not all two-seaters have yet reverted to the GR.1 shape.

Going back to the service history of the trainer, a batch of 12 production aircraft was ordered for the RAF in 1967, and these were later supplemented by nine more. Deliveries of the T.2 began in July 1970 (a year after the GR.1), making it possible to send first-tour pilots to Harrier squadrons. In due course the aircraft received the Pegasus Mk 102 and became the T.2A, then the T.4 with Pegasus 103, LRMTS and RWR. To assist in sales promotion, HSA constructed the slightly modified Mk 52, registered G-VTOL, with equipment supplied free of cost by the various manufacturers. In the hands of John Farley (chief test pilot, at time of writing), this aircraft was to produce some of the most dramatic displays ever seen at air shows, its nose-high ascents from VTO becoming a Farley trade-mark. In order to retain good VTOL performance, some RAF two-seaters intended purely for flying training were not given the laser nose, these 'lightweight' aircraft being designated T.4As.

Subsequent to the Falklands conflict, four additional T.4As were ordered for the RAF.

Harrier Exports

It was clear from the outset that RAF orders for the Harrier would be far smaller than those for the preceding Hunter, hence, if the Kingston plant was to survive on anything like the same scale, the new aircraft would have to be exported in large numbers. Unfortunately, there was little experience at Kingston of marketing in the modern sense. The tradition was that the RAF 'sold' the aircraft by its example, and the manufacturer sent out a man with a contract for the prospective purchaser to sign. Frank Murphy, supported by George Anderson (PR manager) had sold the Hunter very successfully, but the company failed to appreciate that the real lesson of this experience was that the market wanted a high performance, low-cost multi-role aircraft. This lack of feel for the combat aircraft market led to completely false assumptions regarding Harrier sales prospects: exports of 2,000 aircraft were confidently predicted in the late 1960s.

Throughout most of the 1960s sales efforts were handled by a technical sales manager, John Crampton, who was later to play a key role in selling the Harrier to the Spanish Navy (and the Hawk to Finland). Then in 1967 Bill Bedford retired as chief test pilot, and was made overall sales manager. Sales were expected to be triggered by the Harrier's entry into RAF service in 1969, so a handful of experienced ex-RAF pilots were recruited as senior sales executives, each dealing with a different part of the world. The US was excluded, as a special case.

To date, export sales of the Harrier have been disappointing, although they have rivalled domestic sales. The principal reason for the failure (relative to the initial target) has been the combination of high price, subsonic performance, and limited warload-radius capability. Short field performance is widely regarded as a matter of technical interest, but not as an operational necessity. Most air forces see little prospect of going to war, and those in potential war zones generally believe that air bases can be defended against conventional runway bombing. Even within NATO, the possibility of nuclear war is not seen as demanding a dispersable aircraft. If the USAF had accepted the Harrier, the sales story might have been different, since the aircraft has always lacked a convincing endorsement by a major overseas operator. Even the RAF bought twice as many CTOL Jaguars as V/STOL

The rocket climb from VTO has no operational significance, but dramatises the absence of forward roll. John Farley in G-VTOL lifts off from the hardstanding area of Las Palmas AB, near Lima

Harriers. Several navies (notably that of Italy) would have liked a V/STOL fixed-wing element, but had only rotary-wing pilots, and were thus unable to man Harriers.

The V/STOL aircraft's advantage from thrust vectoring in forward flight (VIFF) appeared only in the mid-1970s, and was then generally seen only as a last-ditch defensive manoeuvre in a one-on-one situation with the attacker using guns. Against this slender gain had to be reckoned the lack of rear view, due to those elephant-ear intakes. The Harrier was also criticized for its 22 ft (6.7 m) wide outrigger track, which raised problems in road operations and deck handling. The idea of trestling the fuselage and lifting the wing off before the engine could be removed was not well received (which is why the engine was to have removed dowards on the P.1154 and HS.1170).

In addition, in its early days the Harrier suffered an extremely high accident rate. Salesmen pointed out that the number of accidents did not seem so high in relation to sorties flown (rather than basing the calculation on flying hours), but this served only to emphasize the aircraft's short

TOP RIGHT
Rounding-off the two-seater story, this T.4N is one of three ordered after the Falklands conflict. The design corresponds roughly to the RAF's T.4A

Eight TAV-8As (or Harrier Mk 54s) were ordered as part of the final US Marine Corps batch of FY74. They played a major part in reducing the service's accident rate, which at one time had been horrific

It was never feasible to establish AV-8A production in the US, hence they were all built and tested in Britain. One is seen here alongside a C-133, before transport to the States

endurance. One genuine reason for the losses was birdstrikes in RAF low level operations, the massive intakes (fed also with birds bouncing off the front fuselage) giving a high ingestion rate, and the Pegasus being prone to surge. This situation was improved considerably by a manual fuel control system (MFCS), which gave a far higher probability of a successful relight.

However, it must also be admitted that the simplicity of V/STOL had been exaggerated. It may have been 'a natural extension of conventional piloting techniques' to Hawker test pilots, but for the operator it demanded high quality pilots with fast jet experience, and training on the two-seat Harrier. Any attempt to cut down on student pilot standards produced an instant surge in accidents, an unusually high proportion of which proved fatal.

On paper it can readily be shown that forward basing makes possible more sorties per day, giving the Harrier an ordnance delivery rate that more than justifies its high cost, but such arguments proved futile. Aircraft are still chosen for their maximum speed and flyaway cost; operational studies are only of value at a later stage in justifying the choice to the accountants. It can also be argued that HSA made a mistake in attempting to sell the RAF version of the Harrier with its full TSR.2 avionics kit. This rule was finally broken in the case of Tanzania, where even the salesmen recognised that a simpler avionics fit was called for.

Sell It To The Marines

Postwar studies of the prospects for the British aerospace industry have invariably made the point that there is no possibility of selling military aircraft to the US. No combat aircraft had been imported into America from foreign production lines since WWI, and the only post-WWII military aircraft to be adopted by the US had been the Canberra bomber, which was heavily modified and built under licence by Martin. National pride played some part in this situation, but so did

A Marine Corps AV-8A (or Harrier Mk 50) about to touch down on a carrier deck. The Marines have made many carrier deployments with these aircraft, although they were not intended for lengthy use at sea

A Marine pilot enters his AV-8A. Front fuselage details shown in this Rolls-Royce photograph include the built-in steps, the row of auxiliary inlets, the sideslip vane, and the formation light

A Matador undergoes ground checks on the ramp in southern Spain. Though based at Rota, these aircraft make deployments to the carrier Dédalo, *which is to be replaced by the new* Principe de Asturias

wartime attrition and support considerations.

Nonetheless, in the early 1960s the US Army saw the chance to acquire its own close support aircraft, and showed serious interest in the P.1127 as a replacement for the Grumman OV-1 Mohawk. Hawker accordingly signed an agreement with Northrop, under which the US corporation paid for British V/STOL know-how and an option to build a derivative of the P.1127 under licence. It is interesting to note that Northrop was chosen because it was of a similar size to Hawker Siddeley: the Kingston management had no intention of being swallowed up by a partner such as Boeing or McDonnell Douglas. In the event, the programme was terminated by a US inter-service 'roles and missions' agreement that severely limited the scope for US Army fixed-wing aircraft, CAS being provided by the USAF. From a Northrop viewpoint, this may have been no great loss, as the US Army had stated that, in the event of the P.1127 being chosen, the service would have made its own selection of licensee.

The USMC purchase of Harriers was almost too good to be true, although it had little influence elsewhere, since few countries are interested in amphibious operations. The catalyst in this totally unexpected sale was a Harrier marketing film that Maj Gen Keith McCutheon, USMC Deputy Chief of Staff (Air) happened to see. Two Marine pilots, Col 'Tom' Miller and Lt Col 'Bud' Baker, consequently arrived uninvited at the HSA chalet at Farnborough in September 1968 and spoke the historic words '*We want to fly the Harrier*'.

The two pilots stayed in England several weeks, making a preliminary evaluation of the aircraft. They said in their debriefing that it was a fine aircraft, that had demonstrated a high level of serviceability. They found a striking resemblance to the A-4 Skyhawk, although the Harrier had far more acceleration and better handling at altitude. They felt transition from the A-4 would be easy. Features they praised included the nosewheel steering ('one of the finest we have ever experienced'), the engine life recorder, STO ('very impressive'), 'beautiful' lateral control, the built-in starter, the cockpit design and field of view (to HSA's surprise, they felt the rear view was no

worse than on their existing aircraft), and the simple systems, although they would have preferred the manual reversion capability of the A-4 flying controls to minimize wartime losses.

Their criticisms were relatively minor. They felt the Harrier taxied rather fast, and the brakes chattered. They did not like the number of straps that needed to be fastened when sitting in the Martin-Baker ejection seat, or the tailplane vibration at low speeds. They said they would like to be able to use VIFF over the complete flight envelope, and that the maintenance men were not going to enjoy pulling the wing off to get the engine out ('They'll really tear their hair over that!').

Despite these reservations, the Harrier was clearly the right aircraft to provide quick reaction close support in amphibious landing operations. Before the Harrier, the best the Marines could do was to construct a 4000 ft (1220 m) strip of aluminium planking and install an arrester gear. This would accept an A-4, but it also took time. The Harriers would be ashore quicker, and had ample radius for strikes around the beach-head. They could even provide a limited air defence capability, given the right weapons.

The Harrier or AV-8A (as it was designated) was quickly injected into USMC plans for FY70, which were presented to Congress early in 1969. Although the purchase of foreign-built combat aircraft was politically unpopular, it was eventually accepted on the basis that it would save the five-to-seven years needed to develop the equivalent aircraft domestically. The fact that the USMC was willing to forgo the planned procurement of 17 Phantoms to get the first 12 Harriers was taken as evidence of a real need for the aircraft. This first buy was followed by 18 aircraft in FY71, 30 in FY72, 30 in FY 73, and a final 20 in FY74, this last batch including eight two-seat TAV-8As. The manufacturer's designations were Harrier Mk 50 for the AV-8A, and Mk 54 for the TAV 8A.

Anticipating that most of the USMC Harriers would have to be built in America, in 1969 HSA signed a licence agreement with McDonnell Douglas Corporation (MDC) of St Louis. The agreement was to run 15 years, gave MDC exclusive sales rights for the Harrier and its derivatives in the USA, and also covered the mutual exchange of 'data and drawings on vectored thrust V/STOL configurations stemming from the Harrier during the same period'. However, because the USMC purchase was approved on a year-by-year basis, the cost of starting up production at St Louis remained unacceptably high. All 110 aircraft were consequently built at Kingston, and delivered by USAF transport aircraft.

The original concept was for the Marines to have virtually an off-the-shelf Harrier, with a few essential changes such as radios and the introduction of the AIM-9 Sidewinder, and special clearance for USN ordnance. However, more changes were brought in later. The biggest surprise was that the standard 30 mm Aden cannon was adopted, on the basis that 'with 20 mm we can knock the leaves off a tree, but with 30 mm we can blow the whole tree down'. The only basic armament change was the addition of AIM-9, which required the outboard pylons to be permanently attached.

The radios were much admired on the British side: Magnavox UHF and UHF homing, and Sylvania VHF and Tactical VHF, this last unit accounting for the large antenna over the centre fuselage. A radio altimeter was added, and a different form of IFF installed. The AV-8As were initially delivered with the full Ferranti FE541 nav-attack system, but this was deleted from the 60th aircraft as providing unnecessary capabilities and thus involving excessive maintenance demands. All the Marines wanted to do was to fly a few miles and carry out simple dive attacks, so they abandoned the idea of automatic dead-reckoning navigation and the associated moving map display, and replaced the inertial platform with a two-gyro attitude and heading reference system (AHRS). To the Smiths HUD was added a WAC (weapon-aiming computer), giving a roll-stabilized depressed sightline for ground attack, lead angle computing for guns air-air, and later CCIP (continuously computed impact point) for bombs and RP in ground attack. The early AV-8As were also modified to this standard.

Other changes included the replacement of the Martin-Baker Mk 9A seat with the Stencel SIIIS-3, which employs ballistic deployment of the parachute to permit low level escape in adverse attitudes at low speeds, eg aircraft inverted at only 140 ft (43 m). However, HSA test pilots refused to fly the aircraft with a seat that clearly had far less background experience than the Mk 9A, so the AV-8As were initially fitted with Martin-Baker seats, then these were replaced with Stencels before delivery.

The first AV-8A (serial 158384) had its maiden flight on 20 November 1970 and was delivered to Marine attack squadron VMA-513 in the following March. The type now equips three 15-aircraft 'gun squadrons' and a training unit, VMAT-203, which has eight AV-8As and the remaining seven TAV-8As. Like VMA-231 and -542, VMAT-203 is currently at Cherry Point, North Carolina, while VMA-513 is based at Yuma, Arizona. Marine Corps AV-8As have operated from the USS Guam and Franklin D Roosevelt in the Mediterranean, and detachments have visited Japan, Korea, the Philippines, and Australia.

Although there is a story that an RAF pilot pioneered VIFF and was court-martialled for

The first flight of a Sea Harrier took place on 20 August 1978, with chief test pilot John Farley at the controls. This aircraft (XZ450) was later shot down by Argentine flak during an attack on Goose Green

'endangering his aircraft', most of the development work was done by the USMC, notably by Lt Col 'Harry' Blot. Early NASA tests with a Kestrel had shown that VIFF was worth only ½G, but it was associated with a strong deceleration and a nose-up pitch, giving a 'square' turn. Having been made responsible for USMC tests, Blot, apparently only loosely strapped in to his AV-8A, decided to start out by assessing the deceleration produced at 500 knots (925 km/hr). He reported that *'the airplane started decelerating at an alarming rate, the magnitude of which I could not determine because my nose was pressed up against the gunsight. I was now straddling the stick, with my right hand extended backwards between my legs, trying to hold on for dear life'*. The USMC concluded that VIFF was

an effective means to dislodge an enemy fighter from the six o'clock position, although the AV-8A pilot should be tightly strapped in. After appropriate checks on the strength of the airframe, engine and RCS, it was said that VIFF was limited by none of these, but only by *'a lack of intestinal fortitude on the part of the pilot'*.

Approximately 47 of these aircraft have been converted at Cherry Point to AV-8C standard, which includes the installation of an RWR, a chaff/flare dispenser in the rear fuselage, the lift-improvement devices (LIDs) developed for the AV-8B, on-board oxygen generation system (OBOGS), and formation lights.

The sale to the Marines made nonsense of all the early market predictions for the Harrier, which had ruled out the US, along with a list of politically impossible countries, including Spain and China. The British Labour Government had just cancelled a Spanish order for frigates to be built at UK yards when a Harrier demonstration

This photograph by BAe's Philip Boyden shows the pre-Falklands paint-schemes of the three RN squadrons: No 899 in the foreground, No 800 Sqn in the middle, and No 801 Sqn at the rear

was arranged on the carrier *Dédalo*, hence no great hopes were entertained. The situation was made more embarrassing by Spain's refusal to permit an overflight, which meant that HSA had to persuade the *Armada* to reposition the ship from south of Portugal to off Barcelona. Nonetheless, Farley's demonstration was well received, and in due course Spain purchased 11 AV-8As and two TAV-8As via the US Navy. These aircraft were given the name *Matador*, and formed *Escuadrilla* 008, based at Rota.

At the time of writing the Harrier has not been sold to China, but the stumbling block having been the years taken by Britain's Conservative Government to approve the sale, which delayed matters until China had entered a period of cutbacks in defence spending. The sale was to have been worth several hundred aircraft in the longer term, although they would mostly have been built at Shenyang. The Chinese Harrier would have been based on the Sea Harrier (because it was in production and offered an improved cockpit and rear view), but with a revised nav-attack system to suit Chinese requirements for land and sea-based operations.

Sea Harrier

Royal Navy studies of a possible carrier-based variant of the Harrier began in 1969, but it was not until 1972 that HSA was awarded a study contract. Since this was a minimum change programme, the airframe was to be virtually unaltered, but magnesium had to be deleted from those components of the engine where it might pose a corrosion problem due to salt water ingestion, and a forward-looking radar was required for the air defence role. In consequence, Rolls-Royce (Bristol) and Ferranti were given the go-ahead in 1973 to proceed with development of the Pegasus 104 and Blue Fox radar respectively, since these were clearly to be the pacing items.

In May 1975 it was formally announced that the RN was to acquire 24 Sea Harriers. Three years later an order for a further 10 Sea Harriers and four trainers to RAF T.4 standard was placed, to provide enough aircraft for a training squadron and three (later reduced to two) front-line units. These were to have been numbered 800, 801 and 802, but the third squadron was formed only for a few months in 1982, and numbered 809 (the rumour being that some admiral wanted to see his old squadron reborn). In 1983 three T.4Ns were ordered differing only in minor respects from the RAF T.4A.

From an RN viewpoint, the case for the Sea

The extra dark sea grey and pale undersurfaces of the pre-conflict RN Sea Harriers was followed by dark sea grey, postwar. No 800 in the foreground, No 801 centre, and No 899 at the rear

Harrier was that it could be added to a relatively low cost helicopter carrier without the need for catapults and arrester gear, although it later became clear that a ski-jump was essential if the full performance potential of the aircraft was to be exploited while helicopters operated from the rear of the deck. As its designation FRS Mk 1 implies, the primary role of the Sea Harrier was to be that of a fighter, specifically in destroying large shadowing aircraft that would typically be flying as singletons, at medium level and subsonically. The secondary role was to be anti-shipping strike, which in a NATO context implies the use of nuclear weapons. As a tertiary role, it would carry out reconnaissance, mainly by using its radar to detect large enemy ships.

From an export viewpoint, the Sea Harrier represented a chance for smaller navies to have a high performance fixed-wing element operating from relatively low-cost ships. Unlike the 'Ground Harrier', which only justified its high cost in wartime, the Sea Harrier thus offered economies in peacetime, and once again the Kingston marketeers predicted large export sales. There is little doubt that these forecasts, presented by the trades unions to the Labour Government, played a significant role in the decision to proceed with the project. Whether the aircraft will live up to these predictions remains to be seen: the Falklands conflict proved the effectiveness of the Sea Harrier, but it also eliminated any potential South American market. In addition, the AV-8B is clearly going to have a major impact on Sea Harrier prospects.

In external appearance, the Sea Harrier differs from the RAF aircraft mainly in having a raised cockpit and a radar nose. The floor of the cockpit is raised 10 inches (25.4 cm), giving a vast improvement in rear view over the intakes, and more equipment space. Most magnesium components have been deleted from the airframe and engine, and replaced by aluminium alloys. The reaction control system has been further improved, and a simple high-speed autopilot added to reduce pilot workload in conventional flight, especially in regard to the reconnaissance mission.

Aside from the addition of the Ferranti Blue Fox radar, which is derived from the Sea Spray of

OVERLEAF
A Sea Harrier of No 800 Sqn in post-Falklands dark sea grey, on the flight deck of HMS Hermes. *Following the withdrawal of* Hermes, *the RN will have three carriers and two operational Sea Harrier units*

A Sea Harrier takes off from the seven-degree ski-jump of HMS Illustrious, *which was the first of the* Invincible *class to be armed with the CIWS (close-in weapon system) against sea-skimming missiles*

the RN Lynx helicopter, the nav-attack system has changed with the deletion of the inertial platform (which is difficult to level and align with north on a moving deck), and its replacement by a twin-gyro platform and Decca 72 Doppler radar. A typical navigation error is only 1.5 nm (2.78 km) after a 50-minute flight. A new Smiths HUD/WAC has been installed, a radar altimeter added, and presentation of radar-warning information has been improved. The Martin-Baker Mk 9A seat has been superseded by the Mk 10. Provision is made for two AIM-9 Sidewinders on the outboard wing pylons.

The performance provided is typified by a HI-LO-HI reconnaissance probe of 450 nm (835 km) radius, an anti-shipping strike with two Sea Eagles and two cannon of up to 280 nm (520 km) on

internal fuel, and a medium level combat air patrol (CAP) of 90 minutes at 100 nm (185 km) radius with two drop tanks, two AIM-9s and two cannon. The reconnaissance and air defence sorties are based on the use of two 100 Imp gal (454 lit) tanks.

The first flight of a Sea Harrier was made by XZ450 on 20 August 1978, piloted by John Farley. This was the first production aircraft, but it was used initially on clearance trials, supplementing the work on the three DB aircraft (XZ438-440). The first delivery took place on 18 June 1979, when XZ451 was flown from Dunsfold to RNAS Yeovilton, where No 700A Sqn formed the Intensive Flying Trials Unit (IFTU). On 31 March 1980 this unit became the Headquarters Squadron, No 899, which was to use seven (later eight) Sea Harriers for pilot training and further trials. The two operational units initially formed had five (later six) Sea Harriers each (the normal complement for an *Invincible*-class carrier being these five, plus nine Sea Kings). The first such

Though not available during the Falklands conflict, the long-range BAe Sea Eagle sea-skimming missile is to be employed by RN Sea Harriers in the anti-shipping role

squadron, No 800, was commissioned in April 1980, and served briefly on HMS *Invincible* before transfering to *Hermes*. The second squadron, No 801, was commissioned in January 1981, and normally goes to sea in *Invincible*. The third, No 809, was commissioned in April 1982 in response to the demands of the Falklands conflict, and possibly in the hope that the reserve aircraft used to form it would be replaced by new purchases. This unit was split between *Hermes* and *Invincible* during the conflict, but transfered to the newly-completed *Illustrious* shortly afterwards. On the completion of the third of the series, HMS *Ark Royal*, it is understood that No 800 Sqn will serve in her, and that *Hermes* will be pensioned off. In December 1982 No 809 Sqn was stood down, leaving two operational squadrons to equip three carriers.

Training for RN Sea Harrier pilots follows the RAF course, ending with 13 weeks at Wittering for 27 hours of operational conversion flying on Harriers, before 21 weeks at RNAS Yeovilton for 90 hours on the Sea Harrier. Of the four Navy Harrier T.4s, two are normally based at Yeovilton, one at Wittering, and one is held in reserve. These T.4s are used only for V/STOL training, instruction on the weapons system being carried out on two Hunter T.8Ms (XL602-603), which were earlier used as testbeds for the equipment. Yeovilton's facilities include a variable-angle ski-jump, which came into use at the end of 1980.

Sea Harrier operations differ from those of CTOL naval aircraft in a number of respects. For example, instead of using arrester gear, the Harrier lands vertically, and instead of a catapult take-off, the Sea Harrier makes an unassisted STO up a curved ramp. This ski-jump take-off permits a significant reduction in take-off run (or increase in take-off weight for a given run), and improves the pilot's chance of ejecting successfully in the event

Future Sea Harrier development options include a new pulse-Doppler radar, LERX, zero-scarf nozzles, twin medium-range air-air missiles on each outboard pylon, tip-mounted Sidewinders, and intake strakes

RIGHT
An Indian Navy Sea Harrier Mk 51 flown by John Farley blasts off the concrete at Farnborough. The undercarriage is going up as the engine nozzles rotate aft for acceleration to wingborne flight

of the engine failing during take-off. Ski-jump take-off performance is also much less affected by deck pitching than an unassisted take-off from a flat deck.

Although publicised as another great British invention in the tradition of the steam catapult and the angled deck, the ski-jump take-off is a straightforward extension of the technique used in marginal take-offs before runways were available. Rather than risking the disintegration of his flying machine in an indefinitely long take-off, the pioneer aviator would aim for the biggest bump in the field, which would throw his machine into the air, releasing it from the drag of the ground and giving it a few seconds to reach flying speed.

The ski-jump gives the Sea Harrier a vertical velocity component by inclining its path upward, thus buying time to reach a speed at which its weight can be supported by a combination of wing lift and jet lift. A high-powered CTOL aircraft such as the F/A-18 Hornet could get some benefit from a ski-jump (relative to its unassisted take-off performance from a flat surface), but the margin between deck-end speed and flying speed is limited by the fact that it lacks the Harrier's RCS, which provides effective control regardless of speed.

Ski-jump trials were carried out at RAE Bedford, beginning in August 1977 and covering a range of ramp angles from 6 to 20 degrees. At the higher angles, the aircraft required only half the take-off run, or could take off 3,000 lb (1,360 kg) heavier from the same run. In practice, carrier ski-jump angles are restricted by such factors as undercarriage strength, the sheer height of the

ramp, and the presence of other deck installations. The *Invincible* was originally designed as an anti-submarine cruiser for helicopters only, with a Sea Dart missile launcher on the forecastle, which restricts the ski-jump angle to 7 degrees over a 90 ft (27.4 m) ramp, corresponding to a rise of only 6.5 ft (2.0 m). The ski-jump on *Illustrious* is similar. However, *Hermes'* modification was restricted only by the captain's forward view, hence it has a 12 degree ramp 150 ft (45.7 m) long, giving a deck rise of 15 ft (4.6 m). Benefiting from a later start, the last of the new carriers (*Ark Royal*) will also have a 12 degree ramp.

Like the RAF (but unlike the USMC), the RN does not use water injection in STO from safety considerations, preferring to hold this thrust boost in reserve against any possible shortfall in thrust or slowness in engine acceleration. Nonetheless, it is recognized that water injection may eventually

be required for STO at high weights and temperatures. For stream take-offs, aircraft are parked with as little as 25 ft (7.6 m) between them: there is some buffeting from jet blast, but no harm results. The standard crosswind limit prior to the Falklands operations was 15 knots (28 km/hr), although trials on *Hermes* had gone to 20 knots (37 km/hr) without difficulty.

Take-off procedure includes an engine acceleration check between 27 and 55 per cent fan RPM with nozzles pointed aft. The pilot then moves the nozzles to the angle calculated for unstick, to check RCS duct pressure and allow the flight deck officer (FDO) to check nozzle angle. The FDO also confirms that the tailplane is correctly set. Take-off is performed between painted 'tramlines' with the nozzles depressed 8 degrees to eliminate tailplane buzz, the pilot selecting nozzles down to the preset stop as the

deck edge disappears past the lower edge of the quarterlights.

Typically, a Sea Harrier comes off *Invincible*'s 7 degree ramp at a climb rate of 1,000 ft/min (5.0 m/sec), this rate falling to 300 ft/min (1.5 m/sec) during the initial phase of acceleration. At around 130 knots (240 km/hr) the climb rate starts to increase again, and the pilot then begins rotating the nozzles aft, transition being completed at approximately 165 knots (305 km/hr).

On returning to the ship at the end of a sortie, the aircraft flies a conventional rectangular landing pattern, but at the end of the downwind leg the nozzles are lowered to start a descending decelerating transition on the crosswind leg. This brings the aircraft to the hover abreast of the chosen landing spot, at a height of 100 ft (30 m) and 30 ft (9 m) to the left of the deck. This technique gives a better view of the deck than

The second Indian Navy Sea Harrier, its fin bearing the emblem of No 300 Sqn ('Sea Tigers'). The Mk 51 differs from the RN version in avionics, and in having gaseous oxygen and Matra Magic provisions

approaching straight over the stern, and facilitates an overshoot. Having checked the area around the landing spot, the aircraft is translated over the deck and landed vertically. If the carrier is not steaming into wind, the Sea Harrier's landing pattern is turned round to face relative wind. Landing spots subject to deck turbulence must be avoided.

Approach aids are necessary only in bad visibility. Considering the case of a bad weather recovery at night, the Sea Harrier is brought

corrections and range data, from which the pilot can deduce height errors. The PIA uses the ship's response from the Blue Fox radar (either alone, or in combination with the aircraft's navigation system) to generate range data and azimuth and height corrections on the HUD. In the near future transponder-equipped aircraft will be able to make PIAs to vessels equipped with MADGE (Microwave Aircraft Digital Guidance Equipment).

For the second phase of the approach a decelerating transition is made down a $2\frac{1}{3}$-degree glideslope indicated by red and white lights on the deck edge, an equipment known as HAPI (Harrier Approach Path Indicator). On reaching 0.5 nm (0.9 km) from the carrier, the nozzles are lowered to the hover position, and the aircraft is sidestepped to port, passing the stern at around 40 knots (75 km/hr). Its height is controlled by reference to the forward HAPI lights and a similar array designated CAI (Close Approach Indicator) mounted on the island. A 'Christmas tree' of lights on the rear of the island assists the pilot in positioning over the chosen landing spot and provides a height reference for the start of let-down.

Future developments for RN Sea Harriers (aside from MADGE) include a thrust increase, a reconnaissance data link, an audio-AOA system, a speed-trim device that will facilitate hover positioning (the pilot will be able to 'blip' the nozzles through 10 degrees forward or aft, using the airbrake switch on the throttle), the BAe Sea Eagle air-surface missile, a medium range radar-homing air-air missile, and various armament and radar changes arising from experience in the Falklands conflict. Following the conflict, seven replacement Sea Harriers and seven additional aircraft were ordered for the RN.

Export Sales

At time of writing the only export order for Sea Harriers has come from the Indian Navy, which in December 1979 signed for six Mk 51s and two T.60 trainers, this sale following seven years after Farley's demonstration of G-VTOL from the Indian carrier *Vikrant*. The Mk 51 differs from the FRS.1 in having the Matra Magic missile in place of Sidewinder, and gaseous oxygen in place of LOX, in addition to which there are various modifications to the radio fit, IFF, Blue Fox, RWR, etc. The Mk 60 is based on the RAF T.4, but has the pre-laser nose and most of the operational systems of the Mk 51 aside from the Blue Fox radar. The maiden flight of a Mk 51 took place on 6 August 1982, and the first aircraft was formally handed over at Dunsfold on 27 January 1983 for use by No 300 ('Sea Tigers') Sqn.

within range of the ship's visual landing aids either in a carrier-controlled approach (CCA) or in a pilot-interpreted approach (PIA), guiding the aircraft down a 3-degree glideslope from an altitude of 1,000 ft (300 m) at 3.3 nm (6.1 km) from the ship to a position 0.8 nm (1.5 km) astern at 200 ft (60 m). This glideslope is flown at around 130 knots (240 km/hr) with the nozzles 60 degrees down.

For the CCA a precision approach radar is not required; the controller simply reads off azimuth

Chapter 4
The Falklands
Conflict

Throughout the 13 years from its introduction into service in April 1969 until the first day of May 1982, the Harrier family had never been operated in anger. Its military potential had been the subject both of outspoken claims and of outrageous abuse, but it remained an unproved quantity. In simulated close combats the various types of Harrier had performed well, even against the latest US fighters, but it was clear that if the enemy had medium-range air-air missiles and rules of engagement to match, then the Harrier might never get close enough to prove its value in a dogfight.

In air-to-ground operation, the Harrier GR.3 behaved well enough, but its old analogue nav-attack system was due for replacement by a modern digital one. The Sea Harrier represented an improvement in many respects, but its BAe Sea Eagle anti-ship missile was still years away, and a medium-range air-air missile a distant pipe-dream.

In the early months of 1982 both the GR.3 and Sea Harrier still suffered from years of cost-paring and delayed decisions on equipment. The GR.3 lacked any form of air-air missile, and neither series had provisions for dispensing chaff or IR flares, or for jamming enemy radars. Although part of a mobile force that might have to operate in any part of the world, the GR.3 was still seen by the planners in Whitehall as limited to firing 68 mm rockets and dropping 1,000 lb (454 kg) HE bombs or 625 lb (283 kg) BL755 cluster weapons. It was not cleared to deliver laser-guided bombs or anti-radar missiles (ARM). While its release documents enabled it to operate from aircraft carriers, the planners had seen no requirement for equipment to permit its inertial system to function on a moving deck.

In short, the Harrier family had remained little more than a technological flag-waving exercise for

A Sea Harrier, painted in pre-conflict markings of No 801 Sqn, about to land on Invincible. *It is fitted with gunpods, drop tanks, Sidewinder rails, and an acquisition round on the starboard wing*

13 years. It was still only a tiny element of Britain's armed forces, a type of aircraft on which the bare minimum of defence funds had been expended to keep V/STOL in existence, and that seemed likely to fizzle out in the 1990s without ever having fired a shot or dropped a bomb in any real war. Unless something unexpected happened, V/STOL seemed likely to remain an academic talking-point, a technological concept of practical value only in regard to small carriers and special operations, such as dispersal in Germany's forests or amphibious landings.

What happened to change this situation was a sudden error of judgment by Lieut-General Galtieri, at that time President of Argentina and (as C-in-C of the Army) the senior member of the governing *junta*. Misreading various signs, including the decision to withdraw the RN's ice patrol ship *Endurance*, as indicating an end to Britain's resolve to maintain sovereignty over the Falkland Islands, Galtieri decided to take 'Las Malvinas' by force in what became known as *Operación Rosario*. The first Argentine unit landed near Port Stanley in the early hours of Friday April 2nd, 1982, and the islands were surrendered by the Governor, Rex Hunt, shortly afterwards. Within hours of the invasion the first Sea Harriers had embarked in HMS *Hermes* and *Invincible* at Portsmouth, which throughout the weekend was to be the site of frantic activity as men, supplies and

The Douglas A-4 Skyhawk was the invader's workhorse in the anti-shipping role, flying over half the operational missions launched from Argentine bases. It was operated by both Air Force and Navy

equipment were loaded for the South Atlantic. On Monday April 5th Britain's carrier battle group sailed with 20 Sea Harriers and 45 helicopters, the first phase of a task force that would eventually involve six submarines, over 100 ships, 28 Sea Harriers, 14 RAF Harrier GR.3s, and approximately 175 helicopters. Operation Corporate was under way.

At long last the merits of high performance V/STOL aircraft were thus to be subjected to the acid test of war. If its detractors were right, the Harrier would be found to be an aircraft that could not carry a worthwhile load over a useful distance, a fighter too slow to survive in combat with supersonic adversaries. On the other hand, if its advocates were right, it would prove to have an operational flexibility that would more than compensate for its lack of supersonics, allowing it to perform in ways that no other aircraft could. The academic debates were over: V/STOL was finally to be judged in a shooting war.

The Imbalance Of Forces

What Britain set out to achieve was to persuade Argentina to withdraw her forces by diplomatic pressures, backed by a credible military threat. The decision actually to employ armed force was a fall-back position that was adopted some weeks later, when argument had failed. If Britain's ability to liberate the Falklands by military means was to be credible, then we had to demonstrate not only that an adequate force of men and material could be transported to the South Atlantic, but also that an effective first line of air defence could be provided for the Task Force and for the men to be landed on the islands.

Thus, although the 20 high performance fixed-wing aircraft on the two carriers represented only a very small part of the force, their presence was essential to the British diplomatic and military effort. If there had been no Sea Harrier, there could have been no credible Task Force, and the Falklands would have remained 'Las Malvinas' indefinitely.

The air defence task facing the Sea Harrier squadrons was unquestionably a very severe one, if only because Argentina possessed a far greater force of combat aircraft that could be deployed to the area, and since a large number of these aircraft were members of the Mach 2 Dassault-Breguet Mirage delta-wing family, a series that had attained considerable distinction in Israeli hands in various Middle East actions. Depending on the source of information, Argentina was reckoned to have between 120 and 200 combat aircraft, giving a local numerical advantage of up to six or ten to one!

The basic mathematical equations of combat theory suggest that such odds can easily outweigh any conventional edge in the quality of the smaller side (a qualitative advantage that the French and Israelis would in any event deny). However, the challenge was even worse than the ratio of numerical strengths might imply. The Sea Harrier had been developed primarily to intercept large subsonic, medium level intruders approaching as singletons along a broadly predictable threat axis. Instead of this threat, the Fleet Air Arm had to face the probability of shoals of aircraft coming in, not only at high subsonic speed at low level, but also at high level and possibly supersonic speed, and from all points of the compass.

Aside from aircraft from the four main bases in southern Argentina within 500 nm (925 km) of

Argentine Air Force A-4Ps, photographed by Michael O'Leary at their peacetime base at El Plumerillo, Mendoza. During the conflict, A-4Ps operated mainly from Rio Gallegos, 420 nm (780 km) from Stanley

Port Stanley (bases that had been built up to ensure air superiority over the Beagle Channel in the event of a clash with Chile), British planners had to face the prospect of naval air strikes from Argentina's carrier, the *Veinticinco de Mayo* (25th of May), and of small numbers of aircraft operating from Port Stanley airfield on the eastern tip of the Falklands. Just before the start of the conflict, reports had stated that the Exocet-armed Super Etendards had not yet flown from the carrier, but this was no guarantee that deck trials and crew training could not be rushed through while the British Task Force was in passage to the area.

Similarly, the runway at Port Stanley was only 4,250 ft (1,300 m) long, having been built for use by transport aircraft of LADE (*Lineas Aéreas del Estado*, a public service operation run by the *Fuerza Aérea Argentina*), but it was probable that it would be employed by close support aircraft such as the Pucará, MB.339, and Beech T-34C. It might also be used by the Douglas A-4 Skyhawk and the Mirage, at light weights. The Mirage is, in fact, advertised as the world's only Mach 2 fighter capable of taking off in air defence configuration (ie carrying air-air missiles) with a ground roll of less than 2,500 ft (750 m) and landing in the same distance. For any conventional high-powered aircraft, landing performance is more critical than take-off, but portable arrester gears allow operations from quite short airfields, and hooked

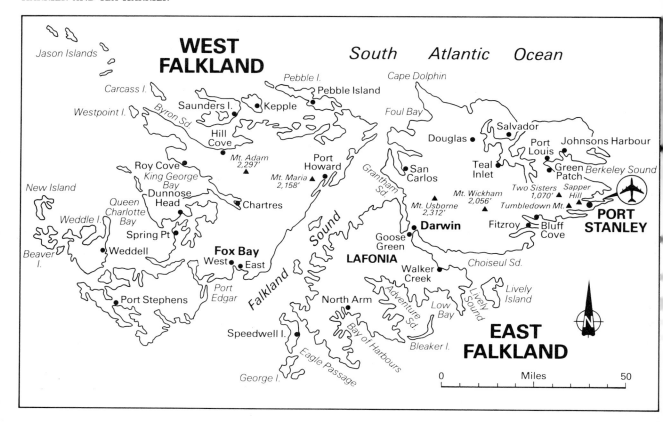

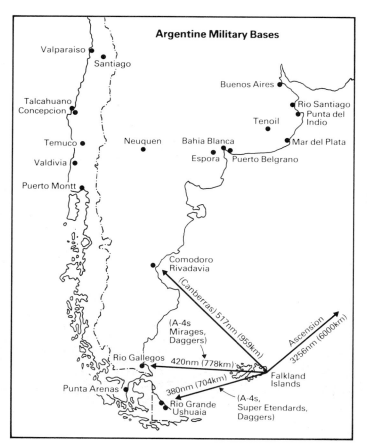

ABOVE
A map of the Falkland Islands showing all the main settlements

This map illustrates how essential organic naval aviation was in the liberation of the Falklands. The proximity of Argentine airbases contrasts strongly with the huge distances involved in operating ground based aircraft fro Ascension Island, the nearest British airfield. The releva Chilean bases are also included

The Argentine Navy A-4Q was operated against British targets from Rio Grande, some 380 nm (705 km) from Stanley. A small number of operational missions were launched from the carrier, but all aborted

naval aircraft require no modifications to use these gears. Hence the basing of A-4s at Port Stanley had to be allowed for, and the possibility of Mirages using the runway (though less likely) could not be ruled out.

In addition to air threats against the Task Force from Argentina, the carrier, and Port Stanley (then renamed 'Puerto Argentina' by the forces of occupation), there was also the prospect of all-aspect attacks by aircraft that had been refuelled in flight. The Argentine Air Force had two Lockheed KC-130H tankers, each with a pair of underwing drogue units, suitable for refuelling A-4s and Super Etendards, both of which types also had a 'buddy' refuelling capability. Fortunately for Britain, those members of the Mirage family operated by Argentina could not be refuelled in flight, although some Daggers may subsequently have been fitted with probes.

Considering the disparity in regional air strength in more detail, Argentina's most potent air combat aircraft was the French-built, AI radar-equipped Mirage III, which formed one squadron of 17 single-seat IIIEAs and two IIIDA trainers. From

Dassault-Breguet brochures, it can be deduced that the type has a HI-LO radius of action of around 500 nm (925 km) with two 1,000 lb (454 kg) bombs, and with 10 per cent of the distance flown at low level for penetration and escape.

Augmenting these all-weather fighters were at least 42 Israeli-built Daggers, (strike fighters with a visual air combat capability) corresponding to the simply-equipped, multi-purpose Mirage 5, and forming two squadrons. The possibility of reinforcements also had to be allowed for: it was later established that the *Fuerza Aérea del Perú* had supplied 10 of its 37 Mirage 5Ps to Argentina during the conflict. This brought the Mirage family total to around 70, a force that Chief of Air Staff Brigadier Lami Dozo must have believed was more than adequate in dealing with 20 subsonic Sea Harriers.

For bombing attacks the *Fuerza Aérea Argentina* also had at least three squadrons of A-4P Skyhawks. The original purchase had consisted of 75 aircraft, with serials running from C-201 to C-275, but published photographs of A-4s numbered C-302 and C-313 indicate that an additional batch had been supplied covertly, although the source is still unknown. From A-4 brochures, it may be estimated that the aircraft has a HI-LO radius of around 500 nm (925 km) with four 500 lb (227 kg) bombs. Further up the bomber scale, Argentina

A manufacturer's publicity photograph of the IA-58 Pucará, which was based in the Falklands for close support duties. Up to 40 were operated from airfields and road sites; some 25 were lost

BELOW
An Israeli-built Dagger of the VIth Brigada Aérea, pictured on the ground at its peacetime base at Tandil. The Dagger had the shortest radius of the various aircraft employed by Argentina

A Canberra B.62 of the IInd Brigada Aérea at BAM
General Urquiza, Paraná. During the conflict Canberras
operated from Comodoro Rivadavia, at 517 nm (960 km)
the most distant base from Port Stanley

BELOW
One of the genuine Argentine success stories was the night-
time resupply missions to Stanley airfield by low-flying C-
130s. Only one C-130 was lost, and that occurred in
daytime to a Sea Harrier

had one Canberra squadron, combining 10 B.62s and two T.64 trainers. The Canberra's radius covered the islands, although its speed and size made it a comparatively easy target.

While not capable of round-trips from Argentina to the Falklands area, the domestically built twin-turboprop Pucará was available in large numbers (at least 70 aircraft). It had proved itself very useful in COIN actions, despite a tendency of the Astazou engine to surge under certain conditions, and could clearly pose a threat to amphibious landing craft and any British troops caught in the open.

Navy aircraft under the *Comando de Aviación Naval Argentina* were numerically less significant. A batch originally of 16 A-4Qs had been used to form one squadron, which could be operated from the carrier. Of the 14 Exocet-armed Super Etendards ordered (the number subsequently being increased to 16 in view of the system's successes), it was known that only five had been delivered, and there were some doubts over whether the unit was ready for war. Finally, to resist any amphibious landing, the Navy could take to the islands its armed trainer force of 10 MB.339s, eight Brazilian-built EMB.326GBs, and 15 Beech T-34Cs.

Aside from dealing with Argentina's large force of combat aircraft, the Sea Harriers could expect to be tasked with intercepting a variety of aircraft pressed into service in maritime patrol duties. The possibilities included the Air Force's two 707-320Bs, eight C-130s and five Learjet 35As (which formed a special *Grupo de Reconocimiento* at Rivadavia), and the Navy's three Electras and three SP-2H Neptunes. Civilian aircraft (eg F.27s) formed '*Escuadrón Fénix*' for reconnaissance and radar spoof missions.

Portsmouth to Ascension

During the weekend that followed the Argentine invasion, the immediate problems facing Britain's Fleet Air Arm were to assemble as many men and aircraft as possible, and find room for them in the ships. Reports from the Falklands had been slow to arrive in the UK (a situation that was to persist throughout the conflict), and it had only been at 1800 hr on Friday April 2nd that HMG finally acknowledged that an invasion had taken place. Nevertheless, at 0430 hr that day the squadron commanders and AEOs (air engineering officers) of Nos 800 and 801 Sqn had been contacted and told to prepare their Sea Harriers and men to embark in *Hermes* and *Invincible*, with extra

Easily distinguished by her 12-degree ski-jump, the size of which was limited only by the captain's forward view, Hermes *carried an impressive complement of fixed- and rotary-wing aircraft*

The author's photograph of an Argentine Army Agusta A.109 with side-mounted machine gun and rocket tubes, similar to the one destroyed by Flt Lt Morgan on 23 May 1982. This example was shown at Middle Wallop

aircraft and men from No 899 Sqn, the headquarters and training unit.

At that stage, No 801, commanded by Lt Cdr Nigel ('Sharkey') Ward, was officially on leave, and No 800 under Lt Cdr 'Andy' Auld was due to start leave at midday on the Saturday. Each of the operational squadrons then had a nominal strength of six aircraft, although it was quite normal for a unit to have one or two in deep maintenance at any time, the operational establishment of five aircraft being required only when the squadron went to sea. The training unit had a nominal strength of eight aircraft, likewise increased by one over the original complement.

Together the three units thus accounted on paper for 20 of the 31 Sea Harriers theoretically available (two of the total of 34 being still on the production line, and one having crashed in December 1980). Of the remaining 11 Sea Harriers, four were still in use as trials aircraft at Dunsfold and Boscombe Down, and the remaining seven were in storage as attrition replacements at RAF St Athan in South Wales. It says a great deal for all concerned that within a week eight additional Sea Harriers had been prepared to the latest modification standard, to augment the 20 that sailed in the carriers on April 5th.

Within the first few hours of the emergency the AEOs of 800 and 801 Sqn (Lt Cdrs Roger Bennett and 'Dick' Goodenough, respectively) had each prepared four aircraft, while No. 899 (AEO Lt Cdr David Chapman) managed the remarkable total of eight plus one 'in-use reserve'. These eight aircraft and pilots from No 899 were divided equally between the two operational squadrons, but during the course of the Saturday No 899 managed to obtain three more aircraft, which were allocated together with the 'in-use reserve' to No 800. These four Sea Harriers were flown by No

899's Co (Lt Cdr Neil Thomas) and three student pilots, one of whom had completed only 30 hr of his 90 hr conversion course. Thus 800 Sqn flew the first of 12 aircraft from Yeovilton to *Hermes* in Portsmouth harbour on the evening of Saturday April 3rd (the 12th actually joined in the Channel), and 801 followed with eight aircraft to *Invincible* on the Sunday morning, their ground parties travelling to Portsmouth by coach and lorry.

Conditions on board ship were crowded both in terms of men and aircraft. Each of the operational squadrons is normally a self-contained unit, with an on-board establishment of five Sea Harriers (here reduced to four), seven pilots, two engineering officers and 107 ratings. To these No 899 had added eight aircraft, eight pilots, and around 50 'maintainers' in the case of *Hermes*, and four aircraft, four pilots and around 25 'maintainers' in the case of *Invincible*. Since in normal circumstances the extra maintenance personnel were permanently based at Yeovilton, many of them had never been to sea before. *Hermes* left UK waters with 14 Sea Harrier pilots and *Invincible* with 12.

As the larger of the two carriers, it was natural that *Hermes* should receive more aircraft, men and stores than *Invincible*, but the ratio of aircraft was also a reflection of operating procedure, which differed markedly between the two ships. From the outset *Hermes* kept some of her aircraft permanently on deck, partly because of possible restrictions associated with using the deck-edge lift at the forward end of the hangar. In contrast, *Invincible* put her aircraft in the hangar overnight unless they were required at alert status. She had begun her service career with five Sea Harriers and seven Sea King helicopters, and later added two more helicopters, but an assessment made in September 1981 had reported that a combination of eight Sea Harriers and nine Sea Kings could theoretically be housed in the hangar, provided that certain maintenance actions (notably a Sea Harrier engine change and a Sea King rotor head change) were not required. It was on this basis that *Invincible* went to war. As it happened, no Sea Harrier engine change was needed during the conflict, although *Hermes* did change the Pegasus of an RAF Harrier GR.3.

The duties that were to face the Sea Harrier squadrons in the South Atlantic were quite different from those that had been envisaged in the context of an East-West clash, but it probably true to say that their aircraft and men were better prepared than those in many of the units that took part in Operation Corporate. The one respect in which the Sea Harriers were ill-prepared for war was their glossy peacetime paint-scheme, extra dark sea grey on top, white underneath, squadron badge on the fin, and side number and ROYAL

*Dispersed operations are regularly practised by Harrier
units of the Gutersloh wing (No 3 and 4 Sqn) in RAF
Germany. This Harrier GR.3 serves with No 4 Sqn*

At war in the South Atlantic: amid a flurry of condensation, a Sea Harrier departs on a CAP mission from the carrier HMS Hermes. *Two Harrier GR.3s are spotted on either side. Another Sea Harrier looks on*

Typical recovery of a Sea Harrier aboard the cluttered flight deck of Hermes *during the Falklands conflict. A second Sea Harrier, just visible off the carriers' stern, waits for its turn to land*

Two Sea Harriers of No 801 Sqn assigned to the carrier HMS Invincible show that fighter pilots still like to stow maps in the cockpit. The lead aircraft (XZ458/No 000), has two kills to its credit. As 'No 12' it was used by Flt Lt 'Bertie' Penfold to score his victory (a Mirage) and by Lt Cdr 'Fred' Frederiksen, who destroyed a Dagger

BELOW Two Sea Harriers, two camouflage schemes: the No 899 Sqn machine (foreground) wears dark sea grey, while No 809 Sqn evidently prefer light and 'Barley' grey

OPPOSITE BELOW A Sea Harrier of No 800 Sqn clears the 12 degree ski-jump which dominates the bow of Hermes

ABOVE *An AV-8A Matador destined for the Spanish Armada hovers over Dunsfold. This is one of 11 AV-8As delivered to Escuadrilla 008*

BELOW *Surely one of the world's best known demonstration aircraft, G-VTOL is a Mk 52 trainer operated by British Aerospace*

ABOVE *Armed with a cluster of practise bombs, this USMC AV-8A heads for the range. The first of 110 AV-8As bought by the USMC were delivered to VMA-513 in March 1970*

BELOW *Ill-fated Sea Harrier: ZA174 operated from HMS Invincible during Operation Corporate until it slid off the flight deck while being positioned for launch. The pilot, Flt Lt 'Mike' Broadwater, ejected safely*

ABOVE *Six Sea Harriers
Mk 51s and two T.60
trainers have been
delivered to India.
At sea, No 300 Sqn
operates from the carrier
INS* Vikrant, *flagship of
the Indian Navy*

*Eight Sea Harriers
overfly RNAS
Yeovilton in
'Arrowhead' formation.
No 800, 801 and the
'headquarters' unit, 899
Sqn, are all home based
at Yeovilton*

HMS Invincible *with a Sea Harrier about to take off along the 'tramlines' painted on the flight deck and ski-jump. Note the Sea Dart launcher on the forecastle, which limited the size of the ski-jump*

NAVY in white. This scheme looked smart and was easy to keep clean, but it also made the aircraft highly visible. If the Sea Harrier was to go into combat, the white had to be replaced by grey, the badge painted over, and the roundels toned down. In the case of *Hermes* this was all done by hand in the course of one day, although some items (eg Sidewinder launchers) had to be painted in dark blue after the grey paint ran out. Side numbers and serials were replaced on the fuselage in dark blue, omitting the first digit of the side number for simplicity. Aircraft without side numbers (normally allocated by FONAC) generally had the last two digits of the serial repeated on the nose. In the case of *Invincible* the aircraft were given the full treatment, taking advantage of the ship's warm, air-conditioned hangar, although this process took far longer. Nonetheless, by the time she reached Ascension,

all but two aircraft (then in deep maintenance) were looking brand-new.

While the Task Force was steaming south, work proceeded both in the UK and on board the carriers to improve the operational effectiveness of the aircraft. One vital aspect of this programme was the introduction of the AIM-9L version of the Sidewinder air-air missile, which could be launched (if necessary) from the target's forward hemisphere and featured other important improvements over earlier models such as the AIM-9G and -9H. The AIM-9L had been cleared for use on the Sea Harrier and was in the RN inventory, but had not been issued to the squadrons before the conflict. It was accordingly rushed into service specifically for Operation Corporate, and the Smiths HUD/WAC modified accordingly to provide the pilot with firing bracket information. Another HUD/WAC change catered for loft bombing from an offset IP (initial point), since the Sea Harrier system had not been intended for blind weapon delivery against inland targets.

Loft trials were conducted over the bombing range at West Freugh in Scotland, and appropriate

View aft along the Hermes' *crowded deck, from alongside the canopy of the leading Sea Harrier. This photograph illustrates the raised cockpit of the naval version, giving much improved rear view*

software changes signalled to the aircraft carriers. Other Sea Harrier weapon trials featured batteries of two-inch (5 cm) rockets, and the Hunting Engineering BL755 cluster weapon, which was originally intended as an anti-tank device, but was known to be highly effective against parked aircraft, AAA, and troops in the open. Following the US decision to provide military equipment to assist Britain in the conflict, a rear fuselage installation for a chaff/flare dispenser package was quickly developed, and supplied to *Hermes*.

Trials in the UK included clearance for Sea Harriers to operate at increased take-off weights from ski-jumps, carrying 330 Imp gal (1,500 lit) tanks on the inboard pylons. In the course of these tests one aircraft (XZ438) was written off in an accident on May 17th, possibly due to an unplanned asymmetric condition. New configurations cleared for flight included the

combination of the large tanks inboard with empty 100 Imp gal (454 lit) tanks outboard, thus reducing tankering requirements on the ferry flight to Ascension, but having the smaller combat tanks available on arrival. In late May, design work began on a twin-Sidewinder installation to improve combat persistence, but this did not enter service until after the conflict was over, Sea Harriers of No 809 Sqn in *Illustrious* having four Sidewinders in combination with 190 Imp gal (865 lit) tanks originally developed for the BAe Hawk.

When the carriers left Portsmouth, not all their Sea Harriers were equipped with the Blue Fox radar, the remainder being fitted with concrete ballast to maintain CG position. This ballast was referred to unofficially (in tribute to a well-known cement manufacturer) as 'Blue Circle radar – the most reliable piece of kit on the aircraft'. Additional radars were air-dropped from RAF Hercules, and following a considerable amount of work to improve the consistency of Blue Fox performance (ably assisted by Ferranti representative David MacAlpine, who had volunteered to sail with the Task Force) the radar

Deck scene on Hermes *as she steamed down the Channel, with last-minute supplies being brought aboard by a variety of helicopters, including the RAF Chinook HC.1 of No 18 Sqn, based at Odiham*

went into battle in far better condition than ever before.

One of the principal decisions facing the engineers was that concerning wartime servicing procedures. At one extreme, they could try to adhere to peacetime maintenance, which would pay off if the conflict proved to be protracted, but might well involve some penalty in aircraft availability. At the other extreme, they could eliminate all actions aside from defect rectification and preflight checks, giving the greatest possible availability, but with long-term risks. Between these extremes, a modified peacetime routine could be followed with a fixed percentage increase in periodicity, determined statistically by failure probability. Once again, the two ships were operated differently, because their ratios of manpower to aircraft were different, as were the tasks placed upon them. Thus, from mid-April until July *Hermes* adopted a reduced maintenance system, eliminating some routine operations and increasing the periodicity of other by 16 per cent, in line with MoD recommendations. *Invincible*, having proportionally more manpower, did a great deal of major scheduled work en route to Ascension, looking ahead three months, and then continued with normal peacetime practice, though carrying out any major servicing at night. The fact that the air war was largely carried out in daylight was a significant factor in the incredible availability rate on the British side, although this was primarily the result of the sky-high morale that had the maintainers working every alternate eight hours throughout the conflict.

Despite the awesome odds against them, and the realization that a well-coordinated pair of Mirages could give a Sea Harrier a hard time, the British pilots never appear to have been in any doubt as to which side was going to win. In the words of 801's 'Sharkey' Ward, 'We never lacked confidence, or were concerned about the outcome'. Ward had been the principal driving force behind the Fleet Air Arm's training emphasis on air combat, an emphasis that had little direct connection with the aircraft's primary role of shooting down maritime patrol aircraft. In his view, the only way to know a combat aircraft in depth is to practice dogfights. Formerly the CO of 899 Sqn, Ward had found that the switch to command 801 gave him the opportunity to develop the Sea Harrier in the ACM (air combat manoeuvring) area, since 899 was still overloaded with development work and 800 was more concerned with weaponry and reconnaissance trials.

Even today the Fleet Air Arm is not willing to discuss Sea Harrier air combat tactics in detail. What can be said is that, rather than using the 'welded wing' formations that were popular until the 1950s and are still in use in some air forces, the Sea Harriers function as 'coordinated-pairs'.

This is effectively an extrapolation of the USAF 'double attack' technique developed in the 1960s to allow aircraft such as the F-104 Starfighter to deal with far more manoeuvrable, but slower aircraft.

Whereas the traditional role of the No 2 in an element was to stick close behind his leader to guard his tail (which gave the leader all the kills and often sacrificed the No 2), coordinated-pairs operation makes full use of the offensive potential of both aircraft, which are widely separated and in a dogfight attempt to time their attacks to gain the defender's rear hemisphere. Due to the large turning radius of modern fighters, separation between the leader and his No 2 may easily exceed visual range, hence radar becomes an important feature of the operation. Sea Harrier pilots have perfected such tactics to the extent that coordinated-pairs operation is now possible at night.

In air combat the Sea Harrier has a number of valuable features, including excellent control and freedom from departure at the low speeds to which a turning fight usually degenerates. It also has good acceleration at low speeds, fully competitive with that of the latest US fighters. As discussed earlier, thrust vectoring can be used in combat as an airbrake and to increase turn rate and pitch rate, but VIFF is basically a defensive manoeuvre and (despite the predictions of the TV and press pundits) this was to play no part in the conflict, since no Argentine fighter succeeded in making a rear hemisphere attack on a Sea Harrier.

Part of the confidence of the Sea Harrier pilots is attributable to the outstanding performance previously obtained in mock combats with supersonic fighters, using instrumented practice ranges to give unbiased results. A measurable advantage had been established by Sea Harrier squadrons not only over USAF F-5E 'Aggressors', but also over F-15 and F-16 units, a situation confirmed by Ward's 801 Sqn just before the conflict, in an exercise off Norway. This had involved *Invincible* in working close inshore, and the Sea Harriers in taking on land-based RNoAF F-16s and USAF F-15s. The exercise had taken place in very bad weather and low temperatures, and had been followed by atrocious conditions off northern Scotland, an experience that the pilots thought would stand them in good stead when it came to covering an amphibious landing on the Falklands in the winter of the southern hemisphere.

Encouraged by combat exercises with French aircraft, the Sea Harrier squadrons continued south, honing their ACM skills and practising air-surface attacks, this initial period culminating with a firepower demonstration on April 16th (just before arrival at Ascension), which included the firing of an AIM-9 against a Lepus flare target. To

Conditions below deck were crowded both for man and aircraft, this view from Hermes' *rear lift showing how Sea Harriers were packed together in the hangar. Some aircraft remained on deck for several weeks*

improve their effectiveness in coordinated pairs ACM and minimize their reliance on radio contact, pilots flew regularly as two-man teams. In the case of *Invincible*, the pilots were 'paired off' from the evening of April 6th, but in *Hermes* there was a more flexible arrangement, with each element leader flying with two or three No 2s in turn.

After two days of repositioning equipment by helicopter cross-decking at Ascension, the Task Force steamed south again, its progress followed by Soviet Tupolev Tu-20 Bears, probably operating from Luanda in Angola.

Meanwhile At Wittering . . . . .

The initial decision to send all available Sea Harriers to the South Atlantic was a straightforward reaction to the demand for some form of air cover to enable the Task Force to operate in waters that threatened to be dominated by the Argentine Air Force. Sea-based aviation was just as essential to the liberation of the Falklands as it had been during WWII to the Malta convoys and the amphibious landings on the Pacific islands.

It was probably only after the carriers had sailed that the full implications of the proposed action sank in at MoD. It was then clear that, even if the Sea Harrier pilots could achieve a kill ratio of three or four to one, despite far higher adverse odds than they had ever faced in peacetime exercises, their losses would still be proportionally high, and their strength could quickly be reduced to a level at which air cover for the Task Force would be patchy or worse.

Estimates for possible Sea Harrier losses ran as high as one per day (a figure that in the event was reached only in the three-day period May 4th–6th), which would have effectively eliminated RN fixed-wing air power within two weeks of the start of the air war. As a further week's supply, it was decided to send an extra eight aircraft south with the *Atlantic Conveyor*, although this would leave only four Sea Harriers in the UK for any trials of armament and equipment. There remained one RN aircraft on the assembly line, and this did not fly until the following year.

To build further Sea Harriers from scratch would take three years: aircraft production has changed out of all recognition since the Battle of Britain, when fighters were constructed in a few months. (Once the details had been made, a Hurricane could be built in 45 days.) The only

As the ships steamed south, operational trials continued in the UK. Here a Sea Harrier takes off from the Yeovilton ski-jump with RAF ferry tanks and Sidewinders. One aircraft was lost during these tests

way to have obtained additional Sea Harriers in the short term would have been to appropriate those under construction for the Indian Navy, although the first of the six did not fly until August 6th. Nonetheless, the IN representative kept a close watch on the production line, saying to his friends in BAe: '*If your men start working faster, I shall know what you're up to!*'

The only realistic short-term solution to the Sea Harrier attrition problem was thus to use RAF Harrier GR.3s, of which there were approximately 70 in service. On current plans the two Gütersloh squadrons are to be replaced with the McDonnell Douglas AV-8B Harrier II, which the RAF will call the Harrier GR.5. As deliveries of the 60 GR.5s get under way in 1986, GR.3s will be returned to Wittering, which is expected to peak at around 50 aircraft, and where GR.3s will be given some form of update. For the Falklands operation the GR.3 was seen as a poor substitute for the Sea Harrier in the primary air defence role, since it lacked a radar, but it would at least be available in comparatively large numbers.

Rumours of a scheme to deploy GR.3s to the South Atlantic began to circulate during the Easter weekend (April 9th–12th), and plans hardened on Tuesday the 13th, after Sqn Ldr 'Bob' Iveson, a flight commander of No 1(F) Sqn, had inspected the container ship *Atlantic Conveyor* in Liverpool harbour. On the afternoon of the 14th a meeting of service and industry representatives was held at MoD to discuss the technical support required in the operation. The civilians recall being sworn to secrecy, then reading in the evening newspapers that GR.3s were to be sent south in the *Atlantic Conveyor*!

As the world-wide 'fire-brigade' unit of the RAF Harrier force, it was natural that No 1(F) Sqn under Wg Cdr Peter Squire should be tasked with reinforcing the Fleet Air Arm. Since receiving a preliminary order on the 8th, warning that No 1(F) was likely to be involved in carrier operations in the South Atlantic, plans had been made at Wittering to get together 12–16 aircraft with the most powerful engines, ie those that records showed to produce the highest thrust level in routine hover performance checks. Of No 1(F)'s own 12 Harriers, three were in second-line servicing and three others had rather poor engines, leaving only six immediately available and classed as suitable for the air-air role. It followed that anything from six to ten would have to be obtained from the OCU and RAF Germany.

To complicate matters, eight GR.3s (including one from No 1(F) Sqn) were involved in a training

An RAF Harrier GR.3 at the hover alongside HMS Hermes, showing the 'double-chin' and S-band transponder blade antenna that characterized the GR.3s used in Operation Corporate

exercise in Canada, together with pilots from all three squadrons. The aircraft were flown to Goose Bay on April 13th by No 1(F) Sqn, since this was the only Harrier unit qualified for air-air refuelling. The plan had been that Nos 3(F) and 4 Sqn would fly them for two weeks, then No 1(F) Sqn would take over for two more weeks and ferry them back across the Atlantic in mid-May. Suddenly, all Harrier aircraft and pilots were required to be available in Europe, and the Victor tankers were tied up with Operation Corporate. The eight GR.3s were therefore flown back by No 3(F) Sqn to Germany via Greenland and Iceland, without tanker support. Reports that they were air-lifted to Wittering in USAF C-5As are not true.

Based on Harrier fleet records, six aircraft from Gütersloh and the OCU were then chosen (they can be distinguished in Falklands photographs by tail numbers from 30 upwards), giving a total of 12 GR.3s to be prepared for carrier operations in the air-air role. For 12 aircraft, No 1(F) Sqn needed 16–18 pilots, but at that stage had only 12 (omitting one USAF exchange officer, and an RN pilot who had sailed with the Task Force), and of

these a few were inexperienced. In the end 16 pilots were selected, of whom eight were from No 1(F) Sqn, the remainder coming from the OCU, RAF Germany, and miscellaneous postings (in the case of pilots who had just completed their tours with No 1(F)). In the intial deployment only eight pilots continued south from Ascension, all No 1(F) Sqn officers aside from one who had just been posted from Wittering to Chivenor.

Pilot training began with take-offs from the RN's ski-jump at Yeovilton, where the first detachment arrived on April 14th. The initial plan was that each pilot would carry out three such operations, but it was quickly decided the 'there was nothing to it', hence the number was reduced to one. Perhaps surprisingly, although RAF Harriers normally have no air-air role, there was no special air combat training. The feeling appears to have been that they had 'done' the Mirage in the course of NATO exercises, and RAF Harrier pilots were not exactly quaking in their boots at the idea of taking on Argentine-flown Mirages.

Flight trials to prepare the GR.3 for its new task included AIM-9 clearance, the trial installation taking place on April 28th at Wittering, and the first firing two days later over the Aberporth range off the Welsh coast. The standard 68 mm SNEB rocket was judged unsuitable for use on aircraft carriers due to radiation hazard (ie powerful radar emissions might induce voltages in the wiring,

The pale grey Sea Harriers of Lt Cdr 'Tim' Gedge's 809 Sqn at RNAS Yeovilton, before deployment to the South Atlantic via Ascension and the Atlantic Conveyor. *The unit disbanded late in 1982*

RIGHT
A Sea Harrier of 899 Sqn with toned-down roundels and winged fist badge, on the ramp at Yeovilton alongside one of the Hunter T.8Ms used to train Sea Harrier pilots in weapon system operation

causing rockets to be fired inadvertently), hence the GR.3 was cleared to use the RN's two-inch (5 cm) rocket, firings taking place at Holbeach on the edge of the Wash. Tests were later carried out with the 1,000 lb (454 kg) Pave Way laser-guided bomb (LGB).

While RAF pilots were being prepared for battle (and it is only fair to add that seven RAF Harrier pilots had sailed with the carriers, these exchange officers compensating for the RN's pilot shortage caused by the long gap between the Phantom and the Sea Harrier), their aircraft were being modified at Wittering. One set of changes was to make the aircraft more suitable for deck operation with a salt water environment. These modifications included improved sealing and drainage (basically Sea Harrier changes) to minimize corrosion, the addition of outrigger shackles to allow the aircraft to be tied down securely on a highly mobile deck, and an I-band transponder to facilitate radar acquisition by the carrier and thus assist in bad weather recovery. For ease of fitment, the transponder and its blade antenna were added to an access panel under the nose, producing the 'double-chin' that characterized the Falklands GR.3s. Typical of the remarkable speed with which such changes were made during Operation Corporate, the transponder installation was requested by MoD on April 14th, and the first modification kits were handed over by BAe on the 22nd. The first 12 installations were produced at Wittering, followed by 15 at Kingston on access panels sent from Wittering. The aircraft were also given additional wiring to allow their inertial platforms to be aligned on a moving deck, and a nosewheel steering modification. This allowed steering to be selected (and the nosewheel thus prevented from castoring) without the need to keep the button depressed on the control column, a change that gave better position control on a rolling deck.

A second series of modifications had to be developed and installed to improve the aircraft's effectiveness, bringing forward improvements that were planned, but had not previously been funded. The most major of these changes was the AIM-9 installation, which in the longer term will probably take place on the Harrier's wingtips as a defensive measure, but for the Falklands could only be considered as a quick fix for the outboard pylons.

In order to achieve the fastest possible conversion, BAe proposed (on April 21st) to use the existing armament wiring to the outer pylons with minimum modification, although this involved a time delay if the pylons were to be converted back to air-ground stores.

The scheme was approved by MoD on the following day, and on April 27th the first Sidewinder installation kit was taken from Kingston to Wittering. A trial fit of the missile was carried out on the 28th, the system was checked, and the aircraft transferred on the 29th to Boscome Down for a firing on the following day. Aside from the wiring change, the Sidewinder installation included fitting a control box in the cockpit, and an adapter to allow the launch rail to be attached to the pylon. This adapter was an item of Phantom equipment, modified by RAF Wittering. A total of 11 aircraft were given the Sidewinder installation in the first phase (five more were converted later), but BAe produced 18 conversion kits and a further 58 after the conflict.

Like the Sea Harrier, the GR.3 had no chaff/flare dispenser although chaff bundles could be (and were) wedged between the bombs and the pylons, and between the airbrake and the fuselage, producing a cloud of radar-reflective aluminium strips on release. Late in April MoD suggested to BAe the addition of chaff/flare 'scabs', which had been considered some years previously for installation on the Harrier's pylons. However, no

This photograph by Lt Covington shows the Sea Harriers and Harrier GR.3s as they were positioned on the deck of the container ship at Ascension Island, having landed on the forward pad

RIGHT
After leaving Ascension the aircraft were covered in purpose-built plastic bags for protection against the salt water. Note the containers stacked three-high along the sides

satisfactory installation appeared possible and attention switched to an internal dispenser similar to that planned for the GR.5. Following the US decision to support the UK with military equipment, a suitable dispenser became available (the Tracor representative having flown the Atlantic with a complete set of equipment immediately after President Reagan's speech approving such aid). Installation design began on May 4th to add the ALE-40 to a ventral access panel in the rear fuselage. The first converted door was fitted to a Harrier at Wittering on the 11th, and release trials began on the following day, the aircraft operating from Boscombe Down and discharging the cartridges over the Larkhill range. By May 20th all 12 conversion kits had been supplied and 10 Harriers modified.

On the subject of electronic warfare, it has subsequently been announced that GR.3s will be fitted with internal Marconi Zeus jamming equipment. At the time of the Falklands conflict an internal jammer could not be developed on a useful timescale, but it appears that some GR.3s had a gunpod adapted to take a jammer of unspecified type. At least one Harrier was modified to use an ARM, presumably the AGM-45 Shrike employed by the Vulcan in two strikes against radars in the Port Stanley area. However, the possibility of using Harriers in the anti-radar strike role did not arise until late in May, and the first flight with an ARM did not occur until June 3rd, hence this combination did not see active service.

One of the most outstanding examples of industry support for the Harriers during this conflict relates to Ferranti's rapid development of equipment to allow the GR.3's inertial platform to be levelled and aligned with north while on the moving deck of an aircraft carrier. This was of crucial importance to the successful use of the GR.3s, hence some explanation of the problem is in order.

Inertial navigation is a dead-reckoning system in which outputs from three accelerometers are used to calculate velocity components (north, east and vertical) and hence changes in position. For the system to work properly, the accelerometers are conventionally set on a gyro-stabilized platform or 'stable table', which before take-off is levelled and aligned with true north, and is constantly adjusted during flight so that it remains level as the aircraft moves around the earth's curvature. The platform is also used as a reference for the pilot's artificial horizon, showing the aircraft's pitch and roll attitude.

However, on a moving deck an aircraft's inertial platform has difficulty in levelling, since (although its electronics will filter out the effects of wind, and groundcrew walking on the wing) its accelerometers will generate spurious signals corresponding to ship motion. Because of this problem the Sea Harrier had been given a different navigation system, although some modern vessels (including *Invincible*) have their own form of inertial navigation, which is specially developed to filter out ship motion effects, and in principle can be used as a master reference in setting up an aircraft system. Since (a) it was not feasible within the timescale to equip the GR.3s with the Sea Harrier system, and (b) the GR.3s had to be capable of operating from *Hermes*, and (c) their inertial systems could not be left running throughout the conflict (if only because the carrier did not have the necessary electrical power outlets), the only possible solution was a mobile inertial reference that could operate anywhere on the ship and communicate with the GR.3's system. This was FINRAE (Ferranti Inertial Rapid Alignment Equipment), a lightweight stabilized

To provide some air defence capability against long-range Argentine air attack while in transit to the TEZ, one Sea Harrier and one spare were left unbagged at the forward end of the deck

RIGHT
The key to safe operation of RAF Harriers from a moving deck was the Ferranti FINRAE, which allowed their inertial platforms to be aligned with sufficient accuracy for attitude reference purposes

platform that could be run continuously and had special software to allow it to function much as a ship's inertial system and to transmit levelling and heading data to a nearby aircraft.

Ironically, a form of FINRAE had been tested ten years earlier, largely at Ferranti's own expense, but (in the absence of an MoD requirement) had been abandoned and its components used for other purposes. By coincidence, Wg Cdr 'Joe' Sim, the officer now responsible for Offensive Support in the RAF Operations Branch, had taken part as a pilot in the earlier FINRAE carrier trials. He was convinced that the Harrier pilots would need help from their inertial systems in the forthcoming deck operations for several reasons: they would be operating in an unfamiliar environment, carrier operations in any event tend to be disorientating, the winter would give reduced visibility and a low cloud ceiling, and the southern hemisphere (sun in

The FINRAE in operation on the Hermes' *flight deck. At the planning stage it had been hoped to use this equipment in the 'passive' mode from below deck, but this proved impractical*

the wrong position, moving in the wrong direction) and the stresses of combat would add to the pilots' problems.

A requirement was accordingly framed on the basis that attitude and heading information on the HUD was essential, and that navigation and weapon aiming information was desirable, although it was recognised from the outset that the latter facilities were doubtful.

At the meeting on April 14th these demands were made known to Ferranti. At that stage only one FINRAE was required, the ship was not specified, nor was the timescale. The company's representatives phoned their report back to Edinburgh, and scheduled an in-house meeting for the first thing on the 15th, to discuss what became known as FINRAE Mk 2 or Project 2007 (derived from the MoD contract number). At this meeting it was decided to produce a minimum of two systems and hopefully a third, all within a month. In what Ferranti recalls as 'the quickest decision and the shortest contract ever known', the company proposal was accepted by telex from MoD at 1700 hr on the 16th.

One of the first actions at Ferranti was to reassemble the original FINRAE team under the leadership of John Dods (now chief engineer of the Inertial Systems Group), and to give them back their old jobs, although in several cases this involved instant demotion! By the evening of Sunday the 18th (when the Task Force was departing Ascension) the design was complete, and on the following day – a holiday in Scotland – the team began ordering long-lead items, promising to follow up with official orders on the Tuesday. A good example of the cooperation enjoyed concerned the wharehouse trolley on which FINRAE was to be mounted: the manufacturer quoted a normal delivery of six months, but on learning why it was required provided it the next morning!

After the end of the first week, the company decided that, judging by newspaper reports regarding the *Atlantic Conveyor*, the original schedule would not get FINRAE to Ascension before the ship left, and that the remaining three weeks of work would therefore have to be compressed into one week. To make this possible, the company borrowed two Jaguar retrofit inertial platforms (designated FIN 1064) from MoD, and provided a third system from its own resources. This equipment is a very modern digital system

An RAF Harrier GR.3 of No 1(F) Sqn, refuelling from a Victor K.2 en route to Ascension. The flight took over nine hours, and three Victors were required to support each flight of three Harriers

(far in advance of the GR.3's own hard-wired analogue system), and had proved in Jaguar flight trials to be highly reliable.

In order to minimize deck clutter, FINRAE Mk 2 was given a tray of batteries as a self-contained power-pack, which would theoretically provide 24 hours of running time between charges. The fully loaded trolley was quite heavy, so it was planned to operate in a 'passive' mode, with FINRAE below deck but communicating with GR.3s that would be parked in pre-planned positions and aligned with a mark on the deck edge. The alternative 'active' mode had FINRAE on deck with the aircraft pointing at it, and levelling and alignment data again conveyed by umbilical cable.

Trials to test at-sea alignment were held on April 28th and 30th, using an RN tug from Rosyth. Interfacing between the digital FIN 1064 and the Harrier's analogue FE541 was meanwhile checked on XW767, a Wittering aircraft flown to Turnhouse (Edinburgh airport). To catch the *Atlantic Conveyor* at Ascension, FINRAE had to be delivered to Wittering by 1400 hr on Sunday May 2nd for loading in a Hercules that was to take-off the following day. The first complete system was assembled at 1800 hr on May 1st, and after further checks left by road at 0300 hr on the 2nd. The second FINRAE and associated LRUs (line replacement units) were flown to Wittering in the company's HS.125 business jet, departing Edinburgh at 1300 hr on the 2nd. In only 18 days Ferranti had produced and delivered the equipment that was essential to safe operation by the Harrier GR.3 from a moving deck.

Ascension to TEZ

Even before FINRAE was delivered to Wittering, the air war had begun in earnest, with Sea Harriers operating successfully in both the air-ground and air-air roles in a day of intensive sorties on May 1st. These operations followed the first bombing attack against Port Stanley airfield by an RAF Vulcan from Ascension, a mission that called for no less than 16 Victor tanker sorties. Clearly, land-based air power could serve Britain in a limited number of roles and at tremendous expense, but only carrier-based aircraft could provide the air defence and close support missions needed in the liberation of the Falklands.

Preceded by two groups of escorts, one steaming directly to the Exclusion Zone and the other to liberate South Georgia in Operation Paraquat, the two carriers had left Ascension on April 18th, their departure hastened by a submarine alert. The possibility of torpedo attack was a constant danger for the larger ships, and there have been reports that Argentina made a serious effort to intercept the *QEII* on her voyage south, but that this was frustrated by the speed of the troopship. The Argentine Navy had four submarines: two old US-built Guppy IIs and two more modern diesel-engined German Type 209s. Of the former category, the *Santa Fé* (which had been built as the USS *Catfish* and was delivered to Argentina in 1971) was damaged beyond repair by RN helicopters during the retaking of South Georgia on April 25th. Her sister boat, the *Santiago del Estero*, we now know to have been cannibalised for spares before the conflict.

Of the Type 209s, the *Salta* stayed in dock with engine problems, but the *San Luis* made a 36-day patrol in the area of the Task Force. She is believed to have fired her torpedoes to no effect, due to a wiring fault in her fire control panel. In the light of the possible torpedo threat, the carriers

An RAF Harrier GR.3 on the ground at Ascension, its external tanks and flight refuelling probe removed, before the short hop to the Atlantic Conveyor. *In the background are Victor tankers*

maintained a constant ASW screen with the Sea King HAS.5s of *Hermes*' 826 Sqn and *Invincible*'s 820 Sqn, a screen that was to last day and night for the next three months. This called for extremely high utilisation rates: one Sea King is reckoned to have spent a third of one month airborne!

The recovery of South Georgia had been virtually a bloodless operation, and for much of April there remained a hope that President Galtieri would back down and withdraw his troops from the Falklands before large-scale casualties were incurred. However, as hopes of a diplomatic settlement faded, Britain took steps to ensure that effective military action could be undertaken without the conflict escalating into an unlimited war between the two countries. On April 8th notice was given of a Maritime Exclusion Zone (MEZ) to be introduced on the 12th (when the SSNs arrived in the area), covering a circle of 200 nm (370 km) radius, centred on a point at 51°40′ South and 59°30′ West. On the 28th it was announced that this would be extended from 1100 hr GMT on the 30th to include associated

HMS Invincible *was mainly concerned with air defence operations. Two of her Sea Harriers are seen here, armed with Sidewinders and Aden 30 mm cannon. Most ground attack sorties were launched from* Hermes

airspace, thus becoming a Total Exclusion Zone (TEZ).

Wednesday April 21st was one benchmark in the process of escalation. Training by the various RN squadrons was officially declared to be completed, and actual operations began. From this date a pair of Sea Harriers was constantly airborne throughout the daylight hours, each armed with two AIM-9s and 200 rounds of 30 mm ammunition, while another pair were held at Alert 5, ie armed and manned and ready to launch within five minutes.

It was on the 21st that the first contact was made with an Argentine military aircraft, a Boeing 707-320B that was being used to shadow the carrier battle group. The 707 was intercepted approximately 150 nm (280 km) to the south by a Sea Harrier of 801 Sqn, flown by Lt Simon Hargreaves, who escorted it away from the ships, being under orders not to fire. Similar intercepts

A Sea Harrier departs Hermes' *skijump, the angled flight deck leaving the starboard side free for other aircraft and armament of various types*

TOP RIGHT
A mixed bag, lashed down on Hermes' *deck, the flush canopy and laser nose of the GR.3s contrasting with the raised cockpits and radar noses of the Sea Harriers*

Evidently taken as the carrier was preparing to accept stores from an RFA, this deck-scene includes various models of Sidewinder, but all operational firings were made with the AIM-9L

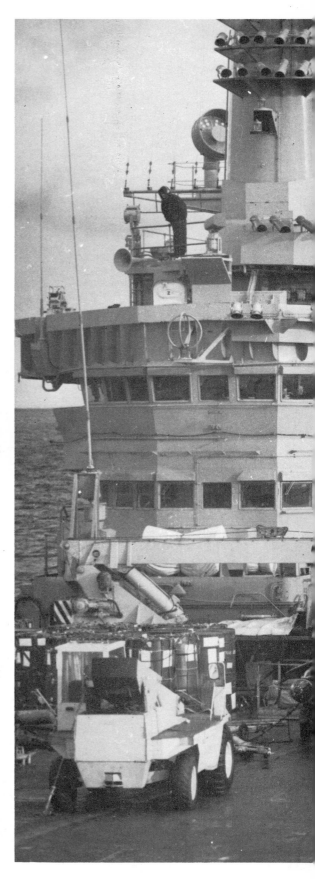

TOP
*Sidewinder-armed Sea Harriers, lashed down at the rear
of the flight deck. Alert status often involved the pilots
sitting in a freezing cockpit for hours at a time*

ABOVE
*A mixture of nose-shapes and colours: an RAF GR.3 in
the foreground, then a pale grey Sea Harrier of 809 Sqn,
and the darker 800 Sqn aircraft that gave rise to the
appellation of 'La Muerta Negra'*

RIGHT
*The flight line of Harrier GR.3s and Sea Harriers on the
deck of* Hermes. *The leading GR.3 is armed with the
BL755 cluster bomb, which was employed as an anti-
personnel weapon with deadly effect*

OVERLEAF CLOCKWISE
A bombed-up Sea Harrier at unstick

*An RAF Harrier GR.3 with empty weapon pylons returns
to land vertically on* Hermes' *deck. Originally tasked with
supplementing RN aircraft in air defence, the Harrier was
employed solely in attack missions.*

*A Sidewinder-armed Sea Harrier is man-handled into
position. With little more than five minutes on station, its
success in air defence probably depended heavily on reports
from the SAS in Argentina*

*On the flight deck, armourers in anti-flash gear prepare a
BL755 cluster weapon (left), and an ASW homing torpedo
for the Sea King helicopter*

took place daily at dawn and dusk up to and including the 24th, following which Argentina was informed that any further repeat would be fatal for the Boeing's crew. The 707 was not seen again within the TEZ, although it did return when the weather was too bad for Sea Harrier operations.

By this stage many of the basic decisions regarding RN aircraft operations had been taken. Despite the fact that there was a four-hour difference between local time and that in London, the Task Force worked on 'Zulu' time, ie GMT. Thus, the first watch went from 0400Z to 1200Z, the second from 1200Z to 2000Z, and the third from 2000Z to 0400Z. Once in the TEZ, daylight lasted from around 1030Z to 1800Z. Most flying was done in the second watch, although strike operations began as early as 0930Z in order to have the sun behind a low flying aircraft attacking from the east, just as the Argentines often attacked at dusk from the west. Most maintenance was done in the third watch.

Under the pressures of war, some of the operating practices that had been developed to ensure safety were to be temporarily abandoned. For example, serviceable aircraft were often placed in *Invincible*'s hangar, fuelled and fully armed, with live Sidewinders, something that would be unthinkable in peacetime. Likewise, aircraft were refuelled and rearmed simultaneously, a practice that ended promptly on June 14th. Harriers were not 'hot-refuelled', simply because the fuelling point is between the two port engine nozzles, and is thus inaccessible with the Pegasus running.

The system of parking aircraft was also changed, due to the need to get airborne quickly, despite deck crowding. In peacetime an armed Sea Harrier is normally parked aft, pointing over the side, to minimize the consequences of an accidental firing. Such parking is safe, but limits the number of alert aircraft and gives an unacceptably long reaction time in war. Once the fighting had begun, aircraft at the rear were therefore parked facing straight ahead or to port, so that they could taxy directly to the take-off position. Additional aircraft were parked further forward at 'Fly 1' and 'Fly 2', respectively just ahead of and inboard of the island. In the case of *Invincible* these aircraft were parked facing forward and to port, so that they could taxy to the runway 'tram-lines' painted on the deck, then reverse to the take-off position by forward use of 100° nozzle angle, giving a rearward thrust component. In the case of *Hermes*, such aircraft were parked facing aft and to port, taxying out in a port turn followed by a U-turn to starboard, in what was referred to as the 'elephant tango'.

The airfield at Port Stanley, looking east toward the township. Built on solid rock and defended by an array of modern weapons, it proved a difficult target for Harrier attacks

Goose Green

Port Stanley

Bluff Cove

Port San Carlos Settlement

Some of the main locations involved in the fighting for East Falkland

Considering the sophistication of the Sea Harrier systems, little difficulty had been experienced during the voyage south. The NAVHARS (navigation, heading and attitude reference system) would not erect properly between 18°N and 18°S, although the system could be re-erected in flight. Once beyond this latitude band the problem disappeared, but it was then found that the software required modification to suit operation in the southern hemisphere. By the time the TEZ was reached, those responsible for the aircraft's avionics were reasonably happy, but the worst of the problems arising from moisture and cold were yet to come.

On April 30th President Reagan bowed to public opinion and announced that the US would side with Britain in resisting Argentine aggression, thus making available not only fuel supplies and

key items of military hardware, but also loaning USAF KC-135 tankers to substitute for RAF Victors in the air defence of the UK. Vulcans had been positioned to Ascension. The RN's submarines were present in sufficient strength to deal with Argentine surface forces. The fight for the Falklands was about to begin.

May Day

Saturday May 1st was not simply the first day of the air war, but a major battle that proved the operational flexibility of the RN Sea Harriers and the professionalism of their pilots. Although losses were comparatively small, the events of that day quite clearly shook the Argentine Air Force to its roots, persuading Lami Dozo to abandon any idea of destroying the Sea Harrier force in the air. If he had ignored those losses of the first day and continued to hurl his Mirages at the Fleet Air Arm, believing that 70 Mach 2 fighters must prevail against 20 Sea Harriers, then Argentina might have reduced the Task Force's outer air

Shorts' Tigercat was one of the guided weapon systems used by the Argentines to defend Port Stanley airfield against air attacks, but it achieved no kills

defences to such an extent that losses of ships would have been far higher, and a successful amphibious landing out of the question.

Instead, Lami Dozo evidently concluded that the Mirage could not win against the Sea Harrier. The legend of 'La Muerta Negra' (The Black Death) had been born, and henceforth Argentine fighters would carry bombs and try to avoid their British counterparts. When intercepted, they would mostly jettison their ordnance and turn for home. A few attempted briefly to combat their opponents, but without success. Not one Sea Harrier was lost in air combat throughout the conflict. After May Day, the defeat of the Argentine air arms was assured, if only by the operational doctrine imposed by their commanders.

The principal target for this and subsequent British air strikes was the airfield at Port Stanley.

The runway itself was a difficult target, being built on solid rock, with hardcore filling the natural depressions. However, it was hoped to damage it sufficiently that Mirages, A-4s and Super Etendards would not be able to use it, and thus to minimize their sortie rate and their chance of penetrating the Task Force defences. In addition, it was hoped to damage aircraft on the ground and the airport facilities, and to force the Argentines to disperse aircraft and supplies around the islands and thus accept reduced operational efficiency. These aims were largely achieved in the weeks that followed, and the Argentines never succeeded in basing fast jets in the Falklands.

The strike that began the air war in the Falklands was the first of five RAF Vulcan sorties (three with HE bombs, two with ARMs) from Ascension, flying over a radius of approximately 3,250 nm (6,000 km). The aircraft, XM607 of No 44 Sqn, descended to 250 ft (75 m) for the last 300 nm (550 km) of the run-in, flying at 340 knots (630 km/hr), and pulling up to 10,000 ft (3,000 m) for the bombing run. The single stick of 21 1,000

The Oerlikon 35 mm twin-barrel Type GDF-003 anti-aircraft cannon controlled by Skyguard, but has a Ferranti standby sight. It carried 238 rounds, and has a cyclic rate of 1,100 rd/min

BELOW
The Contraves Skyguard fire control system (right of centre) is based on a pulse-Doppler radar, and typically controls two twin-barrel 35 mm cannon. A missile launcher may be added, as shown here

lb (454 kg) bombs was dropped at 0745Z by reference to ground-mapping radar and at an angle of 30° to the runway. Although difficult to damage, the airfield was an ideal target for blind bombing, being situated on a distinctively-shaped peninsula. The flashes of the exploding bombs (one of which struck the runway) were clearly visible to the Vulcan crew, and the pressure waves were felt through the aircraft structure. Unseen by the Vulcan, Sea Harriers of No 801 Sqn had flown supporting CAP missions from *Invincible* (which throughout concentrated on the air defence task), but no opposition was encountered. The Sea Harrier was not to be blooded until dawn, in the first British carrier-based airfield strikes since the Suez conflict of 1956.

The two RN carriers were operated quite close together, roughly 150 nm (280 km) to the east of the islands, to minimize the risk of air strikes from Argentina and to combine their ASW and anti-aircraft (AA) defences. As the dawn of May 1st approached, they ran in toward East Falkland, launching at 1050Z from approximately 90 nm (165 km) in a maximum effort mission involving all 20 Sea Harriers.

Although pre-dawn patrols to the north and south of the island had found no air opposition, the possibility could not be ruled out, and Rear-Admiral Woodward was intent on conserving his limited Sea Harrier assets. The eight aircraft of *Invincible*'s 801 Sqn were therefore configured for CAP with two Sidewinders outboard, while *Hermes'* 12 aircraft of 800 Sqn each carried three bombs. All Sea Harrier operational missions were flown with combat drop tanks on the inboard wing pylons.

The plan was for nine aircraft to attack Port Stanley airfield with three reserves, which attacked their secondary target, the grass strip at Goose Green, where some Argentine aircraft were reportedly sited. The main airfield was expected to be heavily defended, hence the attack would take place in two waves, the first of four aircraft tossing thousand-pounders for defence-suppression, and the second of five aircraft carrying out a low level attack on a variety of targets. In order to allow debris from the first wave's bombs to clear, there was a 30-second interval between the attacks, conveniently produced by having the five aircraft make an extra orbit at the hold point en route to the target. By making a low approach and by having the last aircraft clear of the target within 45 seconds of the first explosion, it was hoped to minimize losses due to ground fire.

The first four aircraft (led by Lt Cdr 'Tony' Ogilvy) each carried three thousand-pounders, which were delivered in toss attacks to keep the Sea Harriers outside the envelope of the defences as they came in from the north-east. Three of these aircraft went for reported AAA/SAM sites,

while the fourth delivered its bombs with delayed action fuzes into the middle of the target area. Of the second wave, which approached on either side of Mt Low with 3-sec spacings, four aircraft each had three BL755 cluster weapons, two Sea Harriers attacking the hangars and parked aircraft and two going for targets of opportunity. The fifth aircraft (flown by Flt Lt Penfold) was armed with retarded bombs, which were delivered against the runway. All five aircraft approached low, climbing to 150–200 ft (45–60 m) to release their weapons. They withdrew low until outside the defences, then climbed to medium level to return to the ship.

Typical of subsequent attacks, the pilots of the lead aircraft did not notice much return fire (apparently because most of it was passing behind them, rather than slow reaction by the Argentines), while the pilots of the second wave reported a great deal of AAA and some Tigercat SAM firings. To quote one pilot: 'It was like Fireworks Night – they were hosing it around everywhere!'

Immediate post-strike assessment was provided by two Sea Harriers from the toss-attack section, using the Sea Harrier's starboard oblique camera, Lt Cdr Thomas making a fast low run about 1 nm (1.85 km) to the north, and receiving warning of a radar lock-on (he believed from Roland), while Lt Clive Morrell made a higher pass 2–3 nm (3.7–5.5 km) from the airfield.

The effects of the strike were difficult to asses, but there was certainly some damage to facilities and aircraft on the ground, and some scabbing of the runway, which could cause damage to tyres and engines. At Goose Green, where two Sea Harriers attacked with BL755s and one with retarded thousand-pounders, five Argentine aircraft are believed to have been written off. From Argentine film of the attack on Port Stanley airfield, it appears that a number of the BL755 bomblets detonated before impact, although this would probably not spoil their effectiveness against aircraft targets. It is also known that some bomblets failed to explode. In all, 1,322 are said to have been recovered after the Argentine surrender.

The results achieved by the Argentine defences are much easier to quantify. They claim to have destroyed three Sea Harriers during this first attack, and in reality achieved one strike on the fin of one aircraft, the last over the target, flown by Flt Lt Morgan. The resulting elation back on the British carriers was fully justified in the light of the array of modern air defence weaponry in use by the Argentine Air Force and Army. At the top of the scale, they had Roland, Tigercat and Blowpipe SAMs. Next, both services had the 35 mm Oerlikon cannon on a twin-gun mount, pairs of guns being directed by the very modern Contraves Skyguard pulse-Doppler radar system at both Port Stanley and Goose Green, three or four firing units having been transported to the islands by C-130 and ship during April. The Air Force also had the earlier Super Fledermaus radar fire control system on East Falkland, but this suffered technical problems, and was never used. At the bottom of the AAA scale, the Argentines had optically-directed 20 mm Rheinmetall and 30 mm Hispano-Suiza. The ineffectiveness of Argentine air defences is illustrated by the fact that for this first attack the RN established a line of SAR (search and rescue) helicopters between the islands and the carriers, and that thereafter this mission was left to the ASW Sea King screen.

The Sea Harrier fin strike appears to have been produced by a 20 mm shell, entering from the port side and exploding as it emerged to starboard. A repair was effected in 3.5 hours, although similar damage was later repaired in 1.5 hours. All that was required was for the hole to be cleaned up, then covered with Speedtape, which came as a roll of material, rather like thick aluminium foil with an adhesive backing. Advising on battle damage repairs, each carrier had two technicians from MARTSU (Mobile Aircraft Repair, Transport and Salvage Unit, based at Lee-on-Solent).

All the other Sea Harriers were re-roled within 40 minutes for air defence, in anticipation of a response by Argentine Mirages. For much of that morning the Sea Harrier CAP fenced with Mirages patrolling to the north and south of the islands. The Argentine aircraft were under the control of a brand-new Westinghouse TPS-43 radar at Port Stanley, and had a time-on-station of 30–40 minutes at altitude, thanks to two large subsonic tanks of 374 Imp gal (1,700 litre) capacity. The Mirages repeatedly approached at high level, but each time turned back before they could be engaged. The Sea Harrier pilots were intent on establishing their superiority over the Mirages from the outset, but were not to be drawn to high altitude or too far from the carriers. What followed might be regarded conceptually as a Korean War-style combat, with the Sea Harrier the modern equivalent of the F-86 Sabre, dragging its opponent (the high-flying Mirage being analogous to the MIG-15) down to an altitude at which a high kill-ratio could be achieved.

There is a theory that the Mirage pilots were unable to detect the Sea Harriers with their Cyrano radar, since this had no look-down capability, and that they therefore had to rely (while beyond visual range) on ground control. Armed with the medium-range Matra 530 radar-homing missile, they should theoretically have been able to destroy the Sea Harriers from outside Sidewinder range, but this was not to be.

When, by mid-afternoon, the Argentine pilots began to press home their thrusts toward the Sea Harrier CAP, the Mirages launched their missiles in head-on attacks from well outside maximum firing range (possibly due to faulty ground control) and the 530s, identified by their large size and sustainers, fell short. Such an attack by a section of two Mirages was first made against a pair of 801 Sqn Sea Harriers flown by Lt Cdr Robin Kent (the unit's senior pilot) and Lt Brian Haig, then another with short-range missiles was made against the CO ('Sharkey' Ward) and Lt 'Soapy' Watson. Next came then turn of Flt Lt Paul Barton and Lt 'Steve' Thomas. However, this time the Mirages ventured too close and the killing began.

It was a classic coordinated pairs operation. The Sea Harriers were at 12,000 ft (3,650 m), when Thomas detected on his radar a pair of Mirages in 'sucked echelon', the No 2 set back half a mile (900 m) and slightly off to one side. It is standard RN practice that the first man to make contact controls the intercept, so Thomas directed Barton to pull out to the side and try for a rear hemisphere shot as the Mirages flew through their section. The trail aircraft moved out toward Barton, who fired initially with cannon, then with Sidewinder (all operational firings were with the AIM-9L model). The Mirage, at this stage in a nose-high attitude, presumably trying to out-turn the missile, was hit and pilot bailed out. Meanwhile, Thomas turned into the No 1, but this showed no sign of wanting to tangle with a Sea Harrier and entered a tight spiral dive for cloud cover. Thomas's Sidewinder reached it just as it entered cloud, but the results of the warhead burst were then uncertain.

It is now known from Argentine sources that the pilot of the lead Mirage, finding his aircraft seriously damaged by Thomas' Sidewinder, decided to ignore orders and attempt a landing at Port Stanley. On the approach he jettisoned his drop tanks, and the men on the ground, thinking this was a British aircraft attacking (the Skyguard system at Stanley had no IFF), fired 20 mm, Skyguard/35 mm, and Roland. This kill is listed in British records as an 'own goal'.

The first Sea Harrier kill of the conflict was thus obtained by No 801 Sqn at 1930Z on May 1st. A Dagger was next destroyed, in this case by Flt Lt 'Bertie' Penfold of 800 Sqn, at 1941Z. Probably timed to take advantage of top cover from the Mirages, a flight of six Canberras then approached the Task Force, descending from medium to low level at roughly 100 nm (185 km) distance, where they were spotted briefly by ship's radar. Sea Harriers flown by Lt Cdr 'Mike' Broadwater and Lt Alan Curtiss of 801 Sqn were returning from CAP, and they were asked by the controller on the ship if they could intercept. Given a line of bearing on the last radar contact, they headed out descending to low level. As dusk fell and they let

Test firing of the Euromissile Roland low altitude air defence missile. Argentine sources claim that eight Rolands were fired in the Falklands, destroying four Harriers. In fact they destroyed only one

down through cloud, the Sea Harriers picked up the Canberras on their Blue Fox radars, which (although not designed for low level intercepts) have a useful look-down capability over water. The Canberras were still 150 nm (280 km) from their targets, flying at 50 ft (15 m) in two sections of three, using what the Argentines describe as 'Lincoln tactics', presumably meaning line-abreast formation. On seeing the British fighters diving at them, they broke formation. Curtiss fired a Sidewinder at the lead aircraft, it entered the fuselage, and Canberra went up in a gentle climb. He fired a second, and the aircraft exploded in a ball of flame, although Argentine accounts say that the crew of two ejected.

Broadwater fired two Sidewinders at one of the Canberras receding in the murk, but without visible result. An unconfirmed report suggests that this aircraft crashed on the approach to land at its

base, but this has now been discounted. For the Canberras it had been a disastrous start to the conflict, and the remaining aircraft were immediately switched to night missions against ships, dropping their bombs from 500 ft (150 m), although without radar their effectiveness was limited.

The only other engagement that day occurred with 801's Ward and Watson fired on three small radar contacts (Pucarás or T-34Cs) taking off from Port Stanley. They were first seen briefly at 1.5 nm (2.8 km) as they entered the 800 ft (250 m) cloudbase. Their intention had evidently been to attack some of the British ships that were employed during the afternoon to bombard the airfield, since they came below cloud to jettison tanks and ordnance over the sea. There followed a game of hide-and-seek in the clouds, during which Ward expended 150 rounds to no visible effect. It may be noted that, although the Pucará is manoeuvrable and has a fixed armament of two 20 mm Hispano cannon and four 7.62 mm machine guns, there was no instance recorded of one turning to meet a Sea Harrier head-on.

The elation on the carriers that followed the early morning zero-attrition strike turned to euphoria as the results of the day's sorties came in. The Argentine bombing raid had been broken up so successfully that only one ship suffered splinter damage. At least two Mach 2 Mirages had been lost by the Argentine Air Force to no effect. The Sea Harrier's weapon system had proved its effectiveness in both air-surface and air-air modes, and the ability to switch quickly between roles had been demonstrated. Its pilots' coordinated pairs operations had been proved to work. For the British, it had been a good day.

It is now known that the Argentine air force had flown 56 sorties (12 A-4Bs, 16 A-4Cs, 12 Daggers, 10 Mirages and 6 Canberras) from bases in Argentina, and that 35 had reached the target zone. Two Mirages, one Dagger and a Canberra had been lost.

The view has even been expressed that May 1st was too dramatic a start to the air war, in the sense that the Argentines were so shattered by the results that they decided to conserve their air resources to oppose the amphibious landing, rather than allowing them to be devoured in advance by the meat-grinder of the Sea Harrier CAP system. Another factor in Argentine planning appears to have been the need to hold back some Mirages to defend their cities and bases in the north against possible Vulcan attack, following the Black Buck mission to Port Stanley, in the same way that some fighters were held back against a perceived threat from Chile.

Many Argentines appear to have believed that Britain would respond with nuclear weapons to any major defeat, such as the sinking of the carriers of the *QEII*. Whatever the reasoning, the Mirages were henceforth employed in the air-air role only in the case of escorting night-time resupply missions by C-130s to Port Stanley, none of which was intercepted due to the Sea Harrier's lack of a radar with overland look-down capability.

Harriers South

An earlier section has described how a batch of RAF Harriers was prepared at Wittering, primarily to act as Sea Harrier attrition replacements in the air defence role, and how FINRAE Mk 2 was developed in 18 days and transported to Wittering by May 2nd. The original plan had envisaged these GR.3s joining the *Atlantic Conveyor* before she sailed from Liverpool on April 23rd, but this proved to be impractical. It was decided instead to ferry the available GR.3s to join the ship at Ascension, in parallel with deployment of eight additional Sea Harriers that had been prepared for operational use, mainly from those held in storage at St Athan. These Sea

Harriers included ZA194, which had made its first flight on 23 April.

To digress, although it has never been clear why it was done in this way, the eight Sea Harriers were designated as a separate (and in the event, temporary) unit, No 809 Sqn under the command of Lt Cdr 'Tim' Gedge. The unit was formed on April 6th and began working up on the 12th. Unlike their dark sea grey counterparts already in the South Atlantic, these aircraft were painted a pale grey overall, which made them difficult to see at altitude, but was extremely unpopular with the pilots in low level missions. They had toned-down squadron markings on the fin, which were promptly removed in the case of the four aircraft that later operated from *Invincible*, despite the fact that Gedge flew from the ship.

The distance from the UK to Ascension is approximately 3,670 nm (6,760 km), which is a far greater distance than any member of the Harrier family had previously been flown. If human comfort and efficiency factors are ignored, a flight-refuellable aircraft can generally be kept flying indefinitely, provided that the engine has enough oil and the pilot enough oxygen. In the case of the GR.3 neither posed a problem, and MoD ordered No 1(F) Sqn to fly direct to Ascension. This may have been decided simply on the basis that it was more convenient for the Victor tankers, or in the belief that putting an aircraft on the ground risks unserviceability. Rumours that an Argentine special forces unit was close to the obvious staging point of Gibraltar may also have been a consideration. However, in the case of the Sea Harrier the liquid oxygen container is smaller, and a nonstop flight was out of the question.

The first six Sea Harriers of No 809 Sqn left the UK on April 30th, made a planned stopover at an airfield in Africa (mainly recalled for its jumbo prawns) and continued to Ascension, evidently without incident. They were followed on May 1st by two more. The RAF pilots of the GR.3s were in for a more gruelling experience, with a flight time of anything up to 9 hr 15 min. Positioned at St Mawgan in Cornwall to minimize the agony, the GR.3s were equipped with the big ferry tanks inboard the empty combat tanks outboard, and the standard combat wingtips. Each three GR.3s was to fly with three Victor tankers, two of which did the refuelling and were then in turn tanked up by the third Victor.

On May 3rd the first wave of three GR.3s took off for Ascension, but due to a problem with one of the tankers one GR.3 (piloted by Wg Cdr Squire) had to abandon the flight at around the half-way mark, landing to refuel and then continuing to its destination. On May 4th the second wave departed from St Mawgan, but one GR.3 experienced a technical problem, had to land en route, and returned to the UK. On May 5th

Shorts' Blowpipe SAM was used by both sides. It was originally thought to have shot down Flt Lt Glover's Harrier, but later evidence indicates that 20 mm AAA was responsible

the third wave had a similar problem, but in this case the aircraft was able to continue after an en route landing and defect rectification. By the end of May 5th, there were thus seven GR.3s on the ground at Ascension and another due shortly, together with two FINRAEs, which had been delivered on the 4th by C-130 from Wittering, flying via yet another airfield in Africa.

From the outset of Operation Corporate, MoD had feared an Argentine Entebbe-style raid on Ascension, so two GR.3s (later joined by a third) were left to provide air defence, pending the deployment of Phantom FGR.2s of No 29 Sqn on May 24th. Additional GR.3s were ferried to Ascension later in May, bringing the total to eight aircraft available for combat deployment.

To continue the story of the GR.3 deployment, on May 6th six Harriers were landed vertically on the forward helicopter deck of the *Atlantic Conveyor*, as were the eight Sea Harriers of No 809 Sqn. The aircraft were moved back by tractors into the parking area (protected at the sides by containers stacked three high), an area that they shared with three Chinooks, six Wessex 5s and a Lynx, all the helicopters but one Chinook being fated to be lost in the Exocet attack of May 25th.

After some days spent in servicing checks, the GR.3s and most of the Sea Harriers were put in purpose-built plastic bags (by Driclad of Sittingbourne) to protect them from the elements. A Sea Harrier was maintained at readiness against possible air attack, although once the ship had left the protection of Ascension-based Nimrods it had no radar coverage.

Due to a shortage of accommodation in the container ship, only two of the RAF pilots (Wg Cdr Squire and Sqn Ldr Iveson) travelled south with the aircraft, the remaining six (Sqn Ldrs 'Jerry' Pook and 'Pete' Harris, and Flt Lts 'Tony' Harper, John Rochfort, Mark Hare and 'Jeff' Glover) being embarked with the ground crew in the accompanying *Norland*. Tactics and intelligence information were discussed by Squire and Iveson cross-decking to the *Norland* by helicopter.

The officer responsible for FINRAE was Flt Lt Colin Drew, who had previously been seconded to Ferranti for one week from the Jaguar retrofit programme and was supported by two senior technicians, Sgts Lynch and Patterson, from CSDE and RAF Cottesmore respectively. Their immediate problems were to check that FINRAE would function correctly, and to find accommodation in *Atlantic Conveyor*. Drew became 'the ninth man in a two-man cabin'.

The ships departed Ascension on May 7th, and the RAF team started assembling the equipment immediately. The next two days were spent trying to get FINRAE to work, despite minor problems such as the absence of three-phase electrical supply and the fact that the umbilical cable provided would not reach the only accessible Harrier. It was next found that all the GR.3 wiring modifications to accept FINRAE inputs had been made incorrectly in the rush to prepare the aircraft, but this was soon rectified. The team was then transferred to *Norland*, which was equipped with the Skynet satellite communications system. This was employed to receive software modification intructions from Ferranti, which (on returning to the container ship) allowed FINRAE to be reprogrammed. The equipment was run up, its alignment checked, and a navigation run performed. The system essential to safe Harrier deck operations was ready for the GR.3's war to begin.

The rendezvous with *Hermes* was made at 52° South (roughly the same latitude as Stanley) on May 18th, a lovely day with the CVS clearly in sight from the container ship. Four GR.3s were transferred by VTOL that first day, and one each on the 19th and 20th, when the weather had deteriorated somewhat. The point is worth making, that some of these RAF pilots had never even seen an aircraft carrier before, yet here were transferring from a container ship to a CVS

in the middle of a war zone, ready to fly their first operational missions after only the briefest carrier familiarization. Although totally devoid of drama, it was a reinforcement operation that no other nation on earth was equipped to perform.

Of the eight Sea Harriers, half went with the six GR.3s to *Hermes*, while the remainder transferred to *Invincible*, bringing their fixed-wing totals to 21 and 10 respectively. To complete the story of the Harrier's later deployments, two GR.3s were flown direct from Ascension to *Hermes* in an 8 hr 25 min flight on June 1st, piloted by Flt Lts 'Mike' Beech and 'Murdo' Macleod, followed by two more piloted by Flt Lts Ross Boyens and 'Nick' Gilchrist on June 8th. These were also noteworthy flights, with their inertial systems aligned with great care before take-off from Ascension, a Victor tanker escorting them to within 800 nm (1,500 km) of the carriers, and Sea Harriers picking them up at 200 nm (370 km) radius. The last four GR.3s on Ascension were embarked in the container ship *Contender Bezant* on June 3rd, and their personnel in the MV *St Edmund*. The ships arrived off the islands on June 10th, but did not fly off their aircraft until after the Argentine surrender on the 14th. Thus, although 14 GR.3s went to the South Atlantic during the conflict, only 10 aircraft and 12 pilots took part in actual operations.

Meanwhile the Sea Harriers . . .

While the reinforcements were en route, the 20 Sea Harriers in *Hermes* and *Invincible* were holding the fort, although air activity was substantially reduced by sea fog for much of the time between May 2nd and the 13th. Argentine sources indicate that throughout the air war (May 1st to June 14th) only 24 days were operable in the area of the islands, although the weather was satisfactory for 39 days at their bases at San Julian, Rio Gallegos and Rio Grande.

From May 2nd to the 12th there was no Argentine air interference with the RN's inshore force, but a highly successful strike took place on the Task Force on the 4th, and there was some Argentine air activity on the 9th. During the first half of May, Sea Harrier flying was therefore largely concerned with CAP missions and strikes.

To recap on the position at the end of the first day of operations (May 1st), sorties had been carried out very successfully in both the airfield attack and air-air roles, completely without loss. When the ground attack experts (Flt Lts 'Ted' Ball, 'Dave' Morgan, Clive Morrell and 'Tony' Penfold) had planned the first mission against Port Stanley, they had expected to lose two or three aircraft. The defences had turned out to be stronger than expected (locations of AAA were correctly briefed, but the number of tubes underestimated), yet the attack had been carried out with only one harmless strike on a Sea Harrier. Likewise, when Lt 'Steve' Thomas and Flt Lt Paul Barton had engaged the Mirages, they had been amazed by their opponents' lack of combat awareness. In Thomas' own words: 'It had been a walkover'. The question now was whether the Argentines would improve, and – if so – how quickly.

May 2nd was an important day in the conflict, although Sea Harriers took little part. This was

From the Falklands experience, it can be argued that Britain's defence requirements include modern carriers with a size and displacement similar to that of Hermes, seen here at speed in choppy water. There was a joke that circulated at the time in MoD circles to the effect that if the carriers had been held any further east, the crews would have been in line for the Burma Star!

Though old and rusting, the sheer size of Hermes made her the mainstay of the British naval air effort. From the viewpoint of Harrier operations, she provided excellent take-off weight and stores volume

Sea Harrier XZ458 flying along the Falklands' coastline. The type performed well, though it lacked a look-down radar and medium-range missiles, and carried small drop tanks and only two Sidewinders

the day on which the Argentine Navy made its only attempt to attack the Task Force with both ships and aircraft. The carrier *Veinticinco de Mayo* and her escorting destroyers *Hercules* and *Santisima Trinidad* formed the northern pincer, but bad weather prevented her launching aircraft, and patrolling Sea Harriers (although warned of her presence) were unable to find her. The southern pincer was formed by the cruiser *General Belgrano* with escorts *Piedra Buena* and *Hipolito Bouchard*, while a third group was formed by three Exocet-armed corvettes steaming to the west of the islands. The *Belgrano* was sunk by the RN submarine *Conqueror*, following which all major Argentine ships withdrew to within a few miles of the Argentine coast and took no further part in the fighting.

A smaller-scale engagement took place in the middle of the following night, when two Argentine ocean-going patrol boats (possibly searching for downed aircrew) fired on an RN Sea King, and were promptly attacked by Lynxes from *Coventry* and *Glasgow*, using the brand-new Sea Skua missile. Hit by two pairs of Sea Skuas, the 800-ton *Somellera* sank without trace, while the *Sobral* took two and limped away severely damaged.

May 4th saw the second bombing attack by a Vulcan on Port Stanley airfield, and the first loss of a Sea Harrier. This occurred during a strike by four aircraft of No 800 Sqn against the airstrip at Goose Green, where Lt 'Nick' Taylor was killed when his Sea Harrier was destroyed by AAA. From Argentine film of the wreckage, it appears that a large-calibre warhead (probably 35 mm) exploded inside the integral fuel tank in the wing, resulting in disintegration of the airframe.

On the same day the Argentine Navy enjoyed its only major success, when two Super Etendards, operating from Rio Gallegos and guided by a Lockheed SP-2H Neptune, fired two Exocet missiles against the Type 42 destroyer *Sheffield*, undetected by the Sea Harrier CAP due to their low level approach. One missile hit fuel tanks amidships, starting serious fires, and after four hours the ship was abandoned, some 20 members of her crew having died. It may be noted that after this mission the Argentines decided that the use of the Neptune was too suicidal to continue, and that any future strikes would have to rely on estimates of the British carriers' position supplied by radar fixes from Port Stanley, based on Sea Harrier and helicopter plots. However, this possibility was taken into account by the RN, whose aircraft stayed at low level when within 50 nm (95 km) of the ships. As a result of such measures (and care

with radio transmissions) it has been claimed that no Argentine aircraft ever got within 65 nm (120 km) of the centre of the carrier battle group.

Following the loss of Taylor's aircraft on the 4th, a change of ground attack tactics was decided on to conserve Sea Harrier resources. Henceforth, they would not overfly well defended objectives within the defensive envelope, ie at less than 18,000 ft (5,500 m), unless a vitally important target was found. Instead, 1,000 lb (454 kg) bombs would be tossed from a low approach at a distance of approximately 3 nm (5.6 km), using a mixture

of contact and VT (air-burst) fuzes. Later, releases were made in a level pass using the radar return from an offset IP (initial point), the height gradually increasing with experience up to 20,000 ft (6,100 m).

Despite the fog, some Sea Harrier flying continued, and on May 6th two aircraft were lost in an accident that resulted in the deaths of Lt Cdr John Eyton-Jones and Lt Alan Curtiss. As far as can be established, they were conducting a surface search under the control of a Sea King, and were descending through cloud when they apparently collided. The accident took place well outside the range of Argentine ground defences, and there is no suggestion that there were hostile aircraft in the area.

The loss of two pilots and Sea Harriers was undoubtedly a serious blow, instantly removing a quarter of *Invincible*'s fighter complement, and reviving earlier fears that a loss rate of one aircraft per day might be suffered. By chance, the two Pegasus engines lost were both within a few hours of their extended lives, and this tragic accident thus had the side-effect of eliminating the need for an engine change in *Invincible* during the conflict.

On May 9th the Argentines made an attempt to fly a C-130 into Port Stanley, escorted by two Mirages, and under cover of darkness. Intercepted by Sea Harriers, the Mirages turned back before combat could be joined, the C-130 escaping under the cover of radar ground returns. Later resupply missions were unescorted and more successful, possibly indicating that the C-130 pilots were using night goggles to permit extremely low approaches over the islands. The Argentines claimed that these aircraft flew at only 26 ft (8 m) over the sea.

The 9th also witnessed the detection and destruction of the Argentine fishing vessel *Narwal*, which had been employed to shadow the Task Force. At this stage it had become normal procedure for Sea Harriers going on CAP to carry a single thousand-pounder on the centre-line pylon, and to release it from 18,000 ft (5,500 m) over Port Stanley airfield en route for the CAP area. On this occasion the two aircraft – Sea Harriers of 800 Sqn flown by Lt Cdr 'Gordy' Batt and Flt Lt 'Dave' Morgan – were unable to bomb due to cloud cover (this was later allowed, when the accuracy of medium-level radar bombing had been demonstrated), so they were still 'loaded for bear' on turning away to take up the CAP. As they did so, they found the *Narwal* by radar, and, knowing that the vessel had previously been warned off, asked their controller in HMS *Coventry* for permission to attack.

Thus approved, Morgan (who had done almost 1,000 hours with No 3(F) Sqn in Germany, and should have been the better bomb-aimer) made the first attack, but missed with his bomb, so strafed it with cannon fire until it stopped. Batt released his bomb, and hit the *Narwal* in the forecastle. However, the bombs had been fuzed for medium level release, and it therefore failed to explode. While Morgan climbed to transmit a report on the situation, Batt fired a burst of cannon fire across the ship's bows, and the crew finally stopped engines and took to the lifeboats.

The *Narwal* was boarded by men from a Sea King HC.4 of No 846 Sqn, and the survivors rescued. Of the crew of 25, only one man had died and one suffered serious injuries. The vessel sank on the 10th.

However, *if* Argentine newspaper accounts are to be believed, Britain was not having things all her own way. On the 10th, Lt Daniel Antonio Jukic was lost in action after bombing *Hermes* from his Pucará. The carrier was then reported to be under tow to Curaçao for repairs. Around the same time that HRH Prince Andrew was taken prisoner, and Rear Adm Woodward committed suicide over the loss of the *Sheffield*! Subsequent verbal reports from Argentina indicate that Jukic was actually killed in a take-off accident, when a

Matra Beluga cluster weapon exploded under his aircraft, and that the attack on the *Hermes* was invented for propaganda purposes. Other reports say that Jukic was killed in his Pucará by a BL755 dropped from a Sea Harrier during the May 1st attack on Port Stanley airfield.

Following a week of bad weather, Sea Harrier attacks on Port Stanley airfield resumed on Wednesday May 12th. Meanwhile, evading Sea Harrier CAPs, two flights of four A-4s attacked *Brilliant* and *Glasgow*. The former ship 'splashed' two aircraft from the first wave with Seawolf, while a third hit the water in evading, and the last was destroyed by cooperative Argentine AAA. However, the second wave put a bomb through *Glasgow*, necessitating a temporary withdrawal for repairs.

On the 13th there was no Sea Harrier flying due to fog, but on the following day a further attack was made on the main airfield, and a search was carried out for an Argentine hospital ship reported to be in the area. The night of the 14/15th witnessed landings from No 846 Sqn's Sea King HC.4s of SAS troops for the raid on the airstrip at Pebble Island (known to the Argentines as *Isla de los Guijarros*). Six Pucarás, one Skyvan, and four light aircraft were destroyed without loss, the results being confirmed next morning by a Sea Harrier PR mission flown by Flt Lts 'Ted' Ball and 'Dave' Morgan of 800 Sqn.

On Sunday May 16th the bombing of the main airfield continued all day, and 800 Sqn flew low level reconnaissance sorties over East Falkland and the coast of the Sound, in preparation for the amphibious landings.

The sighting technique used for the starboard oblique camera of the Sea Harrier is to draw a 20° depressed aiming line on the canopy while en route for the target, by simply rolling 20° to port (as shown by the HUD) and drawing the horizon on the perspex with a chinagraph pencil. Official postwar criticism of the effectiveness of photo-reconnaissance in the Falklands probably refers to the fact that the Sea Harrier lens is limited to a focal length of 3 inches (76 mm), which was of little value at the 18,000 ft (5,500 m) needed to clear the defensive envelopes at Port Stanley and Goose Green. The RAF GR.3s used camera pods (two were taken south) with twice this focal length, but there was no equipment available that was suited to medium level photography.

Also on the 16th, a three-aircraft flight from 800 Sqn (pilots Lt Cdr 'Dave' Smith, Flt Lt 'Dave' Morgan and Lt Simon Hargreaves) found two Argentine supply ships on either side of Falkland Sound: the *Rio Carcarania* at Port King, and the *Bahia Buen Suceso* at Fox Bay. The latter vessel was the one that had landed the notorious Capt Alfredo Astiz, his Marines, and the scrap dealers at South Georgia in March, in the affair that had sparked off the whole conflict.

At this stage it was vital to restrict the supplies of ammunition to Argentine outposts (*Alacrity* had blown up the ammunition ship *Cabo de los Estados* in the Sound on the night of the 10/11th), hence two Sea Harriers were scrambled to attack each ship. The *Rio Carcarania* was both bombed and strafed, and her crew were seen taking to life rafts. She was subsequently sunk by Sea Skua attack by a Lynx from *Antelope*. The *Bahia Buen Suceso* was alongside a jetty close to the settlement, and thus could not be bombed due to the possibility of civilian casualties. Instead she was strafed, and reports indicate that a fire started. She defended herself with automatic weapons, and one Sea Harrier took a small hole in the tail. The vessel, which had been loaded with ammunition and eggs, was still there when the Argentines surrendered. She quickly became infested with rats, and was therefore taken out to sea and sunk.

On the 17th the low level reconnaissance missions continued, and on the 18th the carrier battle group joined up with the amphibious landing group and (as discussed earlier) the *Atlantic Conveyor*. The fixed wing replacements of eight Sea Harriers and six Harriers GR.3s brought the total, which had fallen from 20 to 17, back to 31, a relatively healthy figure with which to embark on the next crucial phase of the conflict. Unfortunately, large quantities of Harrier spares and GSE were not transferred immediately, and were lost when *Conveyor* sank on the 28th.

Returning to the subject of the FINRAE equipment for alignment of the GR.3s' inertial platforms, Flt Lt Drew and his team were transferred by helicopter from the container ship to *Hermes* on the 19th, but at the last moment FINRAE had to be left behind (along with their personal gear) because of deck space congestion on the carrier. The next day *Atlantic Conveyor* was 120 nm (220 km) away, and the missing items had to be recovered by use of the ship's Lynx.

By this stage the GR.3s had flown a few sorties without benefit of FINRAE, and the pressure was on to get it working. It was immediately apparent that the 'passive' mode originally planned, with the equipment communicating from below deck to aircraft in known alignment spots, was out of the question, hence the 'active' mode, with FINRAE on deck, had to be used.

Initially the pilots carried out the alignment process, but with up to six aircraft needing alignment for one mission and a minimum of four minutes per alignment, this required them to enter the cockpit 20–30 minutes before take-off. With temperatures around freezing point, this did not improve their operational efficiency, and the job was therefore taken over by RAF engineers. Navigation accuracy proved to be variable, but FINRAE successfully provided the attitude information that was essential to safe deck operation in limited visibility. Pilots navigated in the traditional stopwatch-and-compass manner, from one distinctive point to another, simply ignoring the moving map display of computed position. Weapon aiming was based on a reversionary mode, combining attitude information from the inertial system with aircraft speed from the air data computer.

It is of interest to record that after the conflict FINRAE was tested in *Hermes*, and – with the benefit of one slight modification – gave navigation and weapon-aiming accuracies in line with those achieved in a rapid (2 minute) alignment on land. However, at the time of the conflict the essential requirement was for attitude information, and this was successfully provided.

On the 19th (the day that one of *Hermes*' Sea King HC.4s landed in mysterious circumstances in southern Chile) all eight Harrier GR.3 pilots flew two sorties for carrier familiarization, and two aircraft were vectored out to intercept the Boeing 707 shadower, which still put in a distant appearance in marginal weather. Since it was intercepted outside the TEZ, it was not destroyed.

This was probably the only operational mission flown by the GR.3s with Sidewinder on the outboard pylons. It was evident at this stage that the GR.3 would not be required in the role originally envisaged, ie as a substitute for the Sea Harrier in the air defence task, so the decision was made to reserve the radar-equipped, irreplaceable RN aircraft for air-air work (although it was still employed for loft and medium level bombing) and to use the comparatively expendable GR.3 for ground attack missions. The RAF aircraft was therefore converted back to its standard armament wiring arrangement (a task that took 90 minutes).

For practical purposes, No 1(F) Sqn went to war on Thursday May 20th, attacking a fuel storage depot to the north-east of Fox Bay on West Falkland. In the original intelligence assessment of No. 800's reconnaissance photographs, this target had been dismissed as 'lines of penguins', but then it was noticed that there were exactly ten 'penguins' in each line, and that they were all walking in the same direction! Closer examination showed that the 'penguins' were fuel barrels, probably brought in by the *Bahia Buen Suceso*. The Harriers achieved complete surprise in this attack, receiving no return fire, while destroying the fuel dump in spectacular fashion with BL755 cluster weapons.

May 20th represented the end of the first phase

OVERLEAF
This post-Falklands photograph by Rolls-Royce shows a Sea Harrier of No 800 Sqn in Hermes' *hangar. The dark sea grey paint-scheme is a compromise between the two extremes used during the conflict*

of the Harrier family's war, since the following day was to bring the main landing at San Carlos, with a sudden increase in demand for Sea Harrier CAP and GR.3 ground attack sorties. At this crucial point in the war, the series had proved itself in both the air-air and air-surface roles, and it was now present in worthwhile numbers, although this was due partly to Argentina's decision not to risk a war of attrition in the air, and to the bad weather that had limited sortie rates. On the other hand, despite a comparatively high loss rate on May 1st, Argentina had by far the stronger force. Looking at the situation dispassionately, it is probably fair to say that the air war might have still gone either way at this stage.

The first phase had not only proved the capabilities of the Harrier family, but it had also demonstrated the ingenuity of the men who kept the aircraft flying in appalling conditions. For much of this period, humidity had been around the 100 per cent mark (for up to six days at a time), with condensation streaming off the aircraft. At other times waves had been breaking over the ship's bow, covering the aircraft with salt spray. Although considerable development effort had gone into keeping the aircraft's interior dry, none of the tests in the UK had been as exacting as the conditions now experienced in the South Atlantic. However good the standard of construction, water still found its way in around access panels and the cockpit canopy, the seal of which is not inflated unless the engine is running. Even small amounts of moisture can cause problems with electrical equipment, avionics, and sensitive instruments, and at times the Harrier cockpits were streaming with water.

The environmental protection problem was worse in *Hermes*, with individual aircraft held on the flight deck for up to six weeks at a time, yet availability was maintained at around 95 per cent, thanks to a variety of ingenious and unofficial fixes. Bathroom sealant (supplied by the ship's engineers) was applied lavishly to both interior and exterior surfaces. The computer keyboard was an obvious area for water ingress, so it was covered in clingfilm, as were the instruments. *Hermes'* engineers made 'tonneau covers' to keep the worst of the water off the instruments until take-off. Plugs and sockets were sealed with 'plastic skin' aerosol from the sick-bay. The avionics were kept dry by means of a hot air blower, and some black boxes were actually removed and dried out in the galley ovens! Aircraft reaction time was improved by a rapid avionics warmup modification, devised by Fleet Chief Petty Officer 'Harry' Butler in *Hermes*. The folding nose radome of the Sea Harrier was resealed with rubber taken from the ship's divers' wet-suits. In general, the aircraft survived the conflict in remarkably good condition, although corrosion did occur on exposed parts,

such as the wheels, guns and the Sidewinder missiles, which sat on the wing pylon for up to 50 hours at a stretch.

D-Day

The first large-scale British landing of the conflict was carried out by men of the 3rd Commando Brigade in the early hours of Friday May 21st, on four beaches near San Carlos in East Falkland. The first Argentine air attacks on the ships involved and on the beach-head area took place approximately six hours later, at 10.30 am local time (1330Z).

The air defence of the amphibious objective area was a multi-layer system, with Sea Harrier CAPs at either end of Falkland Sound and sometimes half-way down the Sound, to intercept Argentine aircraft approaching across the two main valleys of West Falkland. In addition, there was a 'missile trap' off the northern end of the Sound, consisting of a Type 42 destroyer with Sea Dart and a Type 22 frigate with Seawolf. Within the Sound there was a 'gunline' of three or four ships, and within the anchorage were the assault ships *Fearless* and *Intrepid* with small calibre guns and Sea Cat missiles, as a last line of naval defence. On shore, there were Rapier fire units and Blowpipe.

On the day of the landing, MoD claims that 15 attacking aircraft were shot down. Of this total, it appears that 800 Sqn accounted for five A-4s (two by Lt Cdr Clive Morrell, and one each by Lt Cdrs 'Mike' Blissett and Neil Thomas, and Flt Lt John Leeming) and one Dagger (Lt Cdr 'Fred' Frederiksen), while 801 destroyed three Daggers (one by Lt Cdr 'Sharkey' Ward and two by Lt 'Steve' Thomas) and one Pucará (also by Ward).

The carriers were maintained well to the east to reduce the danger of air attack, but this also resulted in the Sea Harriers being 20 minutes or more from their CAP stations. In consequence, it was impossible to respond to surge demands from the landing area, and time on station was severely limited. The Sea Harrier brochure quotes 90 minutes endurance at 100 nm (185 km), but a more typical time on station in this conflict was 10 minutes or less, due to the distance from the ships and the low altitude used in searching for Argentine aircraft. This altitude depended on the aircraft's fuel state and the weather, but they generally patrolled either at 10,000–15,000 ft (3,000–4,500 m) or as low as 2,000–3,000 ft (600–900 m). Having taken off with approximately 6,650 lb (3,015 kg) of fuel, they would arrive on CAP with 3,500–4,000 lb (1,590–1,815 kg), and they initially planned to turn back with 2,800 lb (1,270 kg) in order to arrive at the carrier with 1,000 lb (454 kg) remaining. With practice, it was found possible to turn back with only 2,400–2,200 lb (1,100–1,000 kg).

In the vicinity of the carriers, Sea Harriers were normally controlled by the aircraft direction officer in *Invincible*, but at the inshore CAP stations they were under the control of the local anti-air warfare coordinator in a Type 22 frigate (*Brilliant* or *Broadsword*) or one of the Type 42 (Sheffield class) destroyers. The aim was to intercept the incoming aircraft at least 20–30 nm (37–56 km) to the west of the ships' missile engagement zone (MEZ). In principle, friendly aircraft were not supposed to enter the MEZ unless via one of the essential safety lanes, but in the case of 'hot pursuit' the Sea Harrier pilot could request the coordinator to stop the ships firing.

Fortunately, only one Harrier engine change was called for in the course of the Falklands operation, as recorded in this photograph of Hermes' *hangar. The wing is removed and the aircraft trestled*

OVERLEAF
An 800 Sqn Sea Harrier, positioned for a 500 ft (152.4 m) run down Hermes' *tramlines. The circles indicate landing spots for Sea Harriers or helicopters*

On this first day there were six or eight Sea Harriers in the air at all times, with *Hermes* alone launching a pair every 20 minutes. Air defence sorties continued through the following night, though at a reduced rate.

Turning to the Argentine side of the story, all their aircraft were now employed in the air-surface mode with no escorts, although a considerable number of 'spoof' missions were flown in attempts to draw off the Sea Harriers. They generally attacked in fours, cruising with 1,000–2,000 yd (900–1,800 m) between elements, the No 2 aircraft of each element being swept back 60° and separated from his leader by around 250 yd (230 m). For the attack phase they closed up into a form of arrowhead formation, the A-4s at approximately 400 kt (740 km/hr) and the Mirage series at 560 kt (1,040 km/hr). It was felt that, flying at around 30 ft (9 m), there was little danger from any missiles, although this proved to be a false assumption. This low level attack also led to many bombs failing to detonate, and it produced a layer of salt on the windscreen that significantly reduced forward visibility. It may be noted that one A-4 struck *Antelope*'s mast with the fin of a drop tank on May 21st, but recovered to base.

One fundamental problem on the Argentine side was that the Air Force pilots had no prior experience of low level flying over the sea, or of attacking ships. They were therefore given two weeks of special training by the Navy, although the two services differed in their attack techniques. The Navy favoured an approach at 45° to the ship's axis, while the Air Force preferred to come in at 90°. In principle, the former angle is probably better if the bombs are being dropped on the target, while the latter approach is arguably just as good in skip-bombing (although it may bring the aircraft within the field of fire of more weapons on the ship). For weapon aiming, Air Force pilots obtained some measure of range to the ship by drawing on the windscreen two horizontal grease-pencil lines, corresponding to the horizon and the vessel's deck at the correct bomb release distance.

In the list of Argentine priorities, the carriers were the principal target, followed in turn by the logistic support ships, other ships close to land, and finally warships. However, in practice it was often the warships that were encountered first, so they were attacked. The amphibious landing force thus suffered relatively little from air attack at this stage of the conflict.

The Argentines' only countermeasures against the Sea Harriers were their TPS-43 radar at Port Stanley, which provided warnings of aircraft on CAP, and attempts to saturate the CAP position. If intercepted, A-4 pilots would clear their aircraft and turn for home at full throttle, but Mirage/Dagger pilots would sometimes press on, believing themselves to be safe at high speed and low level. Of the various types employed, the Dagger was the one most critical in terms of fuel, having enough for only three minutes in the target area. For those aircraft that could be flight-refuelled, a KC-130 waited 100 nm (185 km) off the Argentine coast. Two badly leaking A-4s were towed back to base by these Hercules.

The first air encounter of the 21st came in the morning, when 801's Lt Cdr 'Sharkey' Ward and Lt 'Steve' Thomas, flying with Lt Cdr 'Al' Craig, who had arrived with the *Atlantic Conveyor*, were on CAP over eight-eighths cloud some 30 nm (56 km) to the west of the landing area. They were advised by the controller in *Brilliant* that the ship was getting fleeting radar contacts with two aircraft, flying at approximately 200 kt (370 km/hr) and 50 ft (15 m) over land to the west of Goose Green. Building up speed, the trio eased down through the cloud, finding it clear below 4,000 ft (1,200 m). Thomas and Craig spotted two light-painted Pucarás, and attacked the nearer one with guns, but without result.

It should be explained that at this stage of the conflict it was standard procedure not to waste the AIM-9L on a relatively easy target such as the Pucará, and that accurate gunfiring was made more difficult by the complete lack of tracer ammunition for the 30 mm Aden. Attacking a low flying target with gunfire is never easy, and in the case of the Sea Harrier (like the F-15) it is made more difficult by the slight upward inclination of the cannon.

By this stage both Sea Harriers had slowed to below 300 kt (560 km/hr) and had full flap down, taking turns at the Pucará, which was weaving to follow the ground contours. They were getting very low on fuel, so Ward (who was not only the CO, but the unit's leading exponent in air combat) came down for a series of gun attacks. His first pass was rather fast at around 400 kt (740 km/hr), but the Pucará's left aileron disappeared and its right engine caught fire. Ward pulled off to the left, dropped his flaps, and came back for a slower pass that left the Pucará's other engine in flames and produced strikes on the rear fuselage. For his third pass, he sat behind at 200 yd (185 m), the radio altimeter showing a height of 15–60 ft (4.6–18 m), 'hosing it'. As the last of his rounds left the guns, pieces flew off the Pucará, the canopy shattered, and the pilot ejected, to land seconds later alongside the tracks left by his aircraft as it skidded over the ground.

The second Pucará had by this time disappeared, its imaginative pilot subsequently claiming to have been fired on by the Sea Harriers. The downed pilot, Major Juan Tomba, had been the leader of the 'Toucan' flight at Goose Green. He was captured by British troops, and later assisted as an interpreter for wounded PoWs.

The port outrigger of this Harrier went over the edge of Hermes' deck, but it was quickly man-handled back to safety. Outrigger track is considerably reduced in the case of the AV-8B

As a memento of this combat, in which his opponents felt that he had displayed an unusually high degree of flying skill in his attempts at evasion, his flying helmet is now preserved in the Fleet Air Arm Museum at Yeovilton.

Moving up the target performance scale, the dispatching of A-4s may be illustrated by an encounter that same day involving a pair of Sea Harriers from 800 Sqn, flown by Lt Cdr Neil Thomas (CO of 899) and Lt Cdr 'Mike' Blissett, the senior pilot of 800. They had been vectored by *Brilliant* after an outbound bogey, first up the Sound, then west on a heading of 290°. Thomas had just flown over the settlement at Chartres, with Blissett out to port and slightly behind, when over the ridge-line to the south came four A-4s heading to the north-east. Blissett saw them and called a starboard break to cut off the A-4s from the amphibious landing area. As the two Sea Harriers broke, the A-4s jettisoned their bombs and turned to starboard, the right-hand pair taking advantage of the fighters' overshoot to achieve a healthy separation, making for home at full throttle.

The left-hand pair of A-4s were less well placed, and having completed a half-turn found themselves with two Sea Harriers behind them and well within the firing range of their Sidewinders. For the first time, Thomas, now doing 540 kt (1,000 km/hr), saw the two A-4s, although he had lost sight of Blissett. He fired a Sidewinder that homed successfully on to an A-4, which descended smoking over low ground, its wreckage being later found by ground forces. Blissett had meanwhile completed his turn, and fired a Sidewinder at the other A-4, achieving a positive kill. They then turned west, hoping to catch the other pair, but failed to find them.

Two of the day's three Dagger kills were produced by 801's Lt Cdr 'Sharkey' Ward and Lt 'Steve' Thomas on their third sortie that day. The two Sea Harriers were on CAP between Pebble Island and Port Howard, roughly 20 nm (37 km) west of the landing area. At this time they were under the control of Lt Cdr Lee Hulme in *Brilliant*, and on asking for 'trade' were first told to wait. When Hulme came back on the air a few seconds later, it was to say that *Brilliant* was being strafed by Mirages (he was wounded in the arm, but went on controlling) and that there were other Argentine aircraft over the Sound. Ward and Thomas then went low, to around 500–1,000 ft (150–300 m) over a flat area north-west of Port Howard, to cut the Argentines' route between King George Bay and San Carlos.

The two Sea Harriers were flying approximately 1,500 yd (1,400 m) apart, completing a turn, when

A Sea Harrier prepares to take-off in an air defence sortie from Hermes. *After the Falklands conflict, the type was given enlarged drop tanks and twin Sidewinder rails*

they saw two Daggers in close battle formation. The two pairs of aircraft turned toward each other, the rear Dagger firing a short-range missile (probably the Matra Magic) at Ward, who passed head-on between the two Argentine aircraft. Thomas continued his turn, rolling in behind the rear Dagger at 1 nm (1,850 m), his target now doing around 480 knots (890 km/hr), and fired a Sidewinder that blew the rear end off. Ward saw the pilot eject as the missile hit (Argentine pilots had considerable respect for the terminal lethality of the AIM-9L), the man escaping successfully, though breaking his leg on landing.

Thomas was more concerned that the fireball from his first kill was preventing him from achieving a lock-on to the lead Dagger. He was just hoping that the pilot would turn gently to one side and climb, so that he could be quite sure what the remaining Sidewinder was locked on to, when the Dagger turned to starboard and pulled up! It was a long-distance shot, but the Sidewinder proximity-fuzed over the Dagger's port wing root in a small, brilliant orange flash. It then disappeared into cloud, but it has subsequently been established that it did not reach its base in Argentina.

Thomas had just completed his second firing, when another pair of Daggers at a lower level flew across in front of the Sea Harriers, which were then at 300 ft (90 m). The Daggers were 1.0–1.5 nm (2–3 km) in front, on a heading of 45° for San Carlos. Ward immediately locked one Sidewinder on, fired, the missile hit, and the Dagger struck the ground.

To complete the story of this mission, they still had a little fuel left, and Ward had one Sidewinder, so they were told by Hulme that there were A-4s over the Sound. They saw three circling opposite San Carlos, then turn south to attack *Ardent.* Trying to reach them before they got to the ship, the Sea Harriers crossed the coast on either side of Port Howard, some 2.5–3.0 nm (4.6–5.6 km) behind the A-4s, all five aircraft going flat out. By now the A-4s were only 5 nm (9.3 km) from *Ardent,* and it was clear that 801's aircraft were not going to catch them in time, so Ward called in *Hermes'* Red Section. Lt Cdr 'Clive' Morrell got one A-4 with a Sidewinder, and his No 2, Flt Lt John Leeming, got one with cannon fire, though this was after they had attacked *Ardent.* The third A-4 was damaged by Morrell's cannon fire, and the pilot ejected over Stanley when his undercarriage failed to lower, the unmanned aircraft being shot down by AAA.

In flying past Port Howard, Thomas had gone over a machine gun nest and his aircraft had been struck by three armour-piercing 0.50-in (12.7 mm) rounds in the rear electrical bay, so he pulled up and went home. Ward, looking round for Thomas, heard the sound of a Sarbe beacon, so he sent a rescue helicopter, but it turned out to be Lt Luna, a Dagger pilot that Frederiksen had shot down earlier.

The A-4 attack on *Ardent* had been one of only 23 combat missions flown by the Argentine Navy, in this case six aircraft having been launched and three lost. This very limited effort was later the subject of bitter criticism by the Air Force, but the Navy pointed out that their missions had had a very high success rate, bearing in mind the destruction of the *Sheffield*, *Ardent*, and *Atlantic Conveyor*.

The losses in the Navy A-4 mission on the 21st were not typical, but attrition of Argentine aircraft was undoubtedly high, and there was serious concern that by the end of the conflict all their experienced pilots would have been lost. The Argentine Air Force assigned three pilots to each A-4, letting them fly operational missions in turn, and rotating them back to peacetime bases in the north after seven or eight sorties. In complete contrast to the British approach, Argentine squadron commanders were withdrawn from operations later in the war.

Although it did not take part in the air defence task, the RAF's No 1(F) Sqn did attack four Argentine helicopters on the ground that day, during a dawn armed reconnaissance mission.

The 'moonscape' of Port Stanley airfield, after weeks of bombardment by Harrier GR.3s, Sea Harriers, Vulcans, and naval gunfire. The runway was subsequently extended to 6,000 ft (1,830 m)

Flown by Sqn Ldr 'Jerry' Pook and Flt Lt Mark Hare, two GR.3s strafed an operating base near Mount Kent. A Bell UH-1H 'Huey' escaped, but a Chinook was destroyed, a Puma exploded, and another Puma was damaged. This last aircraft was repaired, but Pook got another with a BL755 in the same place on the 26th, and another was destroyed nearby by Lt Cdr Braithwaite in a Sea Harrier.

One GR.3 was damaged during the strafing of the Mount Kent site on the 21st. On the same day No 1(F) Sqn sustained its first loss, when Flt Lt 'Jeff' Glover was shot down on his first mission, his GR.3 (XZ963) being hit near Port Howard, probably by 20 mm AAA. Glover's parachute did not deploy fully, and he sustained serious injuries, although he fell in the Sound. Captured by Argentine troops, he was flown to a military hospital in Comodoro Rivadavia, and eventually repatriated on July 8th.

The Falklands conflict provided an excellent opportunity to demonstrate the unique flexibility of No 1(F) Sqn, but it can hardly have been the proving-ground that any of its pilots would have chosen. Although it can be argued that such ground attack aircraft are best employed in battlefield interdiction, the Harrier was mainly to be used in the less cost-effective task of close support. Moreover, FAC (forward air control) was plagued by communications difficulties and lack of effective target-marking, the aircraft had no accurate means of navigation, much of the terrain was featureless, and (having come south to operate

in the air defence role) the squadron lacked the operational planning organization that would characterize ground attack in Central Europe.

Being accommodated in an overcrowded, remote aircraft carrier was better than living under canvas on the Falklands, but it also eliminated any possibility of achieving short reaction times and high sortie rates. A great deal of the squadron's equipment, including airfield matting and BL755 cluster weapons, was lost with the *Atlantic Conveyor*, which further reduced the unit's effectiveness. Morale was hardly improved by the fact that young Navy pilots (averaging only half the V/STOL time of their opposite numbers in No 1/(F)) were getting all the glory of shooting down badly-trained Argentines, while the Air Force's 'expendable' GR.3s were literally taking all the flak!

In the days to come, the GR.3s were to be employed to valuable effect in CAS during the fighting for Darwin and Goose Green, and later in the hills to the west of Port Stanley. They were also used against the main airfield, in some pre-planned attacks on concentrations of troops and equipment, and in PR and armed reconnaissance sorties. Flights from *Hermes* typically lasted 50–70 minutes, and (like those by Sea Harriers) often followed a period of up to three hours with the pilot sitting in a cramped, ice-cold cockpit. As with other combat aircraft, cabin conditioning is not provided on the Harrier series unless the engine is running.

Although No 1(F) Sqn would have preferred a LO-HI sortie to minimize warning time, the ship's position far to the east of the islands dictated a HI-LO-HI, the GR.3s normally descending behind hills to achieve some degree of tactical surprise. Approach to an airfield target would normally be made at around 100 ft (30 m), reducing to 10–30 ft (3–9 m) as they were picked up by Argentine radars, then pulling up to 150 ft (45 m) for weapons release.

Navigation outbound and inbound was assisted by the ship tracking them on radar, and on two occasions GR.3s were guided to their targets by Sea Harriers, when a combined strike was made. Targets were generally designated by grid reference, a six-digit number placing the objective within a square of 100-metre sides.

A postwar count indicates that, aside from small arms, SA-7s and Blowpipes in profusion, the Stanley area was defended by no less than eight radars, four Roland or Tigercat firing units, three Contraves Skyguard units with six twin-barrel 35 mm Oerlikon cannon and nine smaller guns (Hispano-Suiza 30 mm or Rheinmetall 20 mm). In addition, there were eight 20/30 mm guns to the north-west on Wireless Ridge and four to the south-west on Sapper Hill.

The pilots saw little of the missiles fired against them, since the weapons followed pursuit paths

and often detonated prematurely due to ground returns, the result of the GR.3's 'in the weeds' approach level. They were more aware of the mass of tracer produced by small arms, and barrage fire from AAA exploding in front of them. The effectiveness of radar-predicted AAA bears no relation to Argentine claims (they say that in total 11 Harriers were downed by AAA and five by Roland), but the presence of SAMs certainly forced the Harriers to use extremes of altitude, and barrage fire from AAA was undoubtedly a major distraction to attacking pilots.

Due to the nature of its role, the GR.3 took many strikes from small arms and some from 20 mm. All six were hit, the engines, outer wings, and drop tanks receiving many strikes without serious effect. In all, there were 30–40 small arms strikes, but only one GR.3 was lost to such fire. One aircraft, flown by Flt Lt 'Murdo' Macleod on June 12th, received a strike in the rear section of its reaction control ducting. A small fire started when the system was activated by lowering the nozzles to land back aboard *Hermes*, but the aircraft was landed without difficulty and the fire extinguished. Damage was limited to blistering of the paint.

Battle damage repair was one of the success stories of the conflict, due largely to the special kits produced by the RAF and to the initiative of the RN engineers. Notwithstanding its integral-

A Harrier GR.3 on the San Carlos airstrip of aluminium planking. Though delayed by the loss of the Atlantic Conveyor, *it transformed the reaction time of GR.3s and the endurance of Sea Harriers*

machined construction, the outer wing was repaired without difficulty, and it was considered that the fuel-tank area could also have been repaired, although this was not necessary. Fibreglass drop tanks that were supposedly non-repairable had to be repaired since there were no spares. Patches were bonded to these tanks with Araldite. Since the highest probability of a strike is obtained by weapons directly below the line of flight, those parts of the aircraft seen in head-on view were most likely to be hit, the windscreen being a case in point. Three strikes were received, affecting only the outermost laminate, and confirming the windscreen's advertised bullet-proof characteristics. Since replacement of a windscreen takes a considerable time, a temporary repair was effected in at least one case by bonding a small aluminium patch over the hole, again using Araldite. Checked in flight, it was found that above 20,000 ft (6,100 m) the cracks started to spread under cabin pressurisation loads. Below this height the repair proved completely satisfactory, although it may have called for slightly more head movement on the part of the pilot.

Operations Chronology

To revert to the chronology of the fighting, on the 21st the GR.3s had begun by flying airborne alert sorties to provide on-call CAS for the landing forces at San Carlos, in the same way that in 1944 cab-ranks of Typhoons had supported the Allied landings in Normandy. However, little opposition was encountered, so most GR.3s were switched to armed reconnaissance, which was how Pook's section found the helicopters at Mount Kent.

After the intensive Argentine air attacks on the 21st, the 22nd was quieter. Lt Cdr 'Fred' Frederiksen from *Hermes* was flying with Lt Martin Hale (likewise an 800 Sqn pilot) when they sighted an Argentine FPB in Choiseul Sound. They attacked with cannon, and the boat was driven ashore. Near Port Howard the Argentines set up a trap, using Glover's personal locator beacon, and fired a Blowpipe at the Sea King that came to rescue him, but evidently without damage to the helicopter. Meanwhile, the GR.3s made an armed reconnaissance of Weddell airstrip in West Falkland (a suspected C-130 landing site) and attacked Goose Green with BL755s. The latter, known to the Argentines as Pradera del Ganso or *Base Aérea Militar Cóndor*, was much used by the Pucará.

On Sunday the 23rd, Argentine air attacks were renewed, but 10 of their aircraft were shot down.

However, *Antelope* was crippled, and sank on the following day. The GR.3s made attacks with BL755s and retarded thousand-pounders against Weddell airstrip and Pebble Island. The only fixed-wing kill by a Sea Harrier that day was a Dagger shot down by Lt Martin Hale of 800 Sqn, using an AIM-9L.

That day three Argentine helicopters were destroyed in an action involving Sea Harriers from both ships. Flt Lts 'Dave' Morgan and John Leeming of 800 Sqn found four helicopters flying nap-of-the-earth along the coast of West Falkland, from Fox Bay toward Port Howard. They would probably have remained unseen, but for the fact that they made the classic mistake of crossing a stretch of open water. Morgan, leading the Sea Harrier section, dropped low, and identified a Puma at 500 yd (450 m), but was then too close to fire, so broke hard over the top of the helicopter, which appeared to roll into the ground as his wake struck it, and exploded. Later examination indicated that it had been carrying mortar bombs.

Morgan next turned toward an Agusta 109, which was armed with Minipods. It broke left and made for the hills, but both Sea Harriers strafed it, and it eventually caught fire. By this stage the second Puma had landed close to the first, so they pumped their last rounds into it, then handed over to Lt Cdrs 'Tim' Gedge and 'Dave' Braithwaite of 801, who finished it off. Later on the 23rd Lt Cdr 'Gordy' Batt was killed in a night launch accident from *Hermes*.

May 24th was another day of intensive air attacks on ships in the Sound, though 18 Argentine aircraft were shot down. This was the day on which Lt Cdr 'Andy' Auld and Lt 'Dave' Smith shot down three of a section of four Daggers in a low level engagement, with *Broadsword* controlling. Auld was responsible for two of the kills, which were all made with Sidewinders. In the first of two combined GR.3/Sea Harrier strikes against Port Stanley airfield, two Navy aircraft lofted VT-fuzed thousand-pounders for defence suppression, with four GR.3s following quickly in a low level attack.

Tuesday the 25th was Argentina's Independence Day, and was marked by a major air effort, in which the *Coventry* was bombed and capsized at the 'missile trap' station, and the *Atlantic Conveyor* was destroyed by Exocet some 70 nm (130 km) NE of the islands. The attack on the container ship was intended to sink one or both of the carriers, and was a case of mistaken identity, the two Super Etendard pilots simply firing at the largest radar return. It was their longest mission, of 500 nm (925 km) radius, and involved two aerial refuellings. Each carried a 242 Imp gal (1,100 lit) external tank and one Exocet (which left only one for the final strike on *Invincible*), and fired it in a pop-up attack. One missed but the

other struck and set the ship on fire, which cost Britain not only the ship, but three Chinooks, six Wessex, one Lynx, and a great deal of valuable equipment.

Eight Argentine aircraft were lost that day, and GR.3s and Sea Harriers returned to attack the main airfield. Port Stanley's air defences were meanwhile reduced in an incident involving Flt Lt 'Dave' Morgan of 800 Sqn. Morgan was in his Sea Harrier at 18,000 ft (5,500 m), just above the SAM envelope, trying to achieve a lock-on with his Sidewinders against a Pucará orbiting over the bay, when two Rolands were fired against him. He pulled up, and the missiles peaked out before reaching his altitude, the Argentine inventory of Rolands instantly being depleted by perhaps 20 per cent.

On the 26th there were no Argentine air attacks, but GR.3s struck again at Port Stanley airfield, and Sqn Ldr Pook of No 1(F) Sqn destroyed his second Puma on Mount Kent, with BL755s.

Thursday the 27th saw the start of the fighting in which 2 Para defeated Argentine forces at Darwin and Goose Green, with support from the GR.3s of No. 1(F) Sqn. It was during this operation that Sqn Ldr 'Bob' Iveson, flying his second mission of the day (his seventh of the war) was shot down by AAA in Harrier XZ988. Requested by FAC to attack a company position near Goose Green, he had released his bombs on the first pass and, believing that 2 Para was then desperately in need of all the help they could get, made two strafing runs, knowing full well the risks involved in re-attack. Iveson felt his aircraft hit by a shell, then go out of control. He ejected at 100 ft (30 m) a few miles to the west of the settlement, laid low until he was confident that British forces had taken Goose Green, then switched on his beacon and was lifted out by helicopter. At the time he appeared to have suffered only minor cuts and bruises, but subsequent operations (and sitting in the aircraft for hours on the ground) revealed spinal injuries, so he was sent back to the UK for treatment.

May 28th saw the liberation of Darwin and Goose Green by 2 Para, after further attacks by GR.3s with BL755s and 2-inch (5 cm) RN rockets. The Harriers also went to Stanley airfield, where 800's Flt Lt Morgan was still wearing down the defences. Flying a reconnaissance mission at 18,000 ft (5,500 m), he saw a Tigercat fired against him, and explode immediately after launch.

Saturday the 29th was the occasion for further attacks on the main airfield, Sea Harriers alone delivering 18 thousand-pounders. In an accident aboard *Invincible*, Lt Cdr 'Mike' Broadwater slid off the flight deck in Sea Harrier ZA174 (reportedly due to a badly worn anti-skid surface), ejected, and was picked up by a Sea King piloted by one Lt Windsor.

The 30th saw the third loss of a GR.3, when Sqn Ldr 'Jerry' Pook, attacking a gun position on Mount Harriet, suffered small arms damage to the fuel system of his Harrier XZ972. Fuel exhaustion obliged him to eject 30 nm (56 km) short of *Hermes*, but he was picked up after only 10 minutes in the water by a Sea King of 826 Sqn. This was the same day that Iveson was recovered from his evasion exercise in East Falkland. Legend has it that Pook was greeted with the words: '*Good heavens, Jerry, you're all wet! Been for a swim?*' To which Pook replied: '*Something like that, Bob. I gather you've been taking a few days off in the country?*'

The same day saw the Argentine Navy's last Exocet attack on the Task Force, with two Super Etendards (only one with Exocet) and four A-4s (each with two Mk 82 bombs), supported by a KC-130 tanker. Two A-4s were shot down before reaching the ships, and the Exocet missed, but the Argentine Navy insists that the two remaining A-4s successfully bombed *Invincible*. Those who served in *Invincible* (aside from the pilots) are equally adamant that they never even *saw* an Argentine aircraft, and it is rumoured that the only time the ship launched its missiles was at chaff fired by *Hermes*!

Despite the loss of half its aircraft, No 1(F) Sqn managed to attack Stanley airfield on the 31st (with defence suppression by four Sea Harriers), following a report of swept-wing aircraft at dispersal. The targets turned out to be MB.339s, the swept-wing effect being produced by metal planking on the ground. The following day saw the loss of a further Sea Harrier due to ground fire, when Flt Lt Ian ('Mort') Mortimer was shot down by Roland while on patrol over Port Stanley. He ejected into the sea approximately 5 nm (9.3 km) south of the town, then (because of enemy air activity in the area) spent nine hours in his dinghy before being rescued by a Sea King of 820 Sqn.

June 1st was also the day on which the Sea Harriers shot down their only C-130. Lt Cdr 'Sharkey' Ward and Lt 'Steve' Thomas of 801 Sqn were patrolling at around 300 kt (555 km/hr) some 40 nm (74 km) north of Pebble Island, controlled by *Minerva*. They had just decided to go home, wanting to get back with 800 lb (365 kg) of fuel, and were climbing to cruise height, when they were given a contact 40 nm (74 km) north-west from their position. Assured that it was genuine, Ward asked *Minerva* to 'fix decks to land on San Carlos Water' and turned toward the target, which he picked up at long range on his radar. The C-130 was then at 8,000 ft (2,400 m), turning away to the north, then west.

There was a layer of cloud 2,000–3,000 ft (600–900 m) thick, from about 1,800 ft (550 m) upward, and as the C-130 descended through this cloud, Ward told Thomas to stay above, in case

the C-130 pulled up, or it had Mirages for top cover. His first Sidewinder fell just short, but the second started a fire between the starboard engines. However, the C-130 flew on at 100 ft (30 m), so Ward gave it all his 200 rounds of 30 mm, which apparently damaged the flying controls, as it descended in a right-hand spiral into the sea. The C-130 broke up and went straight down, but its life rafts came up with Sarbe beacons transmitting, causing considerable annoyance for the next 24 hours. Although very short of fuel, Ward and Thomas managed the 230 nm (425 km) back to *Invincible*.

The next few days produced sea fog that made flying impossible, and the carriers withdrew from the TEZ until the 5th. On that day a remarkable recovery to *Invincible* was made by Lt Charles Cantan of 801 Sqn in visibility of only 200 ft (60 m). Guided by flares tossed over the stern, he came to the hover alongside, but without visual contact, so he overshot and tried again. On his second attempt he came to the hover, saw the ship's island, correctly estimated his position and chopped the throttle, landing with a mere 150 lb (68 kg) of fuel!

It should be added that finding the ship was no problem for the Sea Harrier, since the pilot was briefed on the ship's previous intended movement (PIM) and it stayed within a relatively small 'box', making radar acquisition easy. At night and in bad visibility, pilots recovered by CCA (carrier-controlled approach), with limits of 650 ft (200 m) visibility and a 100 ft (30 m) ceiling. Daylight operations were normally easier, but the ship might be steaming in any direction due to its ASW manoeuvres.

June 5th also saw the opening of 'HMS Sheathbill', an aluminium planking refuelling strip near San Carlos, this 850 ft (260 m) runway having been transported south in *Stromness*. It had no re-arming facilities, and was intended only to enable the GR.3s to achieve quick reaction in CAS, to allow aircraft running short of fuel to be topped up, and to extend the time of Sea Harriers on CAP. Rather than 10 minutes or less, a Sea Harrier could now stay on station for 30 minutes, then (if its armament had not been used) go up for a further 20 minutes before returning to the ship. Approaches were made down a safety lane with undercarriage down and landing lights on, to minimize the risk from Rapiers.

On the 5th and 6th the GR.3s (which had been reinforced by two aircraft flying from Ascension on the 1st) flew reconnaissance missions in the Stanley area, looking for shore-based MM.38 Exocet firing units, which damaged *Glamorgan* on the 12th. On the 6th GR.3s attacked Argentine troops near Stanley, and on the following day *Exeter* used a Sea Dart to destroy a Learjet at 40,000 ft (12,200 m) leading a formation of

Daggers, which promptly turned for home. Equipped with radar and Omega/inertial navigation system, this was one of four Learjet 35As that had flown 14 such missions, guiding Daggers of the *VIth Brigada Aérea* to within 70 nm (130 km) of their targets.

June 8th saw the last air battle, with Argentine aircraft making a major effort against the Welsh Guards' landing at Fitzroy. In all, 10 Argentine aircraft were shot down, including three by Sea Harriers of 800 Sqn. Flt Lt 'Dave' Morgan and Lt 'Dave' Smith of 800 Sqn were on CAP approximately 10 nm (18.5 km) south of Bluff Cove, about 10 minutes after sunset. Morgan sighted what he identified as a Mirage attacking a landing craft, and as the Sea Harriers dived from 10,000 ft (3,000 m) it became clear that there were four such aircraft, now attempting to escape. Travelling at over 650 knots (1,200 km/hr) and closing fast, Morgan rolled out roughly 1,200 yd (1,100 m) behind the No 4 of this arrowhead formation, and fired a Sidewinder, which produced a quick flash and a fireball. The No 3 started a gentle turn to the left, then, as Morgan fired his second Sidewinder, the enemy aircraft broke hard to starboard, desperately trying to evade it. The Sidewinder promptly cut across the turn and hit the aircraft at 90°, taking the rear end off. The pilot ejected as the aircraft came apart, being narrowly missed by Morgan, who was now down to guns and had just lost his sighting display.

With his options rapidly running out, but two targets in front of him, Morgan put the No 1 in the middle of his windscreen at 1,200 yd (1,100 m) and gave it a squirt. The No 2 then broke hard left in front of him, so he closed to 400 yd (365 m), pulled a lot of lead before relaxing the turn and firing. However, it was clear from the fall of shells in the water that he was not going to get the enemy aircraft without a sighting system, so Morgan pulled up out of Smith's firing line. Smith locked on from 2 nm (3.7 km) with a Sidewinder, which hit the target as it flew across the Sound at 20 ft (6 m), crashing on the southern side. A pilot of 801 Sqn reported seeing an aircraft fly straight off the water into a hillside, and it was at first thought that this was the fourth aircraft, but it may have been Smith's kill. Examination of the wreckage showed that in the fading light they had mistaken A-4s for Mirages.

It was also on June 8th that Wing Cdr Squire's GR.3 (XZ989) was seriously damaged in an accident due to engine failure at the San Carlos airstrip, although Squire was uninjured. Five days later the MEXE matting (laid by the Royal

Shortly after the end of hostilities, the Illustrious *(foreground) took over the Falklands station from her sister ship* Invincible *(rear). The* Ark Royal *will be the third and last of the class*

The Illustrious *turning at speed. Her Phalanx close-in anti-missile system is clearly visible – further evidence of the 'Falklands effect' in UK weapon procurement*

Engineers' Nos 11 and 59 Sqns) was bodily lifted by the downwash from the RAF Chinook, and two Sea Harriers from 800 Sqn had to divert at short notice to the helicopter pads of *Fearless* and *Intrepid*.

The final few days of the conflict saw the last attack on the main airfield on the 11th (800 Sqn tossed eleven thousand-pounders) and a series of attacks by the GR.3s against Argentine positions in the hills around Port Stanley. It was in the course of these missions that No 1(F) Sqn employed with remarkable success laser-guided bombs (LGBs), the conversion kits for which had been parachuted to the Task Force on May 27th.

Produced by fastening a Texas Instruments laser homing head and tail controls to the body of a standard thousand-pounder, the LGB is released in a 'canned' 3G climb from a pre-computed pull-up point, allowing the launch aircraft to remain clear of AAA defences. Only after the bomb has reached the top of its trajectory is the target designated by laser (in this case ground-based), so that the bomb can home on to the reflected energy. Press reports suggest that this Pave Way LGB has a range of approximately 3.5 nm (6.5 km) from a 550 knots (1,020 km/hr) release at a climb angle of 30°, the bomb reaching a height of 1,500 ft (460 m) and requiring a 11 second delay in designation from the instant of release.

These same unconfirmed reports state that No 1(F) Sqn first attempted a high altitude release against Stanley runway, with one GR.3 using its LRMTS to designate for the other's LGB, but that the two systems proved incompatible.

On June 13th Ferranti laser target markers on Two Sisters were employed to designate objectives for GR.3s approaching from behind Tumbledown. In the first attack (by Wg Cdr Squire) against well prepared troop positions, the target was evidently illuminated too soon, as the bomb fell 400 ft (122 m) short, but the second pass produced a direct hit. Sqn Ldr Pook then attacked a 105 mm gun position, likewise scoring a direct hit on his second attempt. The next day Sqn Ldr 'Bomber' Harris was airborne with LGBs, en route to attack the Argentine HQ on Sapper Hill, when the hill was suddenly covered in troops waving white flags, and the mission had to be hurriedly called off. Peace had broken out.

Epilogue

Following the cessation of hostilities, the RAF's No 1(F) Sqn formed a shore-based detachment at Port Stanley, with six GR.3s disembarked from *Hermes* on July 4th joining four aircraft from the *Contender Bezant*. The unit remained in the Falklands in the air defence role until November 11th, when it handed over its aircraft to No 4 Sqn from RAF Germany, and returned to Wittering.

Hermes detached two of her Sea Harriers to *Invincible* on July 2nd and departed the Falklands two days later, having mounted a flypast by 11 Sea Harriers, five GR.3s and 12 helicopters to mark the leaving of Task Force Commander Rear Admiral Woodward, all 16 Harriers being launched in the record time of five minutes. On the 19th as *Hermes* approached UK waters six Sea Harriers were flown off to Yeovilton, to be prepared for service with 809 Sqn in *Illustrious*, *Hermes* thus arriving in Portsmouth two days later with only six fixed-wing aircraft.

Illustrious sailed on August 8th with eight Sea Harriers (two further ex-800 Sqn aircraft having been flown down from Yeovilton), and gained two more aircraft from 801 Sqn on arrival in the Falklands. Two of 809's aircraft served ashore at Port Stanley, providing a radar-equipped air defence element until the airfield could be opened to RAF Phantoms of No 29 Sqn on October 17th. Following the return of *Illustrious* to the UK, No 809 Sqn, which had been informally commissioned on April 19th, was quietly disbanded on December 17th. *Invincible* had meantime returned home with eight Sea Harriers, arriving at Portsmouth on September 17th.

In the three months from April 2nd to July 1st, Sea Harriers had averaged 55 hours/month, compared to 25 hr/month in peacetime. They had flown a total of 2,514 hr in the course of 2,197 sorties, including 1,000 CAPs and 90 for offensive support. On the latest reckoning, they are credited with 20 confirmed and three probable kills without a single loss in air combat. Arriving later and with far fewer aircraft, the RAF GR.3s had managed only 125 ground attack sorties, but they had

performed in a way that no other air force aircraft could have done, thanks to their V/STOL capability. Had the GR.3s been employed in air defence, rather than a role that involved frequent strikes by small arms fire, their sortie total would have been much higher. Virtually free from battle damage problems, Sea Harriers had around 95 per cent availability at the start of each day, and 99 per cent of planned missions were flown.

The comparison with the Argentine air arms is staggering. Out of around 150 jet combat aircraft, the Air Force managed to field (on its own reckoning) only 82 Mirages, Daggers, A-4s and Canberras, plus 40 out of approximately 70 Pucarás. Even this pathetic effort gave a useful numerical superiority over the British, yet the Air Force planned only 505 missions, of which only 445 ever took off, and a mere 272 reached their objectives! Not to be outdone, the Argentine Navy scraped together eight A-4s and five Super Etendards, and flew 23 missions, including some from the carrier (all of which were aborted for one reason or another).

Viewed purely as a testing-ground for equipment, the Falkland conflict had been of incalculable value. On the one hand, it had highlighted shortcomings in equipment, such as the Sea Harrier's lack of look-down radar capability over land, its limited endurance, small number of air-air missiles, and restricted photo-reconnaissance capability. Most of these deficiencies (like its dependence on some form of early warning of incoming aircraft) were well known, but it took a war to dramatize the need for funding to correct them. Other problems, such as a fault in the nose undercarriage, were completely new, since only in a wartime ASW environment would *Invincible* be steamed at maximum speed in the roughest of seas, regardless of the pitching that this produced.

If it showed up some faults, the war undoubtedly brought out far more good points. It bore out everything that had been claimed for the versatility of V/STOL. It proved that the Harrier is capable of quite exceptional serviceability levels. Rather than showing the need for super-carriers, it demonstrated that V/STOL aircraft can operate in sea conditions and in bad visibility that would preclude flying by conventional aircraft. In the worst case, a Harrier can always stop and wait for deck movement to die down for a few seconds, before landing. It also proved what effective a combination the Sea Harrier and AIM-9L make, although the head-on attack capability of this late-model Sidewinder was never exploited. What mattered was the missile's ability to defeat a manoeuvring target, its high probability of a direct hit, and the devastating effect of its warhead. With such an armament the Sea Harrier achieved an outstanding air-air capability.

Chapter 5
Harrier Derivatives– AV-8B and beyond

As indicated earlier, although the overall P.1127/Harrier family development programme involved a not inconsiderable expenditure by the UK (subsidized to some extent by the US and West Germany), the operational performance of the production aircraft has been limited by restrictions on engine development funding. The 21,500 lb (9,750 kg) thrust rating of today's Pegasus is no different from the level achieved in the early 1970s, despite a steady growth in aircraft weight since that time.

The decision to emphasize longer engine life and improved reliability was undoubtedly justified, but the associated hiatus in thrust growth has brought problems for the operators (especially in regard to vertical landing weight at high temperatures), and has made it increasingly easy for any competitor or potential adversary to project an aircraft of far better warload-radius performance.

In the early days of V/STOL it was assumed by Hawker Aircraft that, once the practicality of the single-engine vectored-thrust concept had been demonstrated, others would adopt the same approach, although in the West they might be discouraged by patents that extended into the 1980s. In the event, this form of competition never materialized, since overseas interest in V/STOL had reduced, and since most countries working in this field chose to pursue different technological approaches, which appeared to offer performance gains, but in the event were almost invariably disastrously unsuccessful.

What could not be forseen was that UK spending on further V/STOL development would be so limited that the design of what might be termed a 'Super Harrier' of double the warload or radius would be left to America, and that the possibility of some Western supersonic derivative of the Harrier would hinge largely on the advent of a US Navy demand for a V/STOL fighter around the turn of the century.

Harrier II

The second major phase of Harrier development is represented by the McDonnell Douglas AV-8B Harrier II, which will be known in the RAF as the Harrier GR.5. The AV-8B is the outcome of a long association between MDC and HSA/BAe, beginning with the 15-year agreement signed in 1969, giving the American company licence-manufacturing rights for the Harrier/AV-8A, and providing for the exchange of information on Harrier-derived future projects.

One result of this cooperation programme was the proposed AV-16 or Advanced Harrier of the early 1970s, which was to be equipped with a long-span supercritical wing, and fitted with a Pegasus 15 engine of increased diameter, giving a thrust of 24,500 lb (11,110 kg). In its basic version, the AV-16 was still subsonic, but it offered far better warload and radius than the AV-8A. The principal customer was to be the USMC, but differently-equipped models were also offered to the USN, RAF, and RN. However, this approach failed because there was not sufficient common ground between the four services, and because of the high cost of engine development.

Following termination of AV-16 studies, HSA and MDC pursued independent lines of development, each proposing minimum-cost Harrier derivatives based on the existing engine, but using airframe modifications to achieve much better take-off and cruise performance. The MDC project led the way in terms of improved take-off performance, although in the end the HSA project acquired most of the associated MDC changes. The proposals differed basically in that the MDC aircraft had a lightweight carbon-fibre wing, while the British metal wing design was probably more advanced aerodynamically. The HSA/BAe design required less changes to the fuselage, and might have been applied retrospectively as a part-life update, although it was later decided that all the 'GR.5s' were to be built from scratch. The major disadvantage of this proposal was the weight of the

enlarged 'tin wing', exacerbating the vertical landing performance problem, which was already critical for the Sea Harrier. Aside from the aerodynamics of its wing, the MDC proposal was more advanced, and the scale of production offered the prospect of a reasonably low unit cost. A deal was therefore struck in 1981, by which BAe would be compensated by a share of the AV-8B workload for termination of its own project, while the RAF accepted the American aircraft to replace Harrier GR.3s in Germany.

In order to minimize the cost to the UK of AV-8B procurement, it was decided that, as the new aircraft were delivered, Harrier GR.3s from RAF Germany would be returned to Wittering, and updated, with modifications to extend fatigue life and reliability, small wing leading edge root extensions (LERX), enlarged drop tanks, additional pylons for self-defence missiles, a nav-attack system update, and provisions for ECM equipment and an improved anti-armour weapon.

In USMC service all three AV-8A and five A-4 squadrons will be replaced by the AV-8B by 1989. The principal objective in this very extensive

British Aerospace flight-tested various LERX (leading edge root extensions) on a GR.3 for possible use on the GR.5 and Sea Harrier. The LERX delays wing rock, but is longitudinally destablizing

The AV-16 envisaged a major advance, based on the Pegasus 15, producing an aircraft that would appeal to the US Navy in addition to existing V/STOL operators. Shown here is a supersonic variant

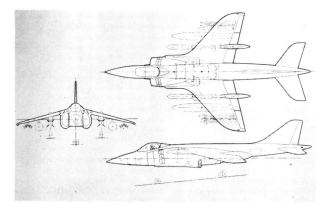

The BAe proposal for a GR.3 replacement, sometimes referred to as the GR.5(K), would have had an enlarged metal wing, LERX and additional sensors and hardpoints. It was dropped in favour of the AV-8B

BELOW
The McDonnell Douglas AV-8B Harrier II at the hover, showing the massive stakes and flaps that enhance take-off performance, and the LERX that were acquired in the course of development

rehash of the Harrier was to achieve a massive improvement in STO performance without resort to expensive engine development work. Firstly, the basic wing area was increased from a nominal 201 sq ft (18.7 sq m) to 230 sq ft (21.4 sq m), although the actual increase was more than these figures suggest, due to the AV-8B's trailing edge kink and the LERX. Secondly, the plain flaps of the Harrier were replaced by much larger, 'positive circulation' single-slot flaps that are specially developed to gain lift from the jet-pump action of the rear nozzles. The installed thrust of the engine was then improved approximately 600 lb (272 kg) by the introduction of a second row of auxiliary inlets. Combined with 15-degree drooped ailerons, the new flaps are estimated to be worth over 6,700 lb (3,040 kg) in STO weight from a 1,000 ft (300 m) run.

As indicated above, VTO performance was less important, but the USMC envisaged for the AV-8B a deck-launch intercept mission in which no forward roll was available, so the ventral strakes were enlarged and a retractable cross-dam (linked to the nose undercarriage) installed at their forward end, to increase ground cushion effect and reduce the recirculation of hot gases into the intakes. (These LIDs are estimated to be worth 1,200 lb (544 kg) in VTO weight). It is perhaps of some historical significance that almost 30 years after the start of the P.1127 design, a member of the Harrier family will be in service, capable for the first time of performing a useful mission from VTO, though admittedly with a very light armament load.

In order to try to preserve the Harrier's relatively high cruise speed in spite of the greater wing area, a supercritical aerofoil shape was employed. The aerodynamic gains are open to question, but this approach certainly provided a much thicker wing, which helped to increase internal fuel from 5,056 lb (2,293 kg) to 7,500 lb (3,400 kg). This clearly played a major role in improving warload-radius performance.

Since empty weight is of crucial importance in

the case of a V/STOL aircraft, the new wing was constructed largely of carbon fibre composites, which give a saving of 330 lb (150 kg) relative to a metal wing of the same size. Advanced composites were also used in the flaps, tailplane, ailerons, rudder, outrigger fairings, ventral strakes, engine access panels, and the new front fuselage. Total weight of carbon fibre is approximately 1,186 lb (538 kg), representing around 26 per cent of the structure and saving 480 lb (218 kg). This is a higher proportion than in any other combat aircraft; in fact the wing of the AV-8B is the world's largest aircraft component made in this material as a production item.

Another significant improvement was the introduction of a Sperry stability augmentation and attitude-hold system (SAAHS), giving a two-thirds reduction in pilot workload in critical flight regimes, and permitting a hands-off vertical landing to be demonstrated.

Aside from its increase in lifting area and fuel volume, the larger wing permitted a significant improvement in the roll power of the RCS (which was accentuated by moving the controls out to the wingtips), and provided extra wingspan to allow two more weapon pylons to be installed, bringing the total to seven, of which four can take fuel tanks. However, the outrigger units were moved

Interior layout of the AV-8B, as planned for the USMC, the RAF version differing in terms of equipment fit. Although largely redesigned, the AV-8B broadly follows the arrangement of the original

Cutaway view of the F402-RR-406 Pegasus engine for the production AV-8B, this model being preceded by the -404 in the four FSD aircraft and the -404A in the following 12. Note the zero-scarf front nozzles

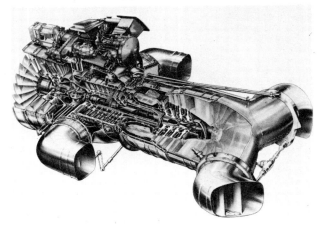

inboard, reducing wheel track from 22 ft to 17 ft (6.7 to 5.2 m), to facilitate road operations and deck handling.

As in the case of the Sea Harrier, the front fuselage of the AV-8B has been redesigned to raise the pilot by 10.5 inches (26.7 cm) and provide more space for equipment. A wrap-around windscreen has been introduced. The new structure benefits from the use of advanced composites, but the extra equipment in the nose creates a CG problem, which has been solved by extending the rear fuselage by 18 inches (45.7 cm). The larger nose is compensated by a fintip extension.

The production engine for the AV-8B will be known as the Pegasus 11-21E or Mk 105, while the US services will refer to it as the F402-RR-406. Whereas previous versions have all four nozzles sawn off obliquely, the front nozzles of the AV-8B engine are extended and sawn off at right angles to reduce the splay angle of the jets. This zero-scarf nozzle also gives a 500 lb (227 kg) increase in static thrust. Combat rating is increased by 2,500 lb (1,134 kg), and VIFF clearance is extended.

The improved engine will operate at lower

turbine temperatures, resulting in reduced maintenance costs and an increase in time between overhauls (TBO) to 1,000 hr, with a hot-end rework at 500 hr. A 'hot-refuelling' point has been added to the left-hand cowling to permit turnrounds with engine running, and provision for a bolt-on, retractable, telescopic flight-refuelling probe has been made higher up on the same side.

Other changes include the introduction of the 25 mm General Electric GAU-12 Equalizer, a five-barrel cannon working on the Gatling principle. In terms of installation it is an unusual arrangement, in that the cannon and its pneumatic drive are contained in the left-hand pod, and 300 rounds of ammunition are housed in a multi-layer magazine in the right-hand pod, the two sides being connected by a crossover fairing.

For the USMC the AV-8B will be equipped with a Litton ASN-130 inertial navigator, a Smiths HUD, an advanced self-protection jamming system (ASPJ) mounted in a pod, an all-weather landing system (AWLS), and a Hughes angle-rate bombing system (ARBS). In the case of the Harrier GR.3 the distance to the target is measured by laser, but this is a technique that is difficult to practice in peacetime and in war might conceivably be subject to jamming. With ARBS a

set of optics combining laser and TV trackers is locked on to the target (daylight attacks are possible using contrast-lock, eliminating the need for laser marking), the outputs of depression angle and sightline spin rate allowing slant range to be computed automatically. Other changes from the GR.3 include a modernized cockpit with push-button up-front control (UFC) panel for such vital functions as communications, navigation, IFF, and weapons control. The AV-8B will also have TV-type multi-purpose displays (MPDs) for ARBS and Maverick presentations, radar warning, navigation data, checklists and stores management. Benefiting from MDC experience on the F-15 and F-18, all the switches required in combat, including controls for the RWR, armament selection, ARBS, manoeuvre flap, and stability augmentation, are grouped on the throttle and control column to permit HOTAS (hand-on-throttle-and-stick) operation.

The RAF version (Harrier GR.5) will have a very high degree of commonality with the USMC aircraft, but it will have Martin-Baker Mk 10L

This sketch of the General Electric GAU-12/U five-barrel 25 mm cannon installation for the AV-8B illustrates the location of the gun in the left ventral pod, and the 300-round magazine on the right

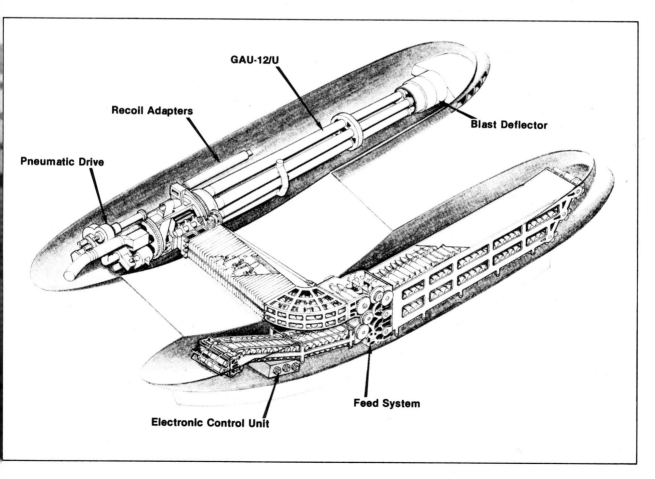

This 'full-scale wind tunnel model' of the AV-8B was a modified AV-8A, tested with engine running in the NASA Ames FST. The tunnel roof was opened periodically to cool the recirculating air

ejection seats in place of Stencels, Marconi ECM and RWR equipment, a moving map display, a panoramic camera in the front fuselage, and BAe Dynamics IRLS. In order to satisfy UK birdstrike requirements (associated with emphasis on low level operation), the GR.5 will have a stronger windscreen, and reinforced structure in the region of intake lips and wing leading edges. At the time of writing the cannon for the GR.5 had not been selected, but it had been decided to locate Sidewinder mounting points ahead of the outriggers.

Although performance data for the GR.3 has remained Restricted, some information has been published on the AV-8B. Maximum speed is quoted as Mach 0.88 at sea level and 0.93 at altitude, both of which are inferior to the corresponding figures for the GR.3 and Sea

Harrier. Radius in a HI-LO-HI mission with seven 1,000 lb (454 kg) is 600 nm (1,110 km). Ferry range with four 250 Imp gal (1,136 litre) tanks is 2,500 nm (4,630 km). Maximum external load is 9,200 lb (4,170 kg). Operating empty weight is 12,750 lb (5,783 kg) and maximum take-off weight is 29,750 lb (13,495 kg).

AV-8B Programme

In order to validate the V/STO performance improvements predicted, tests were begun in 1976 on what was termed a 'full-scale wind tunnel model'. This was basically an AV-8A (BuAer 158385), fitted with a metal replica of the revised wing, the LIDs, the improved intakes, and the enlarged flaps. It had a fully instrumented Pegasus 3, to which could be attached various front nozzle shapes.

This heavily modified aircraft was to be the subject of some of the most remarkable ground tests ever conducted in the field of V/STOL. Mounted on supports in the massive open working section of the NASA Ames FST, a section that is 80 ft (24.4 m) wide and 40 ft (12.2 m) high, this 'model' was tested at various tunnel speeds with its engine running, despite the fact that (like the FST at Langley, used in the original P.1127 model tests) the air in the tunnel is constantly recirculating. To overcome this heating problem, the roof of the tunnel was opened between test runs. Although the results were limited by ground effect and by the strength of the supporting pylons, the results were sufficiently encouraging for MDC to be funded to produce two prototype YAV-8Bs. Again to reduce costs, this was done by converting two AV-8As, 158394 and 395.

Flight tests began on 9 November 1978, but six days later the second prototype was lost following a flame-out of is F402-RR-404 at altitude. Generally representative of the production aircraft except in regard to the retention of the AV-8A front fuselage and unextended rear fuselage, the YAV-8B provided a vast improvement in V/STOL handling and performance, but also demonstrated a dramatic increase in drag. To minimize the drag penalty, the wing-body junction fairing was later enlarged, the inboard wing pylon extended aft to fair into the flap hinge bracket, and the inlet cowl profile revised. To improve instantaneous turn performance, a LERX was added, based on BAe tests.

Encouraged by results obtained on the YAV-8B, the AV-8B programme has proceeded in a series of low-risk stages, beginning in 1979 with funds covering four FSD aircraft, the first of which (BuAer 161396) began hovering checks on 5 November 1981. This phase has been followed by a pilot production batch of 12 aircraft, then a limited production batch of 12 aircraft in FY83. Production for the USMC is expected to peak at six/month in 1986 and run to 336 AV-8Bs, while the RAF will have 60, including two FSD aircraft and a fatigue test specimen. A batch of 12 is to be produced for the Spanish Navy.

The AV-8B will achieve initial operational capability (IOC) with the USMC in 1985. The first DB aircraft (ZD318) for the RAF will fly in May 1985, followed by the first production aircraft in October. Deliveries to the RAF begin in 1986, and the schedule calls for the Harrier GR.5 to be operational by 1987. At time of writing a decision on a two-seat TAV-8B for the USMC was pending; some 27 may be included in the total of 336.

Although it may be regretted that leadership in the development of the Harrier family is passing from the UK to America, BAe has won a massive workload from the AV-8B programme, representing approximately 40 per cent of the airframe work for the combined USMC-RAF production run. In addition to assembly of the RAF GR.5, BAe will supply the centre and rear

fuselages 'plumbed' for both services, together with the centre-line pylon, RCS, fin and rudder. The company will also manufacture (at Warton) the tailplane for the GR.5. In terms of export deliveries, it is anticipated that approximately 75 per cent will be assembled by MDC and 25 per cent by BAe. Most of the engine work will be done by Rolls-Royce, but approximately 25 per cent of Pegasus manhours for USMC AV-8Bs will be done by Pratt & Whitney.

Supersonic V/STOL

Turning finally to the subject of advanced V/STOL developments, it cannot be emphasized too strongly that the technology to produce a supersonic single-engined vectored-thrust fighter has been available in the UK since the 1960s. The fact that no such aircraft exists today is simply the result of a lack of an operational requirement and of development funding. Although R&D costs are notoriously difficult to estimate, there has long been an intuitive feeling in Whitehall that a V/STOL supersonic fighter would cost twice as much to develop as a conventional one, and that such large-scale expenditure cannot be justified in the light of the small domestic market and limited export prospects for such an aircraft.

Notwithstanding their pioneering work in this field, France and Germany appear to have turned their backs on V/STOL, following the advent of the 'graduated response' doctrine of the mid-1960s, reducing the need for dispersal. In the UK the RN is well pleased with the Sea Harrier, and would like to see a supersonic replacement in the mid/late 1990s, if such an aircraft could be developed in conjunction with the USN. The RAF, after initial opposition, has increasingly supported the V/STOL concept in recent years, and has drafted an AST (Air Staff Target) to promote studies of the need for and the cost of STOVL offensive support aircraft with various levels of maximum speed. It seems clear that, provided the AST includes a secondary battlefield air superiority capability, then some supersonic capability will be necessary.

In America, the need for V/STOL aircraft was formally investigated in the late 1970s by the Defense Science Board. Rather than foreseeing (as some earlier USN studies had done) a complete switch from CTOL to V/STOL, the final report advocated a move toward the optimum mix of the two types, a mix that it predicted would tilt toward V/STOL aircraft as engines became lighter. The service that seemed likely to gain

OVERLEAF
Notwithstanding the 'AV-8B' on the cowling, this is one of two YAV-8Bs produced by converting AV-8As. Easily distinguished by their lack of a raised cockpit, the YAV-8Bs also had unextended rear fuselages

This YAV-8B was evidently being tested in ferry configuration, with four 250 Imp gal (1,135 lit) tanks. Trials with the YAV-8B showed significant improvements in V/STOL performance, but increased drag

LEFT
This view of an AV-8B illustrates the GAU-12/U cannon installation and associated strakes, the reduced outrigger track to facilitate road operations and deck handling, and the new wing

most from the use of V/STOL across a broad spectrum of aircraft was the USN, beginning with a comparatively large project (eg, an S-3A Viking with two Pegasus engines) for the ASW, AEW and missiler roles, and followed by a supersonic V/STOL fighter to replace the F-14 and F-18. As an intermediate step, a Mach 1.5 aircraft with a Pegasus with PCB was mentioned as a possibility. The planning of the USAF indicated STOL performance in its tactical fighters, rather than V/STOL, though the Board recommended that the service should evaluate the AV-8B, which satisfied USMC close support needs. Thinking in the US Army stressed extremely low level operation, which favoured what might be termed advanced helicopters (eg, the Bell tilt-rotor concept). Such aircraft could, it was felt, also be usefully employed by the USN.

It is clear that the USN is the only Western service that is likely to fund development of a supersonic V/STOL fighter, although the RN, RAF, and even the USAF might be willing to join in at some stage. However, more recent thinking on the VX or VFMX aircraft to replace the F-14A, A-6A, and EA-6B suggests that this will be a heavy CTOL aircraft, hence supersonic V/STOL is more likely to be seen first in the form of the F-18 replacement, which may be delayed to a later stage.

In designing a supersonic V/STOL fighter, the single-engine vectored-thrust approach has the advantages of engineering and piloting simplicity, coupled with the ability to use VIFF in combat. Its principal disadvantages are high cruise fuel consumption due to poor thrust matching and a compromise engine cycle, and high R&D costs due to the need for a specialized engine. This approach also produces a high temperature and noise environment for the rear fuselage and tailplane (the cold jets tending to press the hot jets against the airframe), and it may suffer from hot gas recirculation when using PCB for take-off. One major deficiency in this line of development is that thrust-reversal for short landing has never been tested on a Pegasus engine, although it has featured in various unsuccessful HSA/BAe project studies, including the proposal for a GR.3 replacement. Without this capability, vertical landing is the norm, placing severe restrictions on landing weight.

In the light of the known shortcomings of the single vectored-thrust engine, various alternative V/STOL powerplant concepts are being studied for possible USN fighter applications, although most are repeats of ideas that were generally rejected in the early 1960s. The tail-sitter, now termed the VATOL (vertical attitude take-off and landing) concept is being proposed in conjunction with tilting platforms on the carrier deck-edge. Despite disappointing results in the past, the jet augmentor is being studied by General Dynamics and Rockwell. Vought is promoting the tandem-fan concept, in which an engine drives by means of a long shaft two axial-flow fans, providing high-pressure air to rotatable nozzles, in a manner reminiscent of the original Wibault patent.

General Electric is meanwhile suggesting a remote augmentation lift system (RALS), also known more dramatically as 'bleed and burn', in which air bled from the propulsion engine is passed through a separate combustor en route to a lift nozzle under the aircraft CG. This is similar to a scheme proposed by Rolls-Royce in the mid-1960s, and it may be relevant to note that this was one of the few that attracted the attention of the late Sir Sydney Camm.

In addition to these alternative schemes, BAe at Warton has proposed the use of two tilting engines pivoting about the wing leading edge, arguing that the improvement in engine reliability over the last 25 years justifies a fresh look at such concepts, which are made more attractive by the possibility of obtaining short, lightweight engines off-the-shelf.

The outcome of the eventual competition between these various V/STOL powerplant concepts cannot be predicted, but the centrally-mounted vectored-thrust engine must surely stand as good a chance as any other. In this context it may be noted that Rolls-Royce has patented a twin-engine, twin-boom arrangement, in which both powerplants would feed vectored-thrust nozzles on the aircraft centre-line, thus simplifying asymmetric problems and making possible the use of much smaller engines than Pegasus.

As building-blocks toward a supersonic vectored-thrust engine, Rolls-Royce has run various tests on a PCB Pegasus, trials that culminate with the engine mounted in an old airframe suspended from a large gantry, to measure hot gas recirculation as a function of height above the ground. To minimize temperature rise at the intakes, the engine manufacturer favours toed-in PCB nozzles, so that the two hot jets strike the ground roughly in the same place, rather than forcing up a hot fountain between them. On the other hand, BAe feels that toed-in jets sacrifice jet lift, and that better results can be obtained by LIDS.

Beyond the ground tests, R-R and MDC would like to see a supersonic technology demonstrator, designated AV-8SX. Based on an AV-8A airframe, this would have a PCB Pegasus of approximately 27,000 lb (12,250 kg) thrust and a Mach 1.6 capability. To allow for the forward shift of thrust centre, the front fuselage would be extended, and the aerodynamic centre moved forward by a leading edge extension for the wing, which would also reduce thickness/chord ratio and hence wave drag. The fuselage would be stretched to permit

To measure ground proximity effects with PCB, Rolls-Royce is running a PCB Pegasus mounted in a Harrier airframe, suspended from a gantry at Shoeburyness, primarily to evaluate hot gas reingestion

RIGHT
This British Aerospace (Kingston) blowing model was used to evaluate ground proximity effects in a possible supersonic vectored-thrust aircraft. The ventral intake was to reduce bird ingestion

FAR RIGHT
A model of the proposed TAV-8B. It was originally agreed that the USMC would use British-built TAV-8s for training for the AV-8B, but MDC later advanced this design, of which the Marines may buy 27

A Rolls-Royce artist's impression of a supersonic naval V/STOL fighter. The canard configuration and three-nozzle engine arrangement are noteworthy, as is the need for lead in the tail-booms!

BELOW LEFT
The MDC Model 279-3 was a study apparently aimed at an F-14 replacement around the end of the century. The front nozzles have been drooped to avoid pressing the rear jets against the fuselage

an increase in internal fuel to 8,400 lb (3,810 kg).

In contrast, BAe (Kingston) regards a supersonic AV-8A derivative as a waste of time and development funds, preferring to go straight to a 'pre-prototype phase' for a new generation V/STOL fighter. Whereas MDC envisages the final production aircraft as using a fashionable canard arrangement, BAe adheres to the traditional tail-aft approach. At time of writing, the Kingston team appears to be advocating the P.1216, a three-nozzle, twin-boom configuration. This avoids the present rear fuselage problems, although it remains to be seen how easy it is to place equipment in the booms. It also reduces the problem of downwash at the tailplane, since the tailplane halves are outboard of the booms. A ventral intake is used to minimize bird ingestion. The engine is not specified, but R-R has referred to an RB.422 of 27,000 lb (12,245 kg) dry thrust and 40,000 lb (18,140 kg) with PCB.

At this stage, the key question is not whether supersonic performance capability can be combined with V/STOL, or even which is the best powerplant approach. What matters if V/STOL is to move ahead in the West (ie, in America and Britain) during the remainder of this century is whether the services that command the necessary R&D funding really see a need for a multi-role V/STOL fighter. Current indications are that the USN did not regard the Falklands conflict as demonstrating any advantage for V/STOL aircraft in comparison with CTOL aircraft operating from super-carriers. This is not to suggest that the USN has lost all interest in V/STOL, but that the

chances for a supersonic V/STOL fighter may now rely more on support for the concept from the USAF.

At first sight, the idea of the USAF supporting the USN in funding the development of a supersonic V/STOL combat aircraft appears to be far-fetched. Historically, the USAF has taken the view that the extremely short airfield performance associated with jet lift would only be necessary in the event of runway bombing of an intensity unthinkable in terms of the total air supremacy on which the service's tactical doctrine is based. *'If we needed V/STOL aircraft because of runway bombing, we would have lost the war anyway'* is the essence of the USAF attitude.

However, two factors may change the USAF stance. One is that the development of highly effective airfield attack weapons, coupled with the availability of chemical and nuclear weapons, may persuade the USAF that there is a case for a dispersable V/STOL element in its tactical forces. The other is that USAF participation in the RDF (Rapid Deployment Force) may cause V/STOL aircraft to be viewed more favorably, due to their ability to deploy quickly to areas where only short airstrips exist, and consequently to minimize congestion at the logistic airhead.

Unless their is an unforseen change of heart in regard to V/STOL aircraft by France or Germany, or unless Japan seeks a partner in the development of such a weapon system, then it seems to be inevitable that Britain's only chance of retaining a foothold in this area of technology is to act as a junior partner to America in a supersonic V/STOL fighter programme. Many in Britain will regret the passing of the lead in this field to the US, after all the pioneering work that was done in this country. On the other hand, as evidenced by the massive UK workload provided by participation in the AV-8B programme, V/STOL is still a branch of technology in which Britain can make a valuable contribution to the defence of the West.

Acknowledgements

The author is pleased to acknowledge the invaluable assistance provided by the following in the preparation of this book:—

British Aerospace PLC:
Robin Balmer, 'Bill' Bedford, John Coombs, John Crampton, Gordon Dare and the staff of BAe (Kingston) Photographic Services, 'Wilf' Firth, John Godden, 'Fred' Hefford, Ralph Hooper, Trevor Jordan, 'Tony' Lewis, 'Danny' Norman, Taylor Scott, 'Mike' Snelling, 'Mike' Stroud, Peter Thompson and the staff of BAe (Aircraft Group) Market Intelligence Unit, 'Ron' Williams, and Colin Wilson.

British Army
Staff Sgt C J Bowman (Int Corps).

Challenge Publications Inc:
Michael O'Leary

Contraves AG:
Peter Blumer, Kurt Moos.

Fleet Air Arm Museum:
Vernon Hillier.

Ferranti PLC:
John Dods, 'Bill' Hare.

McDonnell Douglas Corporation:
'Geoff' Norris, Karen Stubberfield.

Ministry of Defence:
Robin Barrett, Graham Hammond, 'Ted' Knowles, and Michael Pentreath.

Rolls-Royce Ltd:
Alan Brothers, 'Dick' Butcher, 'Tim' Carr, John Hutchinson, and Peter Scott.

Royal Air Force:
Flt Lt John Blenkiron, Flt Lt Colin Drew, Sqn Ldr 'Bob' Iveson, Flt Lt Andrew de Labat, Flt Lt 'Dave' Morgan, Wg Cdr 'Joe' Sim, Wg Cdr Peter Squire.

Royal Navy:
Capt 'Ben' Bathurst, Lt Cdr Roger Bennett, Lt Cdr 'Mike' Blissett, Lt Cdr 'Dick' Goodenough, Lt Cdr Robin Kent, Lt Cdr 'Jan' Larcombe, Cdr Paul Madge, Lt Cdr Brian Morgan, PO F Nowosielski, Lt Cdr Neil Thomas, Lt 'Steve' Thomas, and Lt Cdr 'Sharkey' Ward.

Note: the ranks quoted above applied at the time of the Falklands conflict, this convention having been followed in the main text.

Abbreviations

AA—anti-aircraft
AAA—anti-aircraft artillery
AC—aerodynamic centre
ACM—air combat manoeuvre
AHRS—attitude and heading reference system
AI—air interception
AOA—angle of attack
ARBS—Angle Rate Bombing System (Hughes)
ARM—anti-radar missile
ASI—Ascension Island

ASI—air speed indicator
ASPJ—Airborne Self-Protection Jammer (ITT Avionics/Westinghouse)
AST—Air Staff Target
AWLS—all-weather landing system

BAC—British Aircraft Corporation
BAe—British Aerospace
BAI—battlefield air interdiction

CAI—close approach indicator
CAP—combat air patrol
CAS—close air support
CCA—carrier-controlled approach
CCIP—continuously-computed impact point
CG—centre of gravity
CTOL—conventional take-off and landing
CVS—aircraft carrier, anti-submarine

DB—development batch

EBF—externally-blown flap
ECM—electronic countermeasures
ESM—electronic support measures
FAC—forward air control(ler)
FDO—flight deck officer
FINRAE—Ferranti Inertial Rapid Alignment Equipment
FONAC—Flag Officer, Naval Air Command
FSD—full-scale development
FST—Full-Scale Tunnel (NASA)
FY—Fiscal Year

GMT—Greenwich Mean Time (or 'Zulu' time)

HAPI—Harrier Approach Path Indicator
HF—high frequency
HMG—Her Majesty's Government
HP—high pressure
HSA—Hawker Siddeley Aviation
HSH—High-Speed Helicopter (Hawker Aircraft)
HUD—head-up display

IFF—identification, friend or foe
IFTU—Intensive Flying Trials Unit (RN)
IN—Indian Navy
IN—inertial navigation
IOC—initial operational capability
IP—initial point
IR—infra-red

JPT—jetpipe temperature

L/D—lift/drag ratio
LERX—leading edge root extension
LGB—laser-guided bomb
LIDs—lift-improvement devices
LOH—light observation helicopter
LOX—liquid oxygen
LRMTS—Laser Ranger and Marked-Target Seeker (Ferranti)
LRU–line replacement unit

MADGE—Microwave Aircraft Digital Guidance Equipment (MEL)
MARTSU—Mobile Aircraft Repair, Transport and Salvage Unit (RN)
MDC—McDonnell Douglas Corporation
MDC—miniature detonating cord
MEZ—Maritime Exclusion Zone
MEZ—missile engagement zone
MFCS—manual fuel control system
MID—mentioned in dispatches
MPD—multi-purpose display
MV—motor vessel
MWDP—Mutual Weapons Development Program

NASA—National Aeronautics and Space Administration
NATO—North Atlantic Treaty Organisation
NAVHARS—navigation, heading and attitude reference system
NBC—nuclear, biological and chemical

OBOGS—on-board oxygen generation system
OCU—Operational Conversion Unit (RAF)
OR—Operational Requirement (RAF)

PCB—plenum chamber burning
PIA—pilot-interpreted approach
PIM—previous intended movement
PIO—pilot-induced oscillation
PR—photo-reconnaissance
PR—public relations
RAE—Royal Aircraft Establishment
RAF—Royal Air Force
R&D—research and development
RALS—remote augmentation lift system
RAT—ram air turbine
RCS—reaction control system
RDF—Rapid Deployment Force
RN—Royal Navy
RP—rocket projectile
RPM—revolutions per minute
R-R—Rolls-Royce
RWR—radar warning receiver

SAAHS—stability augmentation and attitude-hold system
SAM—surface-air missile
SAR—search and rescue
SFC—specific fuel consumption
SHAR—Sea Harrier
STO—short take-off
STOVL—short take-off, vertical landing

TACAN—Tactical Air Navigation system
TAR—tactical air reconnaissance
TBO—time-between-overhauls
TET—turbine entry temperature
TEZ—Total Exclusion Zone
T/W—thrust/weight ratio

UHF—ultra-high frequency
UFC—up-front control
USB—upper surface blowing
USMC—United States Marine Corps

VATOL—vertical-attitude take-off and landing
VHF—very high frequency
VIFF—vectoring in forward flight
VL—vertical landing
VSI—vertical speed indicator
V/STOL—vertical or short take-off and landing
VT—vectored-thrust
VTO—vertical take-off

WAC—weapon-aiming computer.

Appendix 1

Sea Harrier Pilots in Operation Corporate

Hermes

Lt Cdr A D Auld	800 Sqn (CO)	DSC
Lt Cdr G W J Batt	800 Sqn (killed in action 24th May)	DSC
Lt Cdr M S Blissett	800 Sqn (senior pilot)	MID
Lt Cdr R V Frederiksen	800 Sqn	MID
Lt Cdr C R W Morrell	800 Sqn	MID
Lt Cdr A R W Ogilvy	899 Sqn	
Lt Cdr N Taylor	800 Sqn (killed in action 4th May)	
Lt Cdr N W Thomas	899 Sqn (CO)	DSC
Lt W Covington	800 Sqn	
Lt M Hale	800 Sqn	
Lt A McHarg	800 Sqn	
Lt D A B Smith	800 Sqn	
Sub-Lt H J George	899 Sqn	
Flt Lt E M Ball	800 Sqn	MID
Flt Lt S Brown	809 Sqn	
Flt Lt J Leeming	809 Sqn	
Flt Lt D H S Morgan	899 Sqn	
Flt Lt B Penfold	800 Sqn	

Invincible

Lt Cdr D D Braithwaite	809 Sqn	
Lt Cdr G J M W Broadwater	899 Sqn	
Lt Cdr A Craig	809 Sqn	
Lt Cdr J E Eyton-Jones	801 Sqn (killed in action 6th May)	
Lt Cdr J J H Gedge	809 Sqn (CO)	AFC
Lt Cdr D Hamilton	801 Sqn	
Lt Cdr R S G Kent	801 Sqn (senior pilot)	MID
Lt Cdr H G B Slade	809 Sqn	
Lt Cdr N D Ward	801 Sqn (CO)	DSC
Lt D A Austin	809 Sqn	
Lt C M Cantan	801 Sqn	
Lt A Curtiss	801 Sqn (killed in action 6th May)	
Lt B D Haig	801 Sqn	
Lt S W Hargreaves	800 Sqn	
Lt S R Thomas	801 Sqn	DSC
Lt M W Watson	899 Sqn	
Flt Lt P C Barton	899 Sqn	
Flt Lt I Mortimer	801 Sqn	MID

Notes:
a) The decorations listed on the right were awarded in recognition of the pilots' active service in the Falklands.
b) Ranks shown were as at the time of the conflict.

Appendix 2

Sea Harriers in Operation Corporate

In view of exaggerated Argentine claims regarding attrition of British aircraft due to ground fire, it is worth noting that of the 28 Sea Harriers that went south, 22 returned to the UK to continue their operations, this figure being confirmed by individual serial numbers. For completeness, the following list covers all the 34 RN Sea Harriers produced at time of writing, showing which aircraft were involved directly in Operation Corporate, what ships they flew from, and how they returned to the UK. Figures shown in brackets indicate aircraft side numbers as applied at the time of the conflict. Sea Harriers flew with different side numbers before and after the conflict, eg XZ455 flew earlier as '102' and '712', then during the conflict as '12', and afterwards as '000' and more recently '715'.

XZ438   First DB aircraft. Retained at Yeovilton for trials. Written off in an accident during a ski-jump take-off with 330 Imp gal (1,500 litre) ferry tanks on 17th May 1982. Pilot ejected.

XZ439   Second DB aircraft. Retained at Yeovilton for trials.

XZ440   Third DB aircraft. Retained in the UK for trials

XZ450   Sailed in *Hermes*. Shot down by automatic weapons over Goose Green on 4th May. Pilot Lt 'Nick' Taylor killed. (No 50).

XZ451   Sailed and returned (17th September) in *Invincible*. (No 006). This was the aircraft in which Lt Cdr Ward shot down a C-130 on 1st June.

XZ452, XZ453   These two aircraft sailed in *Invincible*, and collided in flight in bad visibility on 6th May while conducting a surface search. Pilots Lt Cdr John Eyton-Jones (XZ452) and Lt Alan Curtiss (XZ453) killed. (Nos 007, 009, respectively). It may be noted that XZ452 was the aircraft used by Flt Lt Paul Barton on 1st May to achieve the first kill.

XZ454   Written off prior to the conflict in an accident on 1 December 1980, when the aircraft was carrying out a fly-by of *Invincible*, and the starboard outrigger struck the skijump. Pilot ejected.

XZ455   Joined *Hermes* in Channel on way south, transferred on 2nd July to and returned in *Invincible*. (No 12, later 000). This was the aircraft used by Flt Lt 'Bertie' Penfold to make the second kill (another Mirage) on 1st May, and by Lt Cdr 'Fred' Frederiksen to shoot down a Dagger on 21st May.

XZ456   Sailed in *Invincible*. Shot down by Roland on 1st June. Pilot Flt Lt Ian Mortimer ejected. (No 008).

XZ457   Sailed and returned (21st July) in *Hermes*. Probably the most distinguished Sea Harrier of the war, this aircraft was employed by Lt Cdr Clive Morell to destroy two A-4s on 21st May, and by Lt Cdr 'Andy' Auld to destroy two Daggers on 24th May. (No 14).

XZ458   Sailed from ASI in *Atlantic Conveyor*, transferred to *Invincible*, then to *Illustrious* on 2nd August. (No 007, replacing XZ452).

XZ459   Sailed and returned in *Hermes*, then sailed south again in *Illustrious*. (No 25).

XZ460   Sailed and returned in *Hermes*. (No 26).

XZ491   Sailed from ASI in *Atlantic Conveyor*, transferred to *Invincible*, then to *Illustrious*. (No 002).

XZ492   Sailed and returned in *Hermes*. This was the aircraft used by Lt Cdr Neil Thomas to destroy an A-4 on 21st May (No 23).

XZ493   Sailed and returned in *Invincible*. (No 001).

XZ494   Sailed in *Hermes*, transferred on 2nd July to and returned in *Invincible*. (No 16, later 008, replacing XZ456).

XZ495   Sailed and returned in *Invincible*. (No 003).

XZ496   Sailed and returned in *Hermes*, then sailed south again in *Illustrious*. (No 27).

XZ497   Retained at Yeovilton for trials

XZ498   Sailed and returned in *Invincible*. (No 005).

XZ499   Sailed from ASI in *Atlantic Conveyor*, transferred to and returned in *Hermes*, then sailed south again in *Illustrious*. (No 99).

XZ500   Sailed and returned in *Hermes*, then sailed south again in *Illustrious*. Lost subsequently on 14 June 1983 over Bay of Biscay. Pilot ejected.

ZA174   Sailed from ASI in *Atlantic Conveyor*, and transferred to *Invincible*. Slid off deck on 29th May while being positioned for launch. Pilot Lt Cdr 'Mike' Broadwater ejected. (No 000).

ZA175   Sailed and returned in *Invincible*. (No 004).

ZA176   Sailed from ASI in *Atlantic Conveyor*, transferred to and later returned in *Hermes*, then sailed south again in *Illustrious*. (No 76). This aircraft later hit the headlines as '001', when on 6 June 1983 it was landed by Sub Lt Ian Watson on containers on the deck of the Spanish freighter *Alraigo*, after taking off from *Illustrious* and experiencing a navigation system failure.

ZA177   Sailed from ASI in *Atlantic Conveyor*, then transferred to and returned in *Hermes*. (No 77). Believed to have been the aircraft in which Flt Lt 'Dave' Morgan made his kills, ZA177 was lost on 21 January 1983, when the pilot was forced to eject over Dorset.

ZA190   Sailed from ASI in *Atlantic Conveyor*, then transferred to and returned in *Invincible*. (No 009, replacing XZ453).
ZA191   Sailed and returned in *Hermes*, then sailed south again in *Illustrious*. (No 18).
ZA192   Sailed in *Hermes*. Lost in night take-off accident on 23rd May. Pilot Lt Cdr 'Gordy' Batt killed. (No 92).
ZA193   Sailed and returned in *Hermes*, then sailed south again in *Illustrious*. (No 93).
ZA194   Sailed from ASI in *Atlantic Conveyor*, transferred to and later returned in *Hermes*, then sailed south again in *Illustrious*. (No 94).
ZA195   Not completed until after the end of the conflict.

Appendix 3

Harrier GR.3 pilots in Operation Corporate

Wg Cdr P T Squire		DFC
Sqn Ldr P V Harris		AFC
Sqn Ldr R D Iveson		MID
Sqn Ldr J J Pook		DFC
Flt Lt M D Beech	(flew from ASI 1st June)	
Flt Lt A R Boyens	(flew from ASI 8th June)	
Flt Lt N S Gilchrist	(flew from ASI 8th June)	
Flt Lt J W Glover		
Flt Lt M W J Hare		MID
Flt Lt T A Harper		
Flt Lt M M Macleod	(flew from ASI 1st June)	
Flt Lt J Rochfort		

Notes
a) Unless otherwise stated, the pilots sailed to the TEZ in the *Atlantic Conveyor* or *Norland*.
b) The decorations listed at right were awarded in recognition of the pilots' active service in the Falklands.
c) The ranks shown were as at the time of the conflict.

Appendix 4

Harrier GR.3s in Operation Corporate

The aircraft are listed below in order of tail-code. Harriers '03' to '31' were with No 1(F) Sqn at the outbreak of hostilities, whereas '32' to '37' were obtained from No 233 OCU. Six aircraft sailed from ASI in the *Atlantic Conveyor*, two flew to *Hermes* on 1st June, two more followed on the 8th, and four sailed from ASI in the *Contender Bezant*.

Tail-code	Serial	
'03'	XW919	
'05'	XZ992	
'06'	XW767	
'07'	XZ989	Damaged in heavy landing San Carlos strip 8th June.
'10'	XZ133	
'14'	XZ963	Shot down 21st May. Flt Lt Glover ejected, captured.
'16'	XV778	
'29'	XZ129	
'31'	XZ997	
'32'	XV789	
'33'	XZ972	Shot down 30th May. Sqn Ldr Pook ejected, rescued.
'34'	XZ988	Shot down 27th May. Sqn Ldr Iveson ejected, rescued.
'35'	XW924	
'37'	XV762	

Appendix 5

Provisional Air-Air Kill List

Serial	Date	GMT	SHAR Pilot	Armament	Kill
1	1st May	1930	Flt Lt Barton (801 Sqn)	AIM-9L	Mirage
2	1st May	1941	Flt Lt Penfold (800 Sqn)	AIM-9L	Dagger
3	1st May	1946	Lt Curtiss (801 Sqn)	AIM-9L	Canberra
4	21st May	1510	Lt Cdr Ward (801 Sqn)	Aden	Pucará
5	21st May	1604	Lt Cdr Thomas (800 Sqn)	AIM-9L	A-4
6	21st May	1605	Lt Cdr Blissett (800 Sqn)	AIM-9L	A-4
7	21st May	1735	Lt Cdr Frederiksen (800 Sqn)	AIM-9L	Dagger
8	21st May	1753	Lt Thomas (801 Sqn)	AIM-9L	Dagger
9	21st May	1753	Lt Thomas (801 Sqn)	AIM-9L	Dagger
10	21st May	1753	Lt Cdr Ward (801 Sqn)	AIM-9L	Dagger
11	21st May	1811	Lt Morrell (800 Sqn)	AIM-9L	Navy A-4
12	21st May	1811	Flt Lt Leeming (800 Sqn)	Aden	Navy A-4
13	21st May	1811	Lt Morrell (800 Sqn)	Aden	Navy A-4
14	23rd May	1330	Flt Lt Morgan (800 Sqn)	Wake	Puma
15	23rd May	1330	Flt Lt Morgan (800 Sqn)	Aden	A.109
16	23rd May	1900	Lt Hale (800 Sqn)	AIM-9L	Dagger
17	24th May	1415	Lt Cdr Auld (800 Sqn)	AIM-9L	Dagger
18	24th May	1415	Lt Cdr Auld (800 Sqn)	AIM-9L	Dagger
19	24th May	1415	Lt Smith (800 Sqn)	AIM-9L	Dagger
20	1st June	1346	Lt Cdr Ward (801 Sqn)	AIM-9L + Aden	C-130
21	8th June	1945	Flt Lt Morgan (800 Sqn)	AIM-9L	A-4
22	8th June	1945	Flt Lt Morgan (800 Sqn)	AIM-9L	A-4
23	8th June	1945	Lt Smith (800 Sqn)	AIM-9L	A-4

Notes:
a) At time of writing there was no 'official' kill-list.
b) Some sources credit the Mirage shot down by Stanley airfield defences on 1st May as a kill for Lt Thomas (who damaged it), and discount Flt Lt Morgan's A.109, presumably in the belief that it had touched down before it was destroyed.
c) All times quoted are when the combat was logged on board ship. Local time was three hours earlier.

Index

Accidents 58, 59, 65, 85, 155, 165
Agusta A.109 112
Air Race 74, 76
Angle-rate bombing system (ARBS) 181
Appointments 70
Approach aids 100
ARBS 181
Ark Royal 60
Armstrong-Whitworth Sea Hawk 40
Ascension Island 134, 150
Atlantic Conveyor 126, 130, 132, 151
AV-16 176
AV-8A 86, 89, 90
AV-8B 176, 178, 180, 182, 186
AV-8SX 188

Balzac 24, 25
Bedford, A W 'Bill' 54–58, 65, 84
Bell ATV 32, 33
Bell D-188 27
Bell X-14 32, 33
Bell X-22A 33
Blowpipe 151
Blue Fox 93
Boeing YC-14 21, 23
Bristol BE.52 13, 34
Bristol BE.53 45
Bristol BE.53/2 50
Bristol BE.53/3 54
Bristol BE.53/6 65
Bristol BS.94/5 69
Bristol BS.100/9 65

Camm, Sir Sydney 36, 38, 40, 45, 51, 65, 70, 79
Canadair CL-84 31, 33
Canberra 109, 148
Chapman, Col 49, 50
China 92
Convair XFY-1 16, 18, 19
Curtiss-Wright X-19A 33

Dagger 108
Dassault Balzac 24, 25
Dassault Mirage IIIV 24, 25
DB Harrier 11, 55, 56, 60, 74, 79, 96
Dornier Do 29 28
Dornier Do 31 30, 60, 61
Douglas A-4 Skyhawk 51, 104, 105, 107

East Falkland 144
Engine change 161
Exports 84–92, 101

Falklands 102–175
Farnborough 53
Ferry tanks 126
FINRAE 130, 132, 134, 151
First flights:
    AV-8A 90
    AV-8B 183
    Harrier 74
    P.1127 56
    Sea Harrier 91, 96
    T.2 83
    T.4 84
    YAV-8B 183
Focke-Achgelis Fa 269 32
Fozard, John 42, 45

General Electric GAU-12/U cannon 181
General Dynamics F-16 15
Grumman A2F-1 Intruder 14
Gütersloh 75
G-VTOL 83, 84, 85, 101, 118
Gyroptère 12, 34

Harrier GR.1 71–79
Harrier GR.3 72, 74, 79
Harrier GR.5 183
Harrier GR.5(K) 178
Harrier T.2 79–81, 83
Harrier T.4 84
Harrier T.4N 86
Hawker Aircraft 36, 42, 48, 49
Hawker Fury 39
Hawker Hunter 41
Hawker Hurricane 39
Hawker P.1121 42
Hawker P.1127 13, 46–55, 60–63, 72
Hawker P.1129 44
Hawker P.1150 64
Hawker P.1154 64, 68
Hawker Siddeley Aviation 70
Hawker Siddeley HS.141 26
Hawker Siddeley HS.1170(P.1163) 68
Hawker Typhoon 40
HMS *Ark Royal* 60

HMS *Hermes* 94, 110, 114, 122, 125, 136, 138, 140, 152
HMS *Illustrious* 96, 172, 174
HMS *Invincible* 121, 172
Hummingbird 21
Hooker, Sir Stanley 32, 34, 47
Hooper, Ralph 29, 45–47, 49–51, 56, 70, 79

Indian Navy 99
Inertial navigation system (INS) 73, 129

Jamming 129

Karman, Prof Theodore von 28
Kestrel 60, 62

Laser ranger and marked target seeker (LRMTS) 74
Leading edge root extensions (LERX) 177
Lewis, Gordon 32, 34, 47
Lockheed C-130 109
Lockheed TR-1 14
Lockheed XFV-1 17
Lockheed XV-4B Hummingbird 21

Manned flight 11
Marine Corps 87–91
Matador 89, 118
MBB 25
McDonnell Douglas AV-8B 176, 178, 180, 182, 186
McDonnell Douglas Model 279-3 190
McDonnell Douglas YC-15 21, 23
'McGregor Turn' 65
McKinney, Marion 53
Merrywether, Hugh 55
MWDP 49–51

Natter (Bachem Ba 349) 16
NASA (Langley) 53
NATO 22
Nozzles 48

Oerlikon anti-aircraft cannon 146
Operation Corporate 102–175
OR.329 44, 49
OR.345 57

Pave Way 128, 174
Pegasus 48, 73
Pegasus 2 54, 56
Pegasus 3 60
Pegasus 5 60
Pegasus 6 72
Pegasus 10 72
Pegasus 11-21E 180
Port Stanley airfield 142, 145, 147, 154, 156, 167
Porter, James Robertson 12, 18
Pucará 108, 164

Rockwell XFV-12A 22
Roland 149

Rolls-Royce (R-R) 23
Ryan X-13 Vertijet 16, 19
Ryan XV-5A 21

San Carlos airstrip 169
Sandys, Sir Duncan (White Paper) 44
Sea Eagle 97
Sea Harrier 91–94, 99–101
Shorts SC.1 24
Sidewinder (AIM-9) 121, 129, 137
Simpson, Edgar C 29
Simpson, Duncan 83
Ski-jump 98, 126
Skyguard 146
Sopwith Aviation 36
Sopwith Bat-Boat 37
Sopwith Triplane 37
South Georgia 135
Spanish Navy 89, 91
Squadrons:
    No 1(F) 71, 74, 126
    No 3(F) 75, 79
    No 4 75, 121
    No 20 75
    No 233 OCU 74
    No 300 (India) 100, 120
    No 700A 96
    No 800 92–94, 112, 117, 158, 161
    No 801 92, 102, 112, 117
    No 809 116, 128
    No 899 92, 112, 116, 128
    Tripartite 62
Streamwise tip 61
Supersonic V/STOL 183, 191

TAV-8B 189
Tigercat 145
Tripartite Squadron 62

VAK 191 68
Vectoring in forward flight (VIFF) 85, 90
VFW 25
VFW 1262 30, 66, 69
Victor K.2 134
VJ101C 28
VJ101D 28
Vought XC-142A 33
Vulcan 145, 154

Ward Lt Cdr 'Sharkey' 124, 164
Wibault Gyroptère 12, 34
Wibault/Lewis 12, 35
Wibault Michel 33
Williams, Ron 44
Wolff von 30

Yakovlev Yak-36 *Freehand* 24, 27, 33
Yakovlev Yak-36 *Forger* 24, 26, 33
YAV-8B 184, 186